Cormac McCa

CW00825634

Continuum Studies in Contemporary North American Fiction

Series Editor: Sarah Graham, Lecturer in American Literature, University of Leicester, UK

This series offers up-to-date guides to the recent work of major contemporary North American authors. Written by leading scholars in the field, each book presents a range of original interpretations of three key texts published since 1990, showing how the same novel may be interpreted in a number of different ways. These informative, accessible volumes will appeal to advance undergraduate and postgraduate students, facilitating discussion and supporting close analysis of the most important contemporary American and Canadian fiction.

Titles in the Series include:

Bret Easton Ellis: American Psycho, Glamorama, Lunar Park
Edited by Naomi Mandel

Cormac McCarthy: All the Pretty Horses, No Country for Old Men,
    The Road
Edited by Sara L. Spurgeon

Don DeLillo: Mao II, Underworld, Falling Man
Edited Stacey Olster

Louise Erdrich: Tracks, The Last Report on the Miracles at Little
    No Horse, The Plague of Doves
Edited by Deborah L. Madsen

Margaret Atwood: The Robber Bride, The Blind Assassin,
    Oryx and Crake
Edited by J. Brooks Bouson

Philip Roth: American Pastoral, The Human Stain,
    The Plot Against America
Edited by Debra Shostak

CORMAC McCARTHY

All the Pretty Horses, No Country for
Old Men, The Road

Edited by Sara L. Spurgeon

continuum

Continuum International Publishing Group

The Tower Building   80 Maiden Lane
11 York Road   Suite 704
London SE1 7NX   New York, NY 10038

www.continuumbooks.com

British Library Cataloguing-in-Publication Data
A catalogue record for this book is available from the British Library.

ISBN: 978-0-8264-38201 (paperback)
ISBN: 978-0-82643-2216 (hardcover)

Library of Congress Cataloging-in-Publication Data
A catalog record for this book is available from the Library of Congress.

Typeset by Newgen Imaging Systems Pvt Ltd, Chennai, India
Printed and bound in Great Britain

Contents

Series Editor's Introduction

Each study in this series presents ten original essays by recognized subject specialists on the recent fiction of a significant author working in the United States or Canada. The aim of the series is to consider important novels published since 1990 either by established writers or by emerging talents. By setting 1990 as its general boundary, the series indicates its commitment to engaging with genuinely contemporary work, with the result that the series is often able to present the first detailed critical assessment of certain texts.

In respect of authors who have already been recognized as essential to the canon of North American fiction, the series provides experts in their work with the opportunity to consider their latest novels in the dual context of the contemporary era and as part of a long career. For authors who have emerged more recently, the series offers critics the chance to assess the work that has brought authors to prominence, exploring novels that have garnered acclaim both because of their individual merits and because they are exemplary in their creative engagement with a complex period.

Including both American and Canadian authors in the term 'North American' is in no sense reductive: studies of Canadian writers in this series do not treat them as effectively American, and assessment of all the chosen authors in terms of their national and regional identity, as well as their race and ethnicity, gender and sexuality, religion and political affiliation is essential in developing an understanding of each author's particular contribution to the representation of contemporary North American society.

The studies in this series make outstanding new contributions to the analysis of current fiction by presenting critical essays chosen for their originality, insight, and skill. Each volume begins with a substantial introduction to the author by the study's editor, which establishes the context for the chapters that will follow through a discussion of essential elements such as the writer's career, characteristic narrative strategies, themes and preoccupations, making clear the author's importance and the significance of the novels chosen for discussion. The studies are all comprised of three parts, each one presenting three original essays on three key recent works by the author, and every part is introduced by the volume's editor, explaining how the chapters to follow engage with the fiction and respond to existing interpretations. Each individual chapter takes a critical approach that may develop existing perceptions or challenge them, but always expands the ways in which the author's work may be read by offering a fresh approach.

It is a principle of the series that all the studies are written in a style that will be engaging and clear however complex the subject, with the aim of fostering further debate about the work of writers who all exemplify what is most exciting and valuable in contemporary North American fiction.

Sarah Graham

Acknowledgments

As thousands have pointed out before me, no book is ever the result of solitary labor. I would like to extend my heartfelt gratitude to the McCarthy scholars who contributed their ideas, time, questions, and carefully crafted chapters to this volume. Their work is genuinely outstanding and it was an honor to be involved in bringing their voices together here. I must thank as well my colleagues from Texas Tech who listened patiently to my obsessive ruminations about this book for countless miles on early morning runs through the streets of Lubbock. You kept me healthy and sane (mostly). My thanks, too, for the support of the Western Literature Association, which allowed several of the authors included in this volume the opportunity to discuss their work at the 2009 Western Literature Association Conference before an audience of brilliant, idiosyncratic Western scholars. My gratitude goes also to my husband Greg and our sons, Seth and Ian, for their unfailing support and for never once complaining about missed family outings, late night hours in front of the computer, or piles of papers arranged in unusual places. Special thanks as well to series editor Sarah Graham for her unflappable calm and absolute belief in this project in the face of tragicomic setbacks and obstacles.

Introduction

Sara L. Spurgeon

One of the most controversial and important American writers of the last 100 years, Cormac McCarthy has inspired extravagant (and often extreme) critical and popular responses. In *How to Read and Why* (2000) Harold Bloom judges McCarthy's fifth novel, *Blood Meridian, or The Evening Redness in the West* (1985), to be an epic worthy of Homer, William Shakespeare, and Herman Melville, declaring in a 2000 interview that "there is no greater work by a living American" (7). He deems *Blood Meridian* a masterpiece "not to be surpassed," even by McCarthy himself.

While this would be fine praise for any writer, alone it would not lift McCarthy into the ranks of those authors with whom he is most frequently compared. These literary antecedents commonly include Shakespeare, with whom McCarthy shares a love for the audacious use of language and often elevated, archaic diction; Herman Melville, for McCarthy's idiosyncratic narrators, epic vision, and powerful evocations of a terrifying but beautiful natural world; and Nobel Prize winner William Faulkner, for common roots in the Southern Gothic, a genre known for its fidelity to region, violence, and exaggerated, often grotesque, characters. The comparisons to Faulkner may be especially apt. Like this earlier practitioner of American High Modernism, McCarthy is also fond of complex, 100-word sentences (at least in his early fiction) and manifests a fascination with the roles of race, gender, and violence in shaping American history. What may lift McCarthy into these exalted literary ranks, however, is not simply that in 1985 he wrote a novel "not to be surpassed," but that in 2006, according to many critics, he surpassed it, with the Pulitzer Prize winner, *The Road*. Perhaps most astonishingly, he did so in a prose style strikingly different from that he had employed in *Blood Meridian* 20 years earlier.

South by Southwest: From Southern Gothic to Post-Western Apocalypse

The extraordinary evolution of McCarthy's work will be the focus of this introduction, and three of his most important post-1990 novels, *All the Pretty Horses* (1992), *No Country for Old Men* (2005), and *The Road* (2006), the focus of the following chapters. These three texts were chosen for their literary value, diversity of styles, the growing body of critical work engaging them, and their genre-crossing characteristics. Indeed, debates about placing McCarthy's fiction into genres have engaged critics since the beginning of his career. To hint at the difficulty of this task, consider that *All the Pretty Horses* is typically labeled a Western but has also been called an anti-Western, a post-Western, and a romance; *No Country for Old Men* has been labeled urban Western, detective fiction, hard-boiled, noir, and even horror; while *The Road* is referred to as post-apocalyptic, post-nuclear, environmental fiction, as well as futuristic sci-fi, while Oprah famously called it "a love story" (Winfrey). One contributor to this volume even challenges its classification as a novel (Phillips). And importantly, in light of McCarthy's frequent practice of writing his novels first as screenplays, all three books considered here have been adapted for film.

McCarthy's ability to continually move in new stylistic and thematic directions in his work, now covering nearly fifty years of published fiction, may be one of his most distinctly American characteristics. As John Cant notes, "McCarthy is quintessentially American in two ways. He is an individualist on a heroic scale and he believes in the possibility of moving on to reinvent the self" (21). While F. Scott Fitzgerald is famously rumored to have written, "there are no second acts in American lives," McCarthy has arguably had at least three literary lives, all wildly successful in their own ways. In addition to jumping genres and prose styles, his unerring sense of place spins up locations that ring utterly true, from the Appalachian mountains of the American South and the deserts of the American Southwest, to the small towns of nineteenth-century Mexico and Tennessee. He moves easily from rural to urban spaces, with his depiction of the urban slums of mid-twentieth century Knoxville, Tennessee and its urban river, often compared to James Joyce's evocation of Dublin, while both *The Crossing* and *No Country for Old Men* present compelling visions of crowded modern cities on both sides of the US-Mexico border.

These peripatetic movements across space and time (*Blood Meridian* is set in the 1840s, *No Country for Old Men* in 1980, and *The Road* in some close, but unspecified future) have presented a challenge to scholars seeking to organize or impose structure on McCarthy's large body of work. Despite his frequent literary reinventions, there are common themes and narrative strategies uniting his novels. One characteristic frequently noted by readers and critics is the level of violence. Some assume this indicates that McCarthy holds a nihilistic worldview, while others suggest it is a vehicle through which McCarthy examines metaphysical questions about the capacity for good and evil in human nature and the place of humanity in what appears to be an uncaring universe. While violence is an intrinsic part of all the genres he has worked in (or subverted) thus far, McCarthy's violence does seem to be of a different order. In one of the first scholarly collections of essays on McCarthy, editors Wade Hall and Rich Wallach choose the term "sacred violence" as a descriptor of McCarthy's vision and the title of their Reader's Guide. Many critics have noted the disturbingly beautiful language used in McCarthy's detailed descriptions of torture, scalping, and murder, while others have commented on the objective, almost disinterested voice of the narrator describing the action (McCarthy rarely provides glimpses of his characters' internal monologues). A few have found this use of violence gratuitous or sensationalizing, but McCarthy has responded that "there is no such thing as life without bloodshed" (Woodward, *New York Times*, 29), and scholars admit the violence he describes so vividly is generally historically accurate.

Some readers suggest that it is the very accuracy of McCarthy's obsessive historical research that makes the violence in his work so unsettling, but this is reflective of another theme that runs through McCarthy's oeuvre, the legacy of an American history cut through with racism, slavery, invasion, conquest, the exploitation of poor and working-class people, and the attempted genocide of Native Americans in the United States and Mexico. McCarthy's work can appear reminiscent of Faulkner's comment that "The past is never dead. It's not even past" (Faulkner, *Requiem*, 1.2). In McCarthy's novels, the past and the myths we tell about it shape not only relations between whites, African Americans, Native Americans, Mexicans and Mexican-Americans, but also the ideas we hold about gender, especially masculinity, and how those ideas influence the way humans relate to a non-human world. Indeed, in a body of work fraught with rape, incest, and cannibalism, some readers find McCarthy's depictions of human violence against animals the most horrifying.

This array of literary themes is developed by McCarthy through an equally impressive diversity of narrative strategies. In addition to Shakespearean language, Faulknerian sentence structures, and memorably ambiguous opening and closing scenes, McCarthy is well known for his refusal to utilize commas, quotation marks, apostrophes, and other forms of standard punctuation, claiming that good writing doesn't need such unnecessary distractions (Winfrey). Well written dialogue (for which he is almost universally praised) should make it obvious, McCarthy argues, who is speaking. His ear for regional dialects is so keen, some linguists claim they can identify whether a character is from the eastern or western Appalachians based solely on the character's speech patterns.

McCarthy's work also shows the strong influence of film as a narrative form. His novels are laced with an intertextuality that references both the scene structure and visual quality of film (where, generally lacking an omniscient narrator, we must infer a character's inner thoughts from his or her actions, as is the case in nearly all of McCarthy's published work), with nods to various directors and famous scenes, as well as numerous novelists and their works. When asked about the influence of other writers on his own prose, McCarthy responded, "The ugly fact is books are made out of books. The novel depends for its life on the novels that have been written." (Woodward, *New York Times*, 30).

Scholars have found that the books and authors that underpin McCarthy's writing have changed over the course of his career, reflecting the differing genres, regions, and histories he engages. Madison Smartt Bell suggests McCarthy's work be thought of in phases that include what he terms the Appalachian works, *Blood Meridian* (which he feels stands apart from McCarthy's other novels), and the Border Trilogy—*All the Pretty Horses* (1992), *The Crossing* (1994), and *Cities of the Plain* (1998). I would like to refine, update and expand on those divisions, and offer a larger format for thinking about McCarthy's oeuvre and his place in North American fiction.

"I wasn't going to be a respectable citizen": McCarthy's Early Life and Work

There was no indication in his early life that McCarthy would ever have an oeuvre. He was neither a reader nor a writer before his early 20s, and he claims to have hated school from the first day he set foot in one as a child (Woodward, *New York Times*, 29). Born in 1933 in Rhode Island, his family moved to Tennessee in 1937, where his father Charles (for whom he was named, Cormac being Irish for "son of Charles") worked as an attorney representing the Tennessee Valley Authority. The TVA is the government agency that built most of the major dam projects in the state, many of which remain controversial today due to the thousands of rural poor (the very people who would come to populate McCarthy's early fiction) forced from their homes to make way for the dams, as well as the nearly immeasurable environmental destruction they created in the name of energy production and flood control. The presence of a potent landscape which becomes as vital to the story as its human characters is apparent in nearly all of McCarthy's work, and the death of nature itself is the controlling reality of *The Road*. The fact that McCarthy's father provided legal defence for the TVA's dam-building no doubt laid at least some of the groundwork, as Cant and others have argued, for the fraught father-son relationships that underlie most of McCarthy's fiction until *No Country for Old Men* in 2005 and *The Road* in 2006.

Despite his claim that "I was not what [my parents] had in mind. I felt early on I wasn't going to be a respectable citizen" (Woodward, *New York Times*, 30), McCarthy graduated from Catholic high school in Knoxville in 1951 and enrolled at the University of Tennessee's Knoxville campus, although he dropped out to join the Air Force in 1953. He was posted to a remote station in Alaska where, among other things, he hosted an Armed Forces radio program and, he says out of sheer boredom, began reading seriously for the first time, mainly in the barracks. When he left the Air Force four years later he re-enrolled at the University of Tennessee, majoring in Engineering, but dropped out again without graduating. He did manage to publish two short stories, "Wake for Susan" (1959) and "A Drowning Incident" (1960) in the university magazine *The Phoenix*, and married fellow student and poet, Lee Holleman, in 1961. Their son Cullen, McCarthy's first child, was born in 1962, in the midst of moves between Knoxville, New Orleans, and Chicago where McCarthy worked in an auto parts warehouse and completed his first published novel, *The Orchard Keeper* (1965). (He had begun writing *Suttree* in 1959, but wouldn't finish it for nearly two decades. He is known to take many years to complete manuscripts, often working on two or three books at once.) McCarthy and Holleman divorced in 1964 and that same year McCarthy, who had no agent, famously sent the unsolicited manuscript for *The Orchard Keeper* to the only publishing firm he'd heard of, where it was picked up by Random House's legendary editor, Albert Erskine, champion of William Faulkner and Ralph Ellison. This novel foreshadows rhetorical approaches and characteristics that become hallmarks of McCarthy's future work: generally poorly educated, working class characters presented without romanticization or condescension; the evocation of a vanishing, often rural way of life; the bookending of the text with obscure but related opening and closing scenes; the absence of quotation marks, commas and other standard punctuation and grammatical markers; pitch perfect dialect; and a complex series of father-son relationships overshadowed by violence. While Erskine would edit McCarthy's work for the next 20 years until his retirement from Random House, he would also admit "we never sold any of his books" (Woodward, *New York Times*, 30), leaving McCarthy perpetually short of cash. In fact McCarthy's first four books, the Southern or Appalachian novels—*The Orchard Keeper* (1965), *Outer Dark* (1968), *Child of God* (1973), and *Suttree* (1979)— would all be critically well received and popularly ignored. None sold more than 3,000 hardcover copies (Woodward, *Vanity Fair*, 104). McCarthy was unperturbed, and consistently turned down lucrative offers from universities to teach or speak about his writing.

Instead, following the publication of *The Orchard Keeper*, McCarthy cobbled together funds from odd jobs and various literary awards and sailed to Europe in 1966, ostensibly to research his family's Irish roots (the original Cormac McCarthy, an Irish chieftain, is believed to have built Blarney Castle). The first night onboard ship he met a young British singer and dancer hired to entertain passengers. After a whirlwind romance during which the couple lived in an artists' colony on the Spanish island of Ibiza, he and Anne DeLisle were married in England. While in Europe, McCarthy finished his second novel, *Outer Dark* (1968). Set in an indeterminate time, perhaps the early twentieth century, somewhere in the rural South, this allegorical text follows the desperate search of a young woman for her baby, delivered by her brother who is also the baby's father and then abandoned by him in the woods where it is picked up by an itinerant tinker. It establishes another McCarthy hallmark—the haunting, ambiguous ending. In the final chapter of *Outer Dark*, Rinthy is desperately looking for her baby when she stumbles into the forest clearing and comes across the bones. She, unlike the audience who have witnessed the murder, does not understand what she sees. Terri Witek argues

> in a culmination of the book's plot and structure, the resolution has been reached and then shown to be no resolution at all. The child has been transformed into something elusive and oddly beautiful: the delicate 'calcined ribcage' is somehow not, in the end, Rinthy's baby. The connections . . . are here provided by the plot only to be overthrown, and what we are left with is the poignant sense that all human connections to a world of form, even the most basic, are illusory. (83)

Many of McCarthy's works will echo this bittersweet, futile longing for connections between characters and their often lost families, and between characters and their often lost homes and communities. *Outer Dark*, while generally well-reviewed, like McCarthy's first novel, did not sell well. McCarthy and DeLisle returned to the Knoxville area, living hand-to-mouth in a semi-converted barn, bathing in the nearby lake, and eating beans for dinner each night. McCarthy continued to refuse all offers to speak about or teach writing. Asked by journalist Richard Woodward in 1992 if he ever paid alimony, "McCarthy snorts. 'With what?' He recalls his expulsion from a $40-a-month room in the French Quarter [in New Orleans] for nonpayment of rent." (Woodward, *New York Times*, 31).

Act I: The Southern/Appalachian Novels

Throughout McCarthy's first act, the years of the Southern novels, he built a growing reputation as a "writer's writer," a darkly brilliant novelist, producing works of Southern Gothic in the tradition of Faulkner and Flannery O'Connor. He was also becoming a literary recluse, refusing requests for interviews, readings, book signings, or promotional tours, although Woodward observes that "For such an obstinate loner, McCarthy is an engaging figure, a world-class talker, funny, opinionated, quick to laugh" (*New York Times*, 29). To date, McCarthy has made one public appearance and granted only two interviews since publishing his first novel in 1965—both interviews with critic Richard Woodward—and an appearance on The Oprah Winfrey show in 2007 after she named *The Road* as a pick for the Oprah Book Club. He refuses to attend award ceremonies, sending his agent to the National Book Awards to pick up his prize for *All the Pretty Horses* and an editor from the publisher Knopf to accept his Pulitzer Prize for *The Road*. Madison Smartt Bell notes that in the first half of his career, McCarthy "shunned publicity so effectively he wasn't even famous for it" (9). He did have a small but fervent following, however, mainly among readers and scholars of Southern fiction.

Not all critics, however, praised these early works. McCarthy was awarded a Guggenheim Fellowship in 1969 which he used to support himself as he finished his third novel, *Child of God* (1973), about which critic Richard Brickner wrote "[T]he carefully cold, sour diction of this book—whose hostility toward the reader surpasses even that of the world toward Lester [the necrophiliac serial killer who is the title character]—does not often let us see beyond its nasty 'writing' . . ." (6). While not among McCarthy's most important works, this novel is, despite Brickner's condemnation, generally considered a small, albeit harrowing, gem of a book. Like many of McCarthy's novels, it is a meticulously researched narrative, evocative of the changing world of the rural American South in the mid-twentieth century. It is loosely based on the life of an actual serial killer, the character called by

McCarthy's narrator, a child of god. (In an interesting example of McCarthy's sly sense of humor and love of word play, James Blevins is the name of the man charged with the real life crimes similar to those McCarthy attributes to his character Lester Ballard. Later, in *All the Pretty Horses*, a teenage runaway and possible horsethief, and a popular radio evangelist will both be called Jimmy Blevins.)

In 1976, McCarthy separated from Anne DeLisle (they later divorced), and at the age of 43 abruptly moved to El Paso, Texas, bringing with him his clothing, books (he estimates he owns nearly seven thousand, mainly kept in storage lockers), and the half-finished manuscript for his fourth, and to date most autobiographical, work *Suttree* (1979), the last of the Southern novels. Commonly considered McCarthy's funniest book, *Suttree* ends with its eponymous hero leaving Knoxville to move west, and in retrospect may be read as McCarthy's farewell to the South, the end of his first act. Based in part on the strength of this work, considered by many the strongest of the Southern novels—a masterpiece in its own right, sometimes compared to James Joyce's *Ulysses*—McCarthy was awarded a $250,000 MacArthur Fellowship (the so-called "genius" grant) in 1981. He bought a tiny stone house behind a shopping mall in El Paso in 1982, and used the funds from the MacArthur Fellowship to finance the five years of astounding research that went into the transitional novel of his second act, *Blood Meridian* (1985).

Act II: Southwestern Gothic

Set in the phantasmagorically violent regions on both sides of the US-Mexico border in the mid-1800's and based on historical events, *Blood Meridian* follows the short, violent life of a nameless character known as the kid as he joins first a band of American filibusters attempting to provoke war with Mexico, then a band of American scalphunters hired by the governor of the Mexican state of Chihuahua to scalp Apache men, women, and children for money and who go about their bloody work with such feral glee they eventually cease to demand payment for it at all. McCarthy says he read over three hundred books in preparation for writing *Blood Meridian*, learned Mexican-inflected Spanish in order to write the dialogue, and traveled personally to every location chronicled in this sprawling frontier text that moves from Tennessee to New Orleans to Texas then south into Mexico, north again to Tucson, Arizona and San Diego, California before closing with the horrific death of the main character in an orgy of blood and filth in the jakes behind a tavern in Fort Griffin, Texas, famous in the 1870s mainly for its large number of prostitutes and murders.

Harold Bloom proclaimed *Blood Meridian* "the authentic American apocalyptic novel, . . . a canonical imaginative achievement, both an American and a universal tragedy of blood" (*Modern Critical Views*, 1). Nevertheless, this book, like McCarthy's previous novels, sold poorly. It did, however, expand his profile among scholars. Many, though not all, critics agreed (at least until *The Road*) that this novel was McCarthy's finest achievement, the mature work of an author at the height of his creative powers. Some read it as the Southern Gothic moved West, with the hallucinatory, allegorical violence of Faulkner or O'Connor viciously wedded to the classic Western with more than a little Melville and Joseph Conrad thrown in for good measure. But *Blood Meridian* stands more fully with the Border Trilogy, which follows it, than with the previous four Appalachian books.

While much criticism has categorized McCarthy's work into the Southern, or Appalachian novels, and the Southwestern novels, in part because of the geographic neatness of such a division, what truly makes the Southwestern works distinct from the Southern fiction is something more than geography or setting. It is a reinvention of McCarthy's prose, his focus, and his scope. There are still recognizable elements from the Southern novels (the sensuous, almost erotic joy in language, a keen ear for dialog and dialect, an allegorical feel, and the ever-present violence), but *Blood Meridian* and the Border Trilogy, McCarthy's second act, are at the same time entirely new. All four works are embedded in a complex history far more fully realized than the history underlying the Southern novels, and it is in point of fact a different history of a different place, demanding a different kind of book. One of the roles of the Southern Gothic is to critique the hypocrisy of post-Civil War white Southern culture with its glorification of personal honor, the supposed purity of white bloodlines, chivalry toward (upper-class white) women, and a fondly imagined connection to the aristocracies of Europe, through a carnivalesque revelation of the racism, misogyny, and class violence that underlies it, even as some critics argue the genre some-times subtly reinforces the very cultural structures it criticizes. While McCarthy's Southern novels are seen by many scholars as fulfilling the promise of Faulkner by bringing the Southern Gothic fully into the late twentieth century, the Southwestern novels do not perform the same function for the genre of the Western, which has not historically offered any sustained critique of westward expansion or white settler culture. It may be said that McCarthy's Southwestern novels do the opposite, overturning and undermining the Western, subverting it from within. Rather than glorifying the project of Manifest Destiny—the assumption that an Anglo-American conquest of North America was divinely ordained and racially inevitable—as many traditional Westerns do,

McCarthy's Southwestern novels strip away such ideological dressing, forcing readers to confront the racism, greed, and brutal violence that fueled westward expansion and which lie just beneath the surface of the contemporary American West. Some critics suggest this creates a new genre, a Western or Southwestern Gothic which, like the Southern Gothic, works to expose the bloody but often hidden historical under-pinnings of American culture. And as with some critics of the Southern Gothic, there are scholars who feel McCarthy actually offers a romanti-cized defense of Western icons such as the cowboy rather than a mean-ingful critique of them, especially in *All the Pretty Horses*, which most closely resembles the typical Western.

In the case of *Blood Meridian*, however, a majority of scholars interpret the text as a scathing indictment of Manifest Destiny as an ideology (one that, in its insistence on an American duty to expand democracy, some argue still influences US foreign policy). McCarthy's novel examines Manifest Destiny as an expression of racialized nationalism, and exposes its impact on the nations, peoples, and natural environment on both sides of the US-Mexico border region. Bloom notes this makes *Blood Meridian* and by extension the Border Trilogy both "American and . . . universal." The Southwestern novels are at once intensely local in their descriptions of landscape, languages, dialects, and historical incidents, and almost anti-regional in the scope of their vision. These are books with an even longer historical gaze than the Southern novels. It is no accident that *Blood Meridian* opens with a quotation about a 300,000 year old fossil skull from Ethiopia that shows signs of having been scalped, or that *All the Pretty Horses* begins with the young protagonist riding across his Texas ranch among the ghosts of the Native Americans his ancestors murdered in order to possess that land.

The publication of *Blood Meridian*, however, does more than simply mark McCarthy's move from a first act into a second. It also marks his move from a talented but obscure regional novelist into a legitimate subject for scholarly criticism, although still associated with the American South. In 1988, respected Southern literary scholar Vereen Bell produced the first book-length study of McCarthy's oeuvre, *The Achievement of Cormac McCarthy*, covering all the novels published to that date. Even so, McCarthy remained a darling of scholars and a few hardcore fans, but relatively unknown to the general reading public on both sides of the Atlantic. This would change dramatically with the publication in 1992 of the first novel of the Border Trilogy, *All the Pretty Horses*, which sold widely in the United States and the United Kingdom, winding up on the *New York Times Bestsellers* list and winning the prestigious US literary prize, the National Book Award.

The Border Trilogy

All the Pretty Horses illustrates a change in McCarthy's style nearly as drastic as that between *Blood Meridian* and the Southern novels, one reason it is the first of the novels to be considered in this collection. Three-quarters of the action of this book takes place in Mexico, long stretches of dialogue are rendered in un-translated Spanish, and the impact of Spanish language writers such as Octavio Paz, Pablo Neruda, and Cervantes is at least as strong as that of Melville or Faulkner. Other than the three young Texans, one of whom is absent for long stretches before being killed halfway through, nearly all the major characters in the novel are Mexican, forcefully reminding readers that the march of history across North America as often moved on a north-south axis as on an east-west one. The implicating of the United States in the troubled social and political history of Mexico is directly explained in the Dueña Alfonsa's monologue, but it is implied earlier in the novel in McCarthy's description of the two young Americans preparing to cross illegally into Mexico, who "rode at once jaunty and circumspect, like thieves newly loosed in that dark electric, like young thieves in a glowing orchard, loosely jacketed against the cold and ten thousand worlds for the choosing" (30). In addition, as Cant notes, this book

> reflects a change in the mood and atmosphere of [McCarthy's] work . . . The prose is sparer and more economical than before. There are few of the complex 'run on' sentences and lengthy rhetorical passages of the kind that occur in *Suttree* or *Blood Meridian*. (193)

Often called McCarthy's most accessible work, *All the Pretty Horses* is the first to include an entirely likeable main character and a conventional, albeit doomed love story, one reason, many critics speculate, it was also his first best-seller. In addition, *All the Pretty Horses* is the first of McCarthy's novels to be adapted by Hollywood (the film was released by Miramax in 2000, directed by Billy Bob Thornton, starring Matt Damon and Penelope Cruz).

The impact of film in shaping the vision of the author begins to emerge most strongly in the Southwestern works. Although McCarthy wrote a screenplay for PBS called *The Gardener's Son* that was produced in 1976 and aired in 1977 as part of the PBS series *Visions*, as well as three dramas, *The Stonemason* (written in the late 1980s and published by Ecco Press in 1994), *The Sunset Limited* (staged in Chicago then New York in 2006), and the unpublished *Whales and Men* (this manuscript is with McCarthy's papers in the Wittliff Collection at Texas State University in San Marcos), the *cinematic* nature of his imagery first becomes apparent in *Blood Meridian*. In the now famous "death hilarious" scene, the band of American filibusters who have ridden into Mexico in order to provoke war between the two countries are surprised at dawn by a group of mounted Apache riding across a dry lakebed, the remains of an extinct inland sea. As the riders gallop toward them out of the rising sun, McCarthy uses the common desert phenomenon of a mirage distorted by shimmering heat waves to create an almost hallucinatory image tailor-made for the big screen:

> they rode out of that vanished sea like burnt phantoms with the legs of the animals kicking up the spume that was not real . . . And there began to appear above them in the dawnbroached sky a hellish likeness of their ranks riding huge and inverted . . . the howling antiwarriors pendant from their mounts immense and chimeric. (109)

Director Ridley Scott attempted an adaptation of *Blood Meridian*, but ultimately gave up on the project, telling *Eclipse Magazine* in a 2008 interview, "We got it down as a screenplay and the problem is that it is so savage." Scott may be right, and there is some talk that the level of horror is so great, the violence so brutal, and some characters like the judge so grotesque (although the character is based on an actual person) the book is essentially unfilmable. The novels of the Border Trilogy, even more than the hallucinatory *Blood Meridian*, seem especially conducive to filmic adaptation, despite the generally negative reviews Billy Bob Thornton's version of *All the Pretty Horses* received. In fact, some reviewers suggest Thornton's utter devotion to the novel, resulting in a director's cut rumored to be nearly 4 hours long, contributed to the problems critics identified with the halved version of the film released in theaters. Although all the novels of the Border Trilogy were initially imagined as a single screenplay, originally entitled *Cities of the Plain*, there are some important differences in these works. *The Crossing*, the second novel of the trilogy, is darker and more metaphysical in its inquiries into the nature of identity and culture than *All the Pretty Horses*. Its evocation of the natural world, especially the wolf who dominates the first half of the narrative, is immensely powerful and indicative of the ecocritical concerns which would be fully realized in *The Road*, and the presence of Mexico is even more dominating, closely intertwined with life north of the border. As with *All the Pretty Horses*, much of the action in *The Crossing* takes place in Mexico, just prior to the start of World War II. The protagonists, brothers Billy and Boyd, are raised by their English-speaking American parents and their Spanish-speaking Mexican grandmother on a small ranch in southern New Mexico near the border. The novel opens with the child Billy on horseback carrying his infant brother Boyd in his arms and naming for him "the features of the landscape and birds and animals in both spanish and english" with Mexico symbolically visible in the distance (1). This novel also furthers McCarthy's project in his second act of expanding his narrative reach beyond regionalism, the US-Mexico border country, or even North America, as *The Crossing* ends with the still wandering and now homeless Billy witnessing the terrifying false dawn of the world's first atomic bomb test (at Trinity Site near Alamogordo, New Mexico) on July 16, 1945. In this novel, concludes Cant (who considers *The Crossing*, not *Blood Meridian* or *The Road*, McCarthy's finest work to date), McCarthy "most clearly extends his cultural critique beyond the confines of the New World, to challenge the West as a whole" (202).

The protagonists of the first two texts of the Border Trilogy, John Grady and Billy, are brought together in the Trilogy's final novel, *Cities of the Plain*. While the book which follows it, *No Country for Old Men* (2005), is also set in the south Texas/Mexico border country, I argue *Cities of the Plain* is not only the concluding volume of the Border Trilogy but also of McCarthy's second act. The author's prose style in *Cities of the Plain* has evolved yet again, becoming even more spare, the dialog more eloquent and making up a larger proportion of the text. Almost absent here are the strings of linked independent clauses, the rhythmic run-on sentences, and the elaborate, archaic vocabulary of *Blood Meridian* or the Southern novels. As the title suggests, much of the action takes place in urban spaces on both sides of the international border dividing the twin cities of El Paso, Texas and Juárez, Chihuahua. There is a strongly elegiac quality to this novel. In 1952 small farms and ranches across the American Southwest are failing, overrun by oil drilling, massive agribusiness concerns or, in the case of the ranch where Billy and John Grady are employed, sought by the US government as sites for atomic weapon testing. The result is that working cowboys like Billy and John Grady are becoming obsolete, their formidable skills outdated and largely useless in the shadow of nuclear Cold War technology. While all of McCarthy's novels are woven through with multilayered intertextuality evoking, as many critics have noted, everything from Shakespeare to the Bible to William Butler Yeats, this book is especially cinematic in its intertextuality, engaging John Ford as much as John Milton, and imbued with Ford's signature nostalgia for a vanishing way of life. The sense of finality in this volume is made plain in the dedication which appears on the last page: "I will be your child to hold/And you be me when I am old/The world grows cold/The heathen rage/The story's told/Turn the page." (293).

In 1998, the same year *Cities of the Plain* was published, McCarthy, then 65 years old, married for the third time, to Jennifer Winkley, who gave birth to McCarthy's second child, John Francis, in 1999. The couple bought a home near Tesuque, New Mexico, a small enclave on the outskirts of Santa Fe where McCarthy currently keeps an office as author-in-residence (a post apparently created for him) at the prestigious multidisciplinary science think-tank The Santa Fe Institute. His long history of shunning the literary world extends to other writers, and McCarthy seems to prefer the company of scientists and researchers. The one exception was his long friendship with nature writer and novelist Edward Abbey, most well known for his memoir *Desert Solitaire: A Season in the Wilderness* (1968) and the eco-sabotage novel *The Monkey Wrench Gang* (1975). Born in the Appalachian region of Pennsylvania in 1927, Abbey also moved to the Southwest as an adult and did his finest writing there until his death at his home in Tucson, Arizona in 1989. Interestingly, Abbey wrote a novel, *Fire on the Mountain* (1962) based on the life of New Mexico rancher John Prather (named Jon Vogelin in the book) who fought the US government's attempt to confiscate his ranch as part of the White Sands Missile Range, as well as a post-apocalyptic novel, *Good News* (1980), following a small band of survivors struggling to maintain their integrity in the ruins of what was once Phoenix, Arizona. Abbey, like McCarthy, has sometimes been called a man's writer, concerned with celebrating or (less often in Abbey's case) critiquing masculinity, creating mainly male characters who engage in mainly masculine activities, often far from domestic or feminine spaces. Both men are sometimes presumed to appeal to a mainly male readership, although other critics, including two in this volume, Linda Woodson and Stacey Peebles, challenge that assumption. While Abbey and McCarthy share little in common stylistically, their general distrust of authority (Abbey openly proclaimed himself an anarchist and provided the inspiration for the founding of the radical environmental group EarthFirst! and its UK branch, Earth Liberation Front, or ELF) and almost religious reverence for the natural world seemed to provide a powerful bond. Shortly before Abbey's death, the two men concocted (although reportedly never acted on) a plan to secretly reintroduce Mexican Grey Wolves into their former range in the American Southwest (Woodward, *New York Times,* 31). The last survivor of this subspecies in New Mexico is trapped by Billy in *The Crossing*.

Act III: Moving into New Country

Many critics assumed that *Cities of the Plain* would be McCarthy's final novel and that the writer would settle into retirement resting on his impressive literary laurels, so there was a fair amount of surprise, and some consternation, when *No Country for Old Men* appeared in 2005. The consternation came from critics who consider this book weaker than the previous eight, although other critics vehemently defend it. Kenneth Lincoln writes, "The whole is a spare, clean, objective rendering of unwilled pain and willed endurance, minimalist figures against a staggering backdrop of space and eternity where the chase is seen from above and afar, sniper-fashion" (142). Like the novels of the Border Trilogy, *No Country for Old Men* was originally conceived as a screenplay (the Coen brothers' 2007 adaptation won four Academy Awards, two Golden Globes, and three British Academy of Film Awards), but the similarities to the Border Trilogy end there. This text moves McCarthy from his second act to his third. Indeed, the unorthodox structure of this work and its surprising textual features may be part of what flummoxed literary critics and reviewers accustomed to the prose and stylistic character of the Border Trilogy, as Lincoln's description of the vision of the novel as both minimalist and sniper-fashioned suggests. Was it or was it not, many wondered, a Western? Did it not seem to more closely resemble the related genres of the crime novel, detective fiction, or film noir? Where was the evocation of a past or passing way of life, either Appalachian or Southwestern? *No Country for Old Men* felt disturbingly contemporary with its Mexican cartels, drug deals, and its Vietnam veteran main character, Llewelyn Moss. Or is the main character actually Sheriff Ed Tom Bell whose lengthy interior monologues (also a first for McCarthy) dominate the italicized alternating chapters?

Cant argues that *No Country for Old Men* "is a crime novel; its cars, automatic weapons, motel rooms, corporate offices and city locations are the province of the genre developed by Chandler, Hammett, Cain, Ellroy . . ." (240). (In his chapter later in this collections, Jay Ellis will counter that such a resemblance is only superficial and that the novel is more properly a philosophical meditation.) He also points out, however, that the Oedipal conflict at the heart of nearly all McCarthy's previous works, with their absent and/or violent fathers and the sons who fight and flee them, virtually disappears in *No Country for Old Men* and is entirely reversed in the novel that follows it, *The Road*. Llewelyn Moss has no apparent conflict with his father, and while Sheriff Ed Tom Bell struggles to live up to the memory of his, Bell is a father himself, still grieving over the daughter who died in childhood and to whom he now speaks in the privacy of his thoughts set down in the long italicized sections of the novel. Cant suggests this is due in part to McCarthy finally coming to grips with the overpowering legacy of his literary forefathers (what Bloom calls "the anxiety of influence"), as well as his own second chance at actual fatherhood.

McCarthy's second fatherhood seems to play a major role in the shaping of his tenth novel, *The Road* (2006), his only work thus far to be greeted with almost universal enthusiasm, both in the United States and the United Kingdom. In addition to winning the Pulitzer Prize for fiction in 2007, the novel was awarded one of the UK's most respected literary honors, the James Tait Black Memorial Prize for fiction. Despite the fact that its setting is somewhere in the American South (most critics think the Appalachian region near Knoxville and points southeast along the Atlantic coast) rather than the Southwest or the US-Mexico border region, I argue that *The Road* should be classified with *No Country for Old Men* as part of McCarthy's third act because of several important rhetorical and stylistic characteristics. These characteristics separate it from the Southern novels and from *Blood Meridian* and the Border Trilogy while pointing it in the new direction McCarthy began to explore in *No Country for Old Men*. The prose in *The Road*, as some critics have pointed out, does resonate strongly with earlier works like *Suttree* and *Blood Meridian* in its fiercely creative use of language, although it feels quite different stylistically, spare, deceptively simple, and at times almost monosyllabic. The settings alternate from lifeless farmlands to dead forests to burnt cities where

> the soft black talc blew through the streets like squid ink uncoiling along a sea floor . . . and the scavengers passing down the steep canyons with their torches trod silky holes in the drifted ash that closed behind them silently as eyes. (152–53)

Unlike the relentlessly fast pace of *No Country for Old Men*, however, *The Road*, which has no chapter breaks, moves like its characters— slowly and deliberately, earthbound, irrevocably tied to an utterly burnt and devastated landscape. Some reviewers also label this novel minimalist, rhetorically as different as possible from the exuberant Faulknerian excess of McCarthy's Southern works or *Blood Meridian*, although as Lincoln's description of *No Country for Old Men* suggests, this is a turn McCarthy's prose had already begun to make.

The strongly allegorical atmosphere of *The Road*, with neither the father nor the son identified by name, evokes, at least on the surface, the nameless kid of *Blood Meridian*. At a deeper level however, the son in *The Road* may be seen as the antithesis of Suttree, who rebels against the hypocrisy of his father's wealth and privilege by abandoning his own wife and son, and *Blood Meridian*'s kid, whose only family is the violent, alcoholic father he leaves in order to begin his own life of violence at the age of 14. The son in *The Road*, on the other hand, is nurtured and protected by a loving father, and provides an immovable moral center in a novel deeply concerned with the metaphysical questions of the existence of good, evil, and humanity itself in the cold and dark of an apparently godless universe (although this last can be said to be a central concern in all of McCarthy's work). While the post-catastrophe (the exact nature of the destructive event is left deliberately unspecified) setting of *The Road* might seem to demand a nostalgic look back at a vanished world, this is a novel, quite simply, without nostalgia, although certainly not without sorrow for what has been lost. The ruined cities and the devastated and lifeless landscapes littered with human corpses and the now meaningless artifacts of human cultures seem in emotional tone much closer to the blighted, drug-ridden urban spaces of *No Country for Old Men* than to any of McCarthy's previous works, except perhaps the horrifically violent *Blood Meridian*. This is true despite the fact that Sheriff Ed Tom Bell in *No Country for Old Men* frequently indulges in what the novel suggests is a misplaced nostalgia for a past McCarthy's previous books amply demonstrate was not nearly as rosy as Bell likes to imagine. This nostalgia is at the heart of Bell's humanity and his weakness. The father in *The Road*, however, struggles daily to hold on to his humanity, rejecting nostalgia for the vanished past as dangerously distracting in the unending battle to keep his son alive. The son, who has no memory of (and therefore no nostalgia for) that lost world, nonetheless maintains a purity of moral vision anchored not in a colorful or vanishing lifestyle either Appalachian or Southwestern, but rather in a genuine belief in the potential for human goodness—a startling claim in the face of the frequent accusations of nihilism directed at McCarthy.

The tenderly imagined but unrequited relationship between Bell and his dead daughter in *No Country for Old Men* is brought into full flower in *The Road*, linking these novels through a motif utterly absent in every previous work by McCarthy. Unlike the famous opening line of *Blood Meridian*, which commands readers to "See the child," then explains the child's father "lies in drink" and that in the illiterate child himself "broods already a taste for mindless violence. All history present in the visage, the child the father of the man" (3), *The Road* opens with a scene reminiscent of the one McCarthy describes to Oprah Winfrey as the genesis of the novel, in a hotel room in El Paso when he looked down at his sleeping son then out the window at the desert night and suddenly imagined the surrounding foothills in flames (Winfrey): "When he woke in the woods in the dark and the cold of the night," reads the first line of *The Road* (which is dedicated to John Francis), "he'd reach out to touch the child sleeping beside him . . . His hand rose and fell softly with each precious breath" (3). Winfrey tells McCarthy in his surprise 2007 appearance on her television program that the book seems to her to be "a love story" and asks if it reflects his relationship with his young son, who was at that time approximately the same age as the unnamed boy in the novel. McCarthy, blushing, acknowledges that to be the case. In his interview with Woodward two years earlier, McCarthy wonderingly described John Francis as "the best person I know; far better than I am" (Woodward, *Vanity Fair*, 104).

The central conflict in *The Road* is entirely unrelated to the fate of the father, from whose point of view nearly all of the narrative proceeds. It is made clear early in the novel that the father is dying, and he grows weaker with each passing day. The emotion driving the story is not the father's sorrow at leaving the devastated world (indeed he contemplates suicide many times), rather it is his sorrow at leaving his beloved child, the excruciating, unbearable knowledge that he will be dead before his son (approximately 6–8 years old) is even half grown, leaving the boy utterly alone in a charred world where being gang-raped and eaten by roving bands of cannibals is only one item on a terrifyingly long list of unpleasant ways to die. The parallels to McCarthy's own life are obvious, of course—when McCarthy is 80 years old, John Francis will be 14—but it would be a great disservice both to the book and to McCarthy as a writer to reduce this novel to simply an aging parent's expression of anxiety over the prospect of leaving his child too soon.

The film version of *The Road*, released too late to be fully included in this volume, was directed by John Hillcoat and stars Viggo Mortenson and Kodi Smit-McPhee, with appearances by Robert Duvall and Charlize Theron. Released by 2929 Productions Studio in late 2009 in the United States and 2010 in the United Kingdom, it received generally positive reviews, although some critics noted the difficulty of translating McCarthy's mesmerizing prose to the screen in a novel that lacks the extensive dialog of *All the Pretty Horses* and *No Country for Old Men*. The film takes a more nostalgic tone than McCarthy's book, with a sad, sweet score and an opening scene not in the novel featuring Charlize Theron as the man's wife, napping in an edenic, pre-catastrophe clearing framed by flowers and lush green leaves. Several of the scenes specific to the film are extremely powerful, especially one occurring the morning after the son has asked his father how he can stop thinking about his mother, who had earlier committed suicide rather than risk rape and cannibalism in the ruins of the world. In this scene, while the son still slumbers, Viggo Mortenson as the father drops his wallet, containing a photo of his wife, over the side of a massive gray concrete bridge into the dead black water far below. He then lays his wedding ring on top of the concrete guardrail and we see in close up his battered and dirty hand slowly push the ring to the edge as well. In another harrowing scene intensifying the novel's question about the morality of suicide and mercy killing, the father and son crouch in a room in the old Southern mansion in which they've discovered a cellar full of human captives with multiple amputations who are being slowly eaten by the gang which lives there and whose members have unexpectedly returned. The father, believing they are about to be captured, presses a pistol to his son's forehead with a shaking hand while the boy, terrified, pleads "Will I see you? Will I see you again?"

While most critics agree the film is generally successful, both as a film and as an adaptation of the novel to which it is mainly faithful, there are some puzzling filmic choices. Oddest perhaps is the appearance of the family which in the novel randomly discovers the boy just after his father dies, and takes him with them on their own journey. In the film, they are inexplicably shadowing the boy and his father throughout the narrative. The most shocking alteration, however, is quite short in terms of screen time, but does far more to change the vision of the novel than the extended glimpses of the family as they secretly follow the man and his son. This change involves the appearance of two non-human creatures in a world that is, in the novel, wholly devoid of any life save that of the handful of starving and desperate people the pair encounter on the roads. In the film, however, the son opens a discarded snuff box only to be startled when a brightly colored beetle flies out of it then disappears into the clouded grey sky. Later, when the father has died and the family has come forward to show themselves and take the boy in, they introduce him to their bizarrely well-fed pet dog, a species long disappeared from the world of the novel, but about which the boy has dreamed. Arguably, these changes give the film a more hopeful tone than that of the novel which was likely the filmmaker's intention, and yet many critics argue that the steadfast love between the father and son and the son's unshakeable faith in the possibility of human kindness are made all the more poignant in the face of seeming hopelessness.

Although the father-child relationship is one of the major characteristics by which I would classify this book, along with *No Country for Old Men*, as part of McCarthy's third act, it is by no means the most significant aspect of it. *The Road* is increasingly being talked of as one of the most important environmental novels of the last 50 years. Many of McCarthy's previous works are now being reconsidered as environmental texts, and McCarthy's name linked with authors most often classified as nature writers—indeed at least two full-length studies, Georg Guillemin's *The Pastoral Vision of Cormac McCarthy* (2004) and Wallis Sanborn's *Animals in the Fiction of Cormac McCarthy* (2006), specifically engage McCarthy's texts from an ecocritical perspective. While McCarthy has occasionally been compared to Ernest Hemingway, mainly for his focus on masculine characters rather than any real stylistic similarities, an echo of Hemingway's treatment of the natural world reverberates through *The Road*, especially the image of the silent, burned town of Seney, Michigan contrasted with the vibrantly living trout in Hemingway's "Big Two-Hearted River" (1925). Jennifer Egan writes, "In the fictional realm Hemingway defined and epitomized, since visited by writers like Norman Maclean, William Kittredge, and Rick Bass, the natural world acts as a means of sublimating and exorcising men's emotional states" (Egan, 2006).

While shell-shocked and injured World War I veteran, Nick Adams, finds solace in the sight of trout in the clear waters of a Michigan river, McCarthy's evocation of the fish is far more disturbing. The final lines of *The Road* read:

> Once there were brook trout in the streams in the mountains . . . They smelled of moss in your hand. Polished and muscular and torsional. On their backs were vermiculate patterns that were maps of the world in its becoming . . . Of a thing which could not be put back. Not be made right again. In the deep glens where they lived all things were older than man and hummed of mystery. (241)

Opposite to Hemingway's trout, these fish exist only as memories, and whose memory is uncertain. The father in the novel has already died and the son has never seen a trout. Readers can interpret this image, perhaps, as a visceral restating by the narrator of the symbolism embedded in the image of the ruined library the father visits sometime after the un-named disaster has destroyed both nature and human culture. The things to which the now useless books refer, the truths they once invoked so passionately, the human world they created and recorded are, like the vanished trout, both "maps of the world in its becoming" and narratives of a thing "which could not be put back." But in a move typical of his presentation of the natural environment, McCarthy seems to suggest that the passing of the trout is a tragedy beyond that of the human, perhaps beyond human understanding. Unlike the library—the repository of the record of the relatively brief history of humanity on earth—in the place where the trout once lived "all things were older than man and hummed of mystery." Hemingway's Adams is comforted by the continuance of nature in the face of the violence and death he witnessed on the battlefields of Europe and the destruction of the small Michigan town he remembers. For McCarthy, there is no comfort as there is no longer any nature, and perhaps soon, no longer any humans. "The existence of a moral structure—the will to do good," Egan continues,

> is the soaring discovery hidden in McCarthy's scourged planet. He evokes Hemingway's literary vision in order to invert it, first by eliminating the promise that nature can provide a refuge from human destruction . . . and finally by giving us redemption in the form of the love between a parent and a child—their desire to be good although it serves no purpose. (Egan)

McCarthy and Contemporary Scholarship

Although he is still a working writer, reportedly with two new novels currently under contract, McCarthy's position in the North American literary canon is now well established. Following Bell's *The Achievement of Cormac McCarthy* (the first full-length study of McCarthy's work which was, in part, an attempt to argue that he was important enough to warrant a full-length study), other books engaging McCarthy have broadened from early anthologies like Hall and Wallach's *Sacred Violence*, based on selected essays from the first McCarthy Conference in Louisville, Kentucky in 1993, to works which examine McCarthy in more comprehensive ways. Critics are investigating McCarthy's relationship to literary movements such as modernism and postmodernism, his theories of character development, history and the role of myths, his imagination of place and space, his impact on popular film, literary minimalism, environmentalism, even sci-fi and historical fiction. Rather than seeking to place McCarthy as a regional author, either Southern or Southwestern, or as a genre writer (in any of the half dozen or so genres with which he has been associated), the newest scholarship, as exemplified in the following chapters, embeds his texts in larger literary, cultural, and historical matrices. Among the most interesting trends in this volume is the use of class as a category of analysis in chapters that engage McCarthy's work from the positions of post-Marxist, post-capitalist, and globalization studies. How does McCarthy visualize class issues on the supposedly classless frontiers of the American West? What sort of conflicts does he envision when class intersects with rigid or changing gender roles? With nationalism and racism? With American notions of endless amounts of open land, a culture of hyper-consumerism, and the economics of cocaine's production in the third world and consumption in the first? Linda Woodson's reading of the importance of the presence of Mexico and the feminine in *All the Pretty Horses* asks us to consider McCarthy's portrayal of gender, class, and power from the perspective of the country in which most of the novel takes place, while Andrew Husband's explorations of John Grady's struggles with class issues utilizes McCarthy's portrayal of los hombres del país, or the men of the country, to suggest new ways of thinking about modernity and globalization in McCarthy's texts. In Part II, Steven Tatum will follow the trail of a post-capitalist system in modern industrial farming and ranching, narcotics trafficking, and social change in the borderlands in his chapter on *No Country for Old Men*, and Susan Kollin engages contemporary consumer culture as an artifact of history in post-apocalyptic writing in her chapter on *The Road* in Part III.

The emerging fields of ecocritical theory and post-human and animal studies also play a vital role in this volume. Both Kollin and Dana Phillips engage McCarthy's presentation of catastrophic environmental collapse in Part III, Woodson examines the landscapes of Mexico, especially the fertile valley in which the hacienda where John Grady finds work is located, as intensely powerful and feminine landscapes, while Stacey Peelbes argues that John Grady's character as it is portrayed in multiple versions of the screenplay, film, and early drafts of the novel *All the Pretty Horses* is best elucidated not through his relationship with the other human beings in the texts or film, but rather through his relationship to horses.

From Dan Flory's examination of the philosophical underpinnings of evil in both the novel and film version of *No Country for Old Men*, Donovan Gwinner's analysis of the problematics of morality, religion and personal choice in *The Road*, to Dana Phillips' declaration in Part III that *The Road* has slipped the bonds of any and all classificatory systems, the writers in this collection guide our understanding of McCarthy into genuinely new territory.

PART I

All the Pretty Horses *(1991)*

Introduction

Part I of this study consists of three chapters engaging both the novel
and film versions of *All the Pretty Horses*. Chapter 1, Linda Woodson's
"'This is another country': The Complex Feminine Presence in *All the
Pretty Horses*," challenges the assumption that McCarthy's fiction
appeals mainly to male readers, as well as the stereotype that *All the
Pretty Horses* is misogynistic, lacks a feminine presence, or presents
only shallowly developed female characters. To the contrary, Woodson
insists, "the outcome of its action . . . is determined by women." Further,
Woodson argues that critics and readers must look closely at the
historical role of Mexican women during the Mexican Revolution and
in the 1940s, the time in which the novel is set. Doing so, she argues,
"reveals useful amplifications of the women characters and of the
feminine presence within that very real setting . . . and authenticates
the portrayal of the women characters and their motivations."

Stacy Peebles' "Hang and Rattle: John Grady Cole's Horsebreaking
in Typescript, Novel, and Film" focuses specifically on the differing
versions of the novel's main character, John Grady Cole, as he appears
first in McCarthy's unpublished typescript (on which he based all three
of the novels in his Border Trilogy—*All the Pretty Horses*, *The Crossing*
and *Cities of the Plain*), in the novel *All the Pretty Horses* itself, and
finally in the film. Examining the evolution of this character through
the varied presentations of his relationship to horses, Peebles explains
that while "the horsebreaking techniques described in the novel are
similar in principle . . . to 'horse whispering,' or natural horsemanship,"
McCarthy's early drafts of the screenplay (originally entitled *Cities of the*

Plain), "reveal a very different portrait of John Grady as a tough, stubborn kid who approaches both horses and friends with little skill and even less finesse . . . In many ways," she argues, "the film adaptation of *Pretty Horses* resurrects that earlier image of a macho, bronc-busting John Grady, whose approach to horses and to life is to 'hang and rattle' until he gets thrown off." This analysis of varying portrayals of John Grady's character ranging from hyper-masculine bronc-buster to gentle, sensitive horse-whisperer resonates with Woodson's claim that portrayals of the feminine in McCarthy's works are more numerous, unexpected, and subtle than has generally been acknowledged.

Andrew Husbands's post-Marxist examination of John Grady's struggles with issues of class, a vastly ignored subject in most McCarthy criticism, furthers this part's exploration of new ways of looking at what is perhaps McCarthy's most widely-read novel. Utilizing Michael Hardt and Antonio Negri's groundbreaking 2000 tome, *Empire*, Husband argues that far from furthering the myth of a classless cowboy utopia in the American West, McCarthy deliberately probes the role of class in shaping the lives of characters as seemingly similar as John Grady and his best friend Lacy Rawlins, who experience quite different versions of the same events based on their membership in separate socio-economic classes both in Texas and Mexico. In Part II of this volume, Steven Tatum employs a post-Marxist lens in his examination of class and capitalism as the most powerful forces shaping life on the border in the late twentieth century, directing everything from agribusiness to narcotics trafficking. Capitalism and consumer culture drive Susan Kollin's anaylsis of *The Road* in Part III, in which she compares the vision of a desiccated wasteland traversed by the desperate and homeless with John Steinbeck's vision of the Dust Bowl and the Great Depression in *The Grapes of Wrath*.

CHAPTER 1

"This is another country": The Complex Feminine Presence in *All the Pretty Horses*

Linda Woodson

Criticism of Cormac McCarthy's inability to create believable women characters is widespread. In the author's 2007 appearance on the Oprah Winfrey Show, she reminded him that critics have commented on this, to which he replied, "Women are tough," and later, "I find them mysterious." The criticism generally is benign and concerns the lack of development of the female characters, a characteristic that Ann Fisher-Wirth describes positively, "McCarthy's female characters become more interesting the less he attempts to develop them, for their power is poetic, gestural" (127). Nell Sullivan takes a more aggressive stance: "Each novel in the trilogy ultimately excludes the potentially significant female characters as part of a process of the obviation of women" ("Boys" 229).

Because of the genres in which *All the Pretty Horses* is placed as Western, quest literature, and bildũngsroman—forms dominated by male adventurers—the early reception, as Stephen Tatum notes, raised the issue of "whether the novel's appeal is fundamentally limited to certain types of male readers" (77). On the contrary, *All the Pretty Horses* proved to appeal to male and female readers alike, as evidenced by its selection for the National Book Award in 1992 and for the National Book Critics Circle Award in 1993 and its sustained appearance on bestseller lists (79).

Of all of McCarthy's novels, *All the Pretty Horses* has much to recommend a reading of its feminine presence. It remains McCarthy's only novel where the outcome of its action—the expulsion of John Grady Cole from La Purisima, his and Rawlins's release from the prison, and John Grady's return to Texas—is determined by women, Alfonsa and

Alejandra. Even when John Grady accepts responsibility by saying, "And I was the one that brought it about. Nobody but me" (291), the reader is aware that his temperament and character would not likely have accommodated other alternatives were it not for the will of the two women. Unique among the many male teachers who populate McCarthy's fiction, Alfonsa is given a central place in articulating much of the philosophical position of the novel. Her personal narrative and history of the Maderos is given 14 pages, more if Don Héctor's narrative of her life is added to that page count. Perhaps the reason that Alfonsa and Alejandra have been read as vague, symbolic, and poorly developed is that in the context of the genres mentioned above, they have been assessed using predominantly Western European attitudes and expectations. With the exception of a handful of critics, including among others John Wegner and Daniel Cooper Alarcón, few have placed the novel in the context of the history and traditions of Mexico. This omission seems curious given the fact that the ranch is well across the Texas border into Mexico.

As he did in *Blood Meridian*, McCarthy placed *All the Pretty Horses* within a specific locale and incorporated events from the history of Mexico—the story of the Madero brothers—into the novel. These elements are not used prominently enough to turn the novel into historical romance, but they are significant enough not to be ignored. Certainly they contradict readings of the setting as fantastical or exotic. Additionally, the prominent mixture of languages, including Spanish, both colloquial and formal, and English spoken by a Spanish speaker, reminds the reader consistently of the setting in Mexico. In particular, taking a closer look at the historical role of Mexican women during the Revolution and in the late 1940s, and at attitudes toward women as revealed in Mexican culture and literature provides useful amplifications of the women characters and of the feminine presence within that real setting. Such an exploration both amplifies and authenticates McCarthy's portrayal of the women characters and their motivations. It also uncovers a greater feminine presence in the novel than previously recognized. The features of this feminine presence in space, time, and discursive structures are too numerous not to be considered as playing a significant role.

No one has taken this more material approach to understanding Alfonsa and Alejandra as women of Mexico itself, in spite of Alfonsa's warning that "This is another country" (136), a warning that is repeated by other characters such as the captain and Don Héctor. This study will take such an approach to provide a fuller understanding of the two women and consequently to lend their characters authenticity, thus demonstrating McCarthy's greater skill with women characters than is generally acknowledged. Before I turn to that reading, I will survey some of the previous studies and why I think they prevent a fully-developed understanding of the women.

Previous Approaches to Reading the Novel

Dianne C. Luce in " 'When You Wake': John Grady Cole's Heroism in *All the Pretty Horses*" offers one of the earliest readings of the novel as quest. She establishes three motifs: dreaming, wishing, and a childlike sense of entitlement (156), enacted in John Grady's desire to reestablish "his right and proper place in the world" (156) by acquiring Don Héctor's horses, his daughter, and ultimately his ranch. Luce recognizes John Grady's growth "by abandoning his quest for dominance and coura-geously embracing instead a quest for truth and understanding" (155). Alfonsa, in urging him to understand Mexican culture and the con-sequences of his actions toward Alejandra, becomes one of his mentors in his ultimate acceptance of the value of acting upon what is true instead of what one wishes to be true (164). Luce attributes noble motives to Alfonsa in her assertion that Alfonsa is "less interested in control than in responsible choices" (159), but her development of John Grady as hero necessarily places Alfonsa in a subordinate role, as it does Alejandra, who is seen as his equal in her willfulness (158).

Another identification of quest in *All the Pretty Horses* is in *No Place for Home*, building upon an earlier exploration of John Grady's knighthood (Ellis and Palczynski). Ellis, like Luce, identifies Alfonsa's role in warning John Grady concerning the societal constraints that he should be aware of in his relationship with Alejandra (279). While Ellis asserts that Alejandra never has any intention of marrying John Grady (212), he does suggest the strong hold that the figure of the Virgin has in the minds of the Mexican people: "John Grady has stained the Virgin who was Alejandra" (212).

Robert L. Jarrett in *Cormac McCarthy*, who recognizes the romantic elements of "the quest, a cowboy hero, and a nostalgia toward the frontier past" (100), believes that McCarthy's intention in *All the Pretty Horses* is to subvert the Western, creating instead a postmodern quest. Jarrett calls the novel a "border" novel, identifying the similarities between Alfonsa and John Grady as "uncompromising individualists" (111) and "cultural Others" (111), and he sees the motives for Alfonsa's opposition of the love between John Grady and her grandniece as a "self-critique of her own earlier idealism" (113). Ultimately he names three reasons for Alfonsa's actions as having been shaped by her own past: to establish the same constraints that her father had placed upon her earlier relationship with Gustavo, to achieve power over her life's story through controlling that of her niece, and to acquire metaphysical power in general (144). While attributing agency to Alfonsa in the novel's outcome, Jarrett reads Alfonsa's past more through Don Héctor's description of that past than through her own, as will be clear later in a closer look at the discrepancies between the two narratives. In contrast to Luce, Jarrett not only strips John Grady of any heroic qualities, but he also recognizes a greater self-serving quality in Alfonsa's actions. Of Alejandra, Jarrett makes only brief mention, describing her action in telling her father about the affair as an attempt to control her own fate and free herself of the control of her great-aunt (114).

In "*All the Pretty Horses*: John Grady Cole's Expulsion from Paradise," Gail Moore Morrison acknowledges the centrality of the feminine presence. She describes the novel as "firmly grounded in the details of time" (175), place, and topography. However, her primary focus is on identifying it as a bildûngsroman (178) in which John Grady learns lessons not just as "a modern day horse-taming cowboy" (178), but also as "an unlikely knight errant, displaced and dispossessed, heroically tested and stubbornly faithful to a chivalric code whose power is severely circumscribed by the inevitable evil in a hostile world" (178). Although Morrison identifies Alfonsa, whom she calls "the wily serpent" (182), as the "voice of moral authority at the novel's philosophical center" (182), she suggests the lessons Alfonsa imparts to John Grady are a product of an obsession with the times of Madero (187) and of her despair at witnessing the defeat of moral principles, including "honor, loyalty, courage and constancy" (182). In this largely negative reading of Alfonsa's bitter motives, the great-aunt is living vicariously through Alejandra, bending her will and changing her destiny "without scruple" (189).

As insightful as these interpretations are, they fail to embrace the full complexities of the history and traditions of Mexico, especially the complexities of the feminine presence. As Rosaura Sánchez cautions, "all women do not share the same positions in the world" (8). In the remainder of this study, the feminine presence in the novel, particularly embodied in the characters of Alfonsa and Alejandra, will be placed within the context of the symbols, traditions, and history of Mexico in the years of the Revolution (1910–1913) that the novel describes and the years of the novel's action (1949–1951). Doing so demonstrates that McCarthy achieves more fully-developed women characters in Alfonsa and Alejandra than previously recognized and a significant, complex, feminine presence. Reading Alfonsa's narrative as *testimonio* and a comparison of her narrative to that of Don Héctor's reveals her motives more clearly.

Feminine Spaces, Time, and Discursive Structures

Spaces

Ileana Rodriguez explains in *House/Garden/Nation: Space, Gender, and Ethnicity in Postcolonial Latin American Literatures by Women* that Mexican and Latin American literatures place the identification of landscape and houses with the feminine, and nation-building, revolution, and war with the masculine. Niamh Thornton describes this association: "Woman functions as a symbolic representation of apposite loci. She either represents home as a space of safe, civilized domesticity or the external physical landscape" (39). The domestic woman must be protected, but woman as landscape must be "conquered and tamed in a direct parallel with the need for the man to conquer and tame the external, physical natural world" (39). This identification with place has been explored by others (Sullivan, Morrison, Ellis). As John Grady and Rawlins ride from the dry plain into the region where the Hacienda de Nuestra Señora de la Purísima Concepción is located, clearly we are intended to understand the Bolsón de Cuatro Ciénagas as a feminine landscape.

Bolsón

McCarthy, of course, is fictionalizing, but La Purísima is described as located in an actual geographic region that, in itself, has many characteristics associated with the feminine. The Cuatro Ciénagas Coahuila is a valley in the middle of the Chihuahua desert. Unlike the dry desert surrounding it, Cuatro Ciénagas, with its fresh water springs and streams, nurtures many forms of unique life ("Cuatro Ciénagas"). This region of over 843 miles contains natural crystalline pools and rivers formed by a network of underground rivers ("Cuatro Ciénagas"). At least 77 animal and plant species can only be found there. McCarthy describes this uniqueness: "In the lakes and in the streams were species of fish not known elsewhere on earth and birds and lizards and other forms of life as well all long relict here for the desert stretched away on every side" (97). Isolated within the surrounding desert environment, the unique plant and animal life of Cuatro Ciénagas has provided a natural laboratory for the study of early evolution ("Cuatro Ciénagas"). In addition, indigenous peoples of the Americas have long identified natural springs as feminine sites where the Mother sends forth nurturing waters, and it is to this feminine place that John Grady and Rawlins travel. Although the patriarchal society of Don Héctor's cattle ranch and its 170-year history may temporarily occupy the bolsón, in historical time that society is young compared to the feminine world it occupies. Don Héctor Rocha y Villareal is "one of the few hacendados who actually lived on the land he claimed" (96). This fact is significant because La Purísima has not yet made the transition from the cattle ranch as site of family to productive unit managed by overseers, a transition that Rodriguez argues is part of Mexico's modern state building (34). Instead, according to Rodriguez, "In the rural order, women have more power, for they are seen as a class . . .." (54–55). In this feminine landscape, McCarthy subverts the traditional tropes of Mexican history, society, and literature, by creating the Dueña Alfonsa, who represents a Mexico poised between tradition and modernity, and Alejandra, who represents a more modern Mexico, both of whom make use of available means of resistance to establish their agency in this patriarchal society.

Critics have seen Alejandra's character as stereotypical and exotic. Patrick Shaw suggests that she is the "passionate Latin female" (259) with her hair "black and loose" (259). He goes on to describe her as "arrogant, flirtatious, and temperamental" (259). Nell Sullivan, too, emphasizes her "long black hair" and "blue clothing" ("Boys" 247). Morrison, placing her within the landscape, calls Alejandra a "creature of the lake and lagoons, of the night and darkness" (181) to further her argument about the "fantastical nature" (149) of the Mexico being described. But in Mexican literary tradition, in the patriarchal Mexico of the time where women would not achieve full suffrage until 1953, and in the feminine setting of the bolsón, she is anything but stereotypical. John Grady may have designs on conquering and taming Alejandra, but Alejandra is in control from the start. Perhaps unconsciously, certainly recklessly, she uses her body, "capital" in a patriarchal society (Rodriguez 65), as a site of resistance, controlling her body and her acts. In defiance of her father; against a rural Mexico where there is "no forgiveness" (*Horses* 136) for women; against her grandaunt who cautions about the power of that patriarchy; she "owns" her body, choosing who will take her virginity and initiating the circumstances in which it will happen. Ironically, decades earlier Alfonsa had used her body as a site of resistance against patriarchy in refusing to return to Mexico until after her father's death (145). Alfonsa ultimately did return to the closed society of the ranch, where she hopes to guide the life of her grandniece to a different future. The shared urge to resist patriarchy and her love for Gustavo Madero have been factors in Alfonsa's initially putting forward John Grady's cause "even in the teeth of the most outrageous tantrums on the part of Alejandra's mother" (230). She understands, however, the futility of not recognizing the patriarchal structure around her and the danger to Alejandra that stems from her reckless action. As her more modern counterpart, Alejandra, however, even at the end of the novel appears to continue to exhibit defiance against that structure, first in her boldness in meeting

John Grady secretly in Zacatecas and later when we are told that John Grady "was not prepared for the open glances from older men at nearby tables nor for the *grace with which she accepted them* [italics mine]" (249).

Alejandra is consistently associated with the feminine, life-sustaining waters of the region, and she embodies the strength that the feminine invokes. The first time that John Grady sees her she has been riding the horse in the river or in the ciénagas (*Horses* 94), and she responds to the horsemen in a manner uncharacteristic of the modest behavior required of a young woman of the time in a rural setting. She "turned and smiled and touched the brim of the hat with her crop" (94), a gesture that includes "those who'd pretended not even to see her" (94), behavior more appropriate than hers given the vast difference in social rank. In the next encounter she is riding on the edge of the laguna (109), and she pulls up alongside John Grady and "looked full at him" (109). At the dance "she looked at him with great forthrightness and smiled and put her face against his shoulder" (123). Later when they meet as she is returning down the ciénaga road (129), she "stopped and turned her wide face to him" (130) and then "turned and looked off across the lake" (130). The last time that John Grady sees Alejandra before she returns to Mexico City creates definitively the connection between her and the landscape (131). As she comes down out of the mountains, dark clouds tower above her. Unlike Blevins who earlier hides in terror from a thunderstorm (67–71), Alejandra rides:

> all seeming unaware down through the low hills while the first spits of rain blew on the wind and onto the upper pasturelands and past the pale and reedy lakes riding erect and stately until the rain caught her up and shrouded her figure away in that wild summer landscape: real horse, real rider, real land and sky and yet a dream withal. (131–32)

This coming rainstorm may again signal trouble for John Grady, but the description of Alejandra riding "stately and erect" (131) as the storm literally enshrouds her, illustrates that she is very much a part of the landscape itself. While Nell Sullivan reads these instances of "threatening landscapes personified as female" ("Evolution" 76) to emphasize McCarthy's "narrative misogyny" (76), in the context of the primitive bolsón, with its life-giving water in the midst of the desert, the reader is reminded instead of feminine presence and its strength.

In the lake scene, as if to emphasize the symbiosis of the feminine presence, water, and Alejandra, rain is in the mountains, and John Grady enters the lake where the water is "so dark and so silky" (141), like Alejandra's dark hair. There she asks him directly, "Me quieres

[Do you want me]?" (141). Jay Ellis remarks on how this scene "seems to connect [John Grady] with nonhuman nature as much as it does with her" (*No Place* 24), but the fusion of Alejandra with that landscape makes any separation unnecessary. Whereas Morrison calls Alejandra a "creature of the lake and lagoons" (181), John Grady is the one objectified in the relationship as "mojado-reverso [reverse wetback, referring to his illegal crossing of the Rio Grande to enter Mexico], so rare a creature and one to be treasured" (*Horses* 124), like the other rare creatures of the Cuatro Ciénagas. In telling her father about the relationship before Alfonsa can, Alejandra maintains the only freedom that she can at that stage of her life, albeit with a reckless act that does not consider the consequences.

John Cant asserts that the ideas of Octavio Paz are "consistently reflected in McCarthy's work" (190). With the publication of *The Labyrinth of Solitude* in 1950, Paz's ideas are certainly relevant to the historical setting of *All the Pretty Horses*. Paz explores a symbolic division of woman in Mexican culture by sexual behavior: either virgin or whore, either the Virgen of Guadalupe or Malinche. La Malinche, or Malintzin, was an indigenous slave woman who was given to the Spaniards in their victory. Serving as translator for Cortés, she became his mistress and had his son, thus becoming the mother of the first mestizo, or person of mixed European and indigenous heritage (Paz 84–88). Ironically, she is alternately viewed through history as a victim or as a traitor, but Paz's dichotomy emphasizes the latter where the Mexican woman is either idealized as virgin and respectable, or as sexually experienced and shameful. This latter state is what Alfonsa refers to when she explains to John Grady that for women in Mexico "there is no forgiveness" (136). Although Ellis says that John Grady has "stained the Virgin" (*No Place* 212), McCarthy undermines these symbols to avoid stereotyping of the feminine. Alejandra in her role as aggressor is neither the Virgin without sin, nor Malinche, a victim of rape forever stained, although as Thornton explains, "In Mexico, women who move out of their designated [domestic] space are reviled as Malinche figures, who have betrayed their sex" (2). Alejandra, the modern Mexican woman, has begun to claim her own destiny, to challenge oppressive patriarchy. As I will later explain, she and Alfonsa may be much closer in symbolism to the third dominant feminine symbol of Mexico, La Llorona (the weeping woman).

Alejandra has internalized Alfonsa's lesson to value "what is true" (*Horses* 240) and in the end acts on that lesson. What is true in Alejandra's world is the ongoing patriarchy of post-revolutionary Mexico. She understands that her father's love for her can be withdrawn (252), thus affecting her future profoundly; therefore, she ultimately acquiesces to her father's greater power. As Ellis says, Alejandra never intends to become John Grady's wife (*No Place* 212) and certainly not to accompany him to Texas where she would be in a truly subaltern position. Significantly, during the last time that she and John Grady are together, in Zacatecas, the site of the bloodiest battle of the Revolution, she takes him to the Plazuela de Guadalajarita (*Horses* 253), where her grandfather had died in that struggle. Here she tells him, "There was no mother to cry. As in the corridos. Nor little bird that flew. Just the blood on the stones. I wanted to show you" (253). She is clearly impressing upon John Grady both the patriarchal society to which Mexico returned after the Revolution, as well as the failure of the idealism of that Revolution to make any immediate changes. In the post-Revolutionary years, monuments were erected across Mexico to honor the male heroes, and corridos were written to celebrate their bravery; nonetheless, Alejandra seems to share the same understanding of the Revolution's outcome assessed by Thornton:

> The aim of the Revolution was to shatter the petrified time they had lived in. Instead, their hopes of freedom were soon dashed by personal losses and the political corruption of post-Revolutionary Mexico, far removed from the version as represented in official narratives which claim it as progressive and genuinely revolutionary. (108)

House

If the bolsón is Alejandra's, then the ranch house is thoroughly Alfonsa's. McCarthy subverts the usual symbolic designation of this domestic space in the literary tradition of Mexico—a place of imprisonment for women—to create, as he did for the landscape, a feminine place of significant power. In the history of Mexico, men were involved in the public business of government and the economy, and women were relegated to the private spaces of the home (Thornton 51). Carlos Monsiváis calls these women's spaces "the holy zone":

> The society created by the 1857 Constitution and 1860 Reform Laws rendered inadmissible any female participation outside the "holy zone" (the bedroom, the kitchen, household chores, Mass, the confessional). This, despite the fact that women had been demanding civil rights since 1821, demands invigorated by the liberal cause. But the social gaze did not take them into account, instead erasing and silencing them. (1–2)

Jean Franco describes how the typical Mexican house is even constructed like a domestic prison, with thick outer walls and small windows facing the street and rooms that look inward toward a patio (418). Thornton explains that in Mexican fiction "women are represented as belonging to the private realm of the home and domesticity" (2), but it is there, she argues, that women are able to wield what little power they have. In private spaces, "they can use all their skills to their own ends" (190). In this private space Alfonsa uses her power, but unlike Thornton's assertion that women "do not have any power in public spaces, either intellectually or physically" (190), Alfonsa is able to exert power in the Saltillo prison and over the futures of John Grady, Rawlins, and Alejandra.

The ranch may be the Hacienda de Nuestra Señora de la Purísima Concepción, but the portrayal of Alfonsa and her power do not fit the symbolic Virgin any more than McCarthy's vision of Alejandra does. From the first, the ranch house is associated with Alfonsa. Although John Grady's initial entry into the interior of the house is in the company of Don Héctor, the house is described in feminine contrast to the ranch as "cool and quiet" (*Horses* 112) and smelling of "wax and flowers" (112). As they move down the hallway toward the dining room, the clock standing to the left has a pendulum that "slowly swept" (112), like the slowly changing Mexico that Alfonsa will later describe. And, although the dining room contains portraits of men and horses (112), it is clearly associated with the domestic through the description of the walnut sideboard "with some chafingdishes and decanters set out upon it" (112). Later Alfonsa will claim this space in choosing it for the chess game with John Grady. How completely the hacienda is imbued with the spirit of Alfonsa is described just before this game:

> The Dueña Alfonsa was both grandaunt and godmother to the girl and her life at the hacienda invested it with oldworld ties and with antiquity and tradition. Save for the old leatherbound volumes the books in the library were her books and the piano was her piano. (132)

As if to reinforce her understanding of the relegation of women's lives to the closed domestic spaces, Alfonsa speaks to John Grady of the interchanges with Alejandra within that space: "Here we live in a small world. A close world" (135).

Chapel

On the other hand, Don Héctor chooses as the location for his warning to John Grady the chapel converted to a billiard room, but never deconsecrated. Monsiváis explains the role of the Catholic Church in maintaining the patriarchal society of Mexico and in the oppression of Mexican women (3). Anticlericalism was "fundamental to the feminist perspective" (3) in Mexico:

> In 1901, for example, the ladies of Cuicatlán, Oaxaca, proclaimed to the ladies of Zitácuaro, "The Mexican woman, who up until now has been the instrument of clumsy passions and an insurmountable obstacle to the violent development of progress due to the effects of the cancerous virus hypocritically spread by religious fanaticism, must rise up like the heroic Boer women who repelled the invaders, united and resolved to combat clericalism as the most cunning and fearsome enemy of our honor, our conscience, our family, and our fatherland." (3)

Ironically their feminist fervor didn't extend to gendered language!

In that chapel Don Héctor has the doubled patriarchal authority of Mexican society and the Catholic Church. The room provides Héctor a masculine space within the feminine space of the house. Here Héctor narrates the doomed history of Alfonsa and Gustavo Madero, a failed relationship because her father would not permit it, as well as the doomed history of the Madero brothers because of their failure to understand that the ideas of one country do not necessarily work in another. He also, however, takes the opportunity to assert that God is on his side: "I like to feel that God is here. In my house" (144). He explains that, although "Alfonsa knows about these matters" (145)—perhaps not just the matters of how to desanctify a chapel but also of the patriarchal oppression of the Catholic Church in Mexico—he has not had the priest come to desanctify the room: "Personally I question whether such a thing can be done at all. What is sacred is sacred" (144). Christine Chollier rightly suggests that the chapel also "metaphorically refers to the sanctuary of his daughter's person" (10). The sacredness of the room, the significance of the Virgin in the Catholic Church, and his daughter's virginity are joined metaphorically, reinforcing Héctor's patriarchal duty to ensure protection for them all.

Time

Like the other elements of the novel that can be identified as having a feminine presence, time, too, is presented in a complex way. Many have remarked on the similarity of McCarthy's own statements concerning human nature and those of Alfonsa to John Grady. To Richard B. Woodward in the 1992 interview, "Cormac McCarthy's Venomous

Fiction," for the *New York Times Magazine*, McCarthy commented, "There's no such thing as life without bloodshed." And then,

> I think the notion that the species can be improved in some way, that everyone could live in harmony, is a really dangerous idea. Those who are afflicted with this notion are the first ones to give up their souls, their freedom. (McCarthy)

The similarity to Alfonsa's statements to John Grady is indeed remarkable:

> We weep over the might have been, but there is no might have been. There never was. It is supposed to be true that those who do not know history are condemned to repeat it. I don't believe knowing can save us. What is constant in history is greed and foolishness and a love of blood and this is a thing that even God—who knows all that can be known—seems powerless to change. (239)

This circular, anti-Hegelian (Chollier 15), view of history can easily be read as feminine following Julia Kristeva, who argues that masculine time is linear, whereas feminine time is circular ("Women's Time"). It is important, though, to recognize that a circular view of time is also Mayan and part of Mexican heritage. Thornton explains that Mayan time is based upon "a series of ages, which are governed by the lifetime of a sun" (128), and further, "Within each age, time is circular, man is governed by fate, and events repeat themselves until the end of the age when what can be called the history of the new age starts afresh" (129).

In the context of post-Revolutionary Mexico, however, a material understanding of the feminine nature of Alfonsa's circular view of time is readily available. Following the Revolution in Mexico, many were disillusioned with the results. The temporary interruption of the patriarchal regime, in which power and wealth were in the hands of a few, had been fueled by an idealism like that of the Maderos which Alfonsa describes (233). Following the Revolution, little seemed to have changed: power and wealth still remained with the same few, corruption returned, and those who had held idealistic goals, particularly women, could not logically view history as progressive.

Before the Revolution, middle- and upper-class feminists formed antigovernment clubs and spoke out in opposition to Díaz (Monsiváis 3). For example, Juana Belén Gutiérrez de Mendoza, a journalist, established the anti-Díaz newspaper *Vesper* (Macías 26). Gutiérrez was thrown into jail several times during the Díaz regime, and in 1911, Angela Madero, a politically active sister of Francisco and Gustavo, raised 2000 pesos for Gutiérrez to replace her printing press seized by Dìaz (26). Francisco Madero himself insisted on "effective suffrage" (36), and feminists believed that he would end the tyranny under which they had suffered. Dolores Jiménez y Muro, an unmarried schoolteacher and a member of the editorial staff of the feminist journal *La Mujer Mexicana*, was involved in the "Complot de Tacubaya," a conspiracy to bring Madero to power (29). She actually put together the plan of the leaders. Many women like these were working not only for political reform, but also for social and economic reform (29).

During the post-Revolutionary years, women who had been actively engaged in the struggle, including the many soldaderas, were expected to return to the subordinate roles they had played before the Revolution. As Temma Kaplan explains, "Mexico [sic] women occupied various public realms in the 1920s, 1930s, and 1940s, but they had to fight continuously against masculine domination and patriarchal authority" (271). In this context, then, the circular view of history as expressed by Alfonsa would be shared by many other women of Mexico.

Earlier I suggested that symbolically Alfonsa and Alejandra might fit more closely with the figure of La Llorona, as explored by José Limón in his essay, "La Llorona, The Third Legend of Greater Mexico: Cultural Symbols, Women, and the Political Unconscious." Limón proposes La Llorona as a third major socio-cultural symbol of Greater Mexico, both as a positive symbol for women of the region and as a representation of the "socially unfulfilled utopian longing" (400) of the people who tell her story. The legend of La Llorona, or Weeping Woman, has origins in European narrative and is closely related to the Medea story (400). Stories about La Llorona appear in various versions throughout Mexico and the Southwest. In a region containing as many lakes and reservoirs as Cuatro Ciénagas, her story would likely be told many times. The basic outline is that following the betrayal of her husband or lover, she kills their children, often by drowning, and wanders the night near the waters, weeping for them. Limón argues that her act violates patriarchal norms of what women should do, and as such, her act is, though morally incorrect, an understandable reaction to the "social and psychological contradictions created by those norms for Mexican women" (416). Limón posits three stages in the outcome of her story: first, she destroys the nuclear family as it exists in its patriarchal form; second, she restores her maternal bonds with the water through rebirth; and third, in the process, she restores a world of love without men, or at least men as they had been (416).

Limón's interpretation offers an intriguing symbol for Alejandra in the sorrow that John Grady sees in her (*Horses* 140), her insistence on their visit to the Revolutionary plaza, her statement that the Street of Desire and the Calle de Noche Triste (the Street of the Sad Night) are "but names for Mexico" (253), and finally, her questions to John Grady: "How do I know who you are? Do I know what sort of man you are? What sort my father is? Do you drink whiskey? Do you go with whores? Does he? What are men?" (249). The image of La Llorona also fits Alfonsa in her great sorrow for her lost love, the betrayal of her youthful idealism, and in her belief that little can be changed regarding the constancy of "greed and foolishness and a love of blood" (239), as well as in her determination not to accept a conventional marriage for Alejandra (240).

Discursive Structures

In giving Alfonsa a lengthy philosophical narrative in *All the Pretty Horses*, McCarthy placed her in the unique position of being the first woman among the numerous male teachers who people his fiction. The feminine nature of her narrative is made clearer because her first-person narrative is prefaced by Don Héctor's narrative of her past. In order to understand fully how her narrative differs from his, it is necessary first to look briefly at his earlier account.

As described previously, Don Héctor chooses the chapel/billiard room as the site of his warning likely because of the strengthened patriarchal tradition it holds. Georg Guillemin calls Don Héctor's account a "historiographical approach" (105), whereas he characterizes Alfonsa's as "an allegorical interpretation" (*A Cormac McCarthy Companion,* 105). The former, he suggests, "approaches the historical record with a plethora of models and methods" (105). An allegorical interpretation, on the other hand, sees "history not as an evolutionary progress involving cause and effect but as recurrent enactments of the ever same drama whose individual events are highlighted as exemplary moments within the set course of history" (105). Certainly Alfonsa's view of history is circular, but Guillemin's characterization of Héctor's account may be too charitable since, rather than "models and methods," Héctor seems more intent on persuasive tactics.

His Story

Héctor's masculine narrative is clearly designed to intimidate, to use indirect persuasion, without at that point alienating. His is a class story. He begins his history of Francisco Madero (and indirectly his brother, Gustavo) by placing it geographically, reinforcing his own position as landed aristocracy: "He was born in Parras. In this state. Our families at one time were quite close" (144). He then moves to the politics of the

Maderos that fit so poorly with the position of dominant power, in turn establishing his own conservative position as a member of the dominant class. The story that he tells is hazy on the details of the personal—Alfonsa and Gustavo "may have been engaged" (144) and "whatever were the circumstances she seems to have been very unforgiving" (145)—but sure on the details of the Maderos' misguided views: "The political views of the family were quite radical" (144). His telling emphasizes the power of his male ancestors ("my grandfather would never have permitted the marriage" [144]) and their loyalty ("Madero's grandfather was my padrino. My godfather. Don Evaristo. For this and other reasons my grandfather remained loyal to him" [145]). Although he says that the contents of Francisco's book were not "so terrible" (145), he again reinforces the position of landed patriarchal authority by indicating the seeming contradiction between its contents and the position of the "wealthy young hacendado" (145). Héctor is dismissive of liberal political views by referring to them as "these ideas," repeated three times (145). On two separate occasions he again uses the trope of place, this time in the form of nationhood, post-Revolutionary and patriarchal Mexico where women remained the Other: "Mexico is not Europe" (145) and "even Cervantes could not envision such a country as Mexico" (146). Although these statements are made to explain why the ideas that the Maderos brought back from France could not work in Mexico, they further serve to warn John Grady that he is in a unique and autonomous land, with its separate history, political ideas and culture and that the ideas he brought with him from the United States no longer apply.

Rhetorically, two of the most interesting features of Don Héctor's narrative are the two slippages from his identification with patriarchal power, designed no doubt at this point to lessen the sternness of his warning, while indirectly revealing to John Grady that Alejandra is likely to go to France soon. They are clearly not just diversions, but outright deceptions. The first occurs when he asserts that "Alfonsita was not a child. She should have been left to make her own choice and she was not . . .." (144–45). Alfonsita [the diminutive of Alfonsa] was, of course, 17, the exact age of Alejandra during the time the novel takes place, and over whom he fully intends to exert his power. The second comes near the end of his meeting with John Grady when he melodramatically declares, "Who am I? A father. A father is nothing" (146).

Her Story

When John Grady returns to the ranch following his release from prison, Alfonsa meets with him in the parlor (227). She is dressed elegantly and stands "almost formally" (227). This choice of location, at the social center of the house where her power as a woman is at its greatest, is designed, like Héctor's, to intimidate John Grady. It also, though, demonstrates a respect for him that would not necessarily be expected from a 73-year-old woman of means and offers both a glimpse into her true motive and into her character. Unlike her stated motive for telling him her story to allow him to see who his enemy is (241), at that moment she is not his enemy at all. Her motive is rather to share her narrative and her wisdom with a young man in whom she sees promise and for whom she wishes a better future. As Sara L. Spurgeon describes, Alfonsa "has come to terms with the nature of the world as she sees it" (32), and she hopes to persuade John Grady to share her worldview. Like La Llorona in Limón's reading of the myth, Alfonsa hopes for a future world for Alejandra that contains men who are different from the ones she has known.

As if to reinforce this idea, the tapestry on the wall behind her is of a meeting between two horsemen in a "vanished landscape" (227), and above the double doors to the library hangs the mounted head of a fighting bull, one of the major symbols of patriarchal Mexico, already defeated "with one ear missing" (227). Alfonsa has extended her power into the public space, and as the clock ticks in the hall, marking historical time, she inserts her story into the history of Mexico that John Grady will carry back to Texas as witness.

At the beginning of Alfonsa's narrative, she establishes a masculine position of power (Castillo 168) by separating herself from other women in temperament and life experiences and by explaining that hers is not "an ordinary story" (229). She also describes the disastrous love affairs that other women of her family experienced (229), at the same time that she emphasizes the infidelities of the men involved. She separates herself from Alejandra's mother by saying, "I am not a society person" (230). In spite of this positioning and in spite of her education in Europe and the many books she has read, her narrative has already begun to exhibit characteristics described by Walter Ong as markers of oral discourse, and consequently, of feminine discourse in a country where women had no access to a public voice. She begins, "The affair of the stolen horse was known here even before you arrived" (228), language that suggests an oral story. In addition, the history that she relates is "additive" (Ong 37), with its lessons at the end, another feature described by Ong as characteristic of oral language (37). Her language describing the other women in her family contains what Ong calls "clusters of integers" (38), for example, "disastrous love affairs", "men of disreputable character", "tainted blood", and "family curse" (229), as if the subject has been the focus of family talk, family legend.

Again placing herself in a masculine position, Alfonsa refers to philosophical talks with her father, at the same time that she rejects his belief in the "connectedness of things" (230). In doing so, she positions herself apart from the upper-classes, illustrating her own position as marginalized: "positivism was the ruling class ideology at the end of the *porfiriato*" (Pablos 83). It is then that her discourse moves to feminine discursive structures and *testimonio*. Ileana Rodriguez quotes Francoise Perus in explaining that the function of *testimonio* is to:

> document spheres of reality . . . that dominant discourse usually ignores, hides, or falsifies . . . to restore and explore, to insert them in the absences and the blind spots of the social discourse, dominant or not . . . [and that] the subject of enunciation is usually at the same time a witness and an actor. (36)

Debra A. Castillo emphasizes that the speaker must be "a real witness, who gives evidence about true happenings" (168). In describing the devastating poverty all around her during her childhood and in recounting the history of the Maderos from her personal interaction with them and her relationship to Gustavo (232–33), Alfonsa demonstrates that she has been a witness to the events of the Revolution and the subsequent loss of idealism, both her own and that of her country. It is clear that she intends to correct family stories such as those told by Héctor—"Gustavo and I were never engaged" (236)—and when she describes the poverty that she witnessed, she does so with deep respect for the dignity of those experiencing it: "Their intelligence was frightening. And they had a freedom which we envied" (232). Observations from Stephen Crane verify her testimony to that poverty: "at night many of them [the poor] sleep in heaps in doorways, and spend their days squatting upon the pavements" (Pablos 83). Unlike Don Héctor's account, hers rings true when she admits both her position as a young member of the wealthy upper class and the insular distance that it often afforded her: "To my surprise I found myself quite popular and very likely I'd have been cured of my overwrought sensibilities except for two things. The first of these was the return of the two oldest [Madero] boys" (233). The second, of course, was the hunting accident and her disfigurement. As she describes Gustavo's understanding of the pain the accident caused her and his willingness to endure her "rejection or ridicule" (236) in order to help her, she openly, and with tears, reveals that her love for him has endured for almost forty years (236). This *testimonio*, with its unguarded honesty, affirms an ethos, not seen in Don Héctor's account, that supports her lesson to Alejandra to value "what is true above what is useful" (240) and to John Grady that "we cannot escape naming responsibility" (241).

The ethos developed in Alfonsa's *testimonio* that underscores her philosophy, her strength of will and Alejandra's in a patriarchal Mexico, and the feminine imbued in the space and time of the novel all demonstrate a deliberate and more complex feminine presence in *All the Pretty Horses* than has been generally addressed. The foregoing argument has not been undertaken to undermine the many valuable readings, often metaphorical, that have come before. By moving across the border, however, to view the feminine presence from the other side, I have attempted to demonstrate the material substance of the lives of the women of Mexico that the novel portrays, and in doing so, to take a step toward reassessment of McCarthy's ability in writing women characters. Looked at from the history and symbolism of Mexico, the two women, Alfonsa and Alejandra, are stronger, more appropriately motivated, and more fully realized than has previously been acknowledged, proving that this is indeed "another country" (136).

CHAPTER 2

Hang and Rattle: John Grady Cole's Horsebreaking in Typescript, Novel, and Film

Stacey Peebles

In *The Crossing*, the novel following *All the Pretty Horses*, Billy Parham sits and talks with an ex-Mormon in the questionable shelter of a ruined church. The man speaks of storytelling, and emphasizes that "[o]f the telling there is no end" and that "[r]ightly heard all tales are one" (143). A reader of the Border Trilogy certainly might think so, as the stories told in *All the Pretty Horses*, *The Crossing*, and *Cities of the Plain* repeat, echo, and parallel one another, creating what Edwin Arnold has called a "deep resonance" (232). The story of John Grady Cole's experience in *Cities*, for instance, will seem very familiar to those introduced to him in *Pretty Horses*. "Once again," Arnold notes, "he is characterized by his skill with horses, his innate courage and dignity, his sense of honor" (228). Once again he falls in love with a Mexican girl, and later engages in a vicious knife fight. Once again his story ends sadly, some would say tragically.

Christmas Day, 2000, gave us another portrait of John Grady, this time embodied by Matt Damon in Billy Bob Thornton's film adaptation of *All the Pretty Horses*. On May 18, 2009, even more "resonance" was created, as the archive of the Cormac McCarthy Papers officially opened in the Wittliff Collections at the Albert B. Alkek Library at Texas State University in San Marcos. Here, interested readers can trace John Grady's character through the drafts of *Pretty Horses* and all the way back to his earliest incarnation, in film treatments and screenplay drafts of the *Cities of the Plain* story that McCarthy wrote in the late 1970s, well before the Border Trilogy was published. The John Gradys fairly multiply, but as Arnold notes, his basic character traits seem consistent through these multiple iterations: skill with horses, courage, honor, passion, conviction. Particularly in his skill with horses and the way that skill is depicted do we see evidence of all these other traits.

That horsemanship, however, changes considerably in its differing depictions. In this chapter, trace the variations in John Grady's horse-breaking methods and, correspondingly, his relationship to horses and his character as seen in typescripts of the *Cities of the Plain* screenplay, in the novels *All the Pretty Horses* and *Cities of the Plain*, and in the 2000 film adaptation of *Pretty Horses*. I'll begin with McCarthy's novel *Pretty Horses*, since this is the portrait of John Grady Cole with which many McCarthy readers are most familiar, and show how the horse-breaking techniques described in the novel are similar in principle—though not in method—to "horse whispering," or natural horsemanship. Early drafts of the *Cities* screenplay reveal a very different portrayal of John Grady as a tough, stubborn kid who approaches both horses and friends with little skill and even less finesse. That conception is ameliorated in the novel version of *Cities*, to better reflect the character presented in *Pretty Horses*. In many ways, the film adaptation of *Pretty Horses* resurrects that earlier image of a bronc-busting John Grady, whose approach to horses and to life is to "hang and rattle" until he gets thrown off. The changing versions of John Grady reflect differing visions of what it means to master a skill, an art, or another creature—and the implications of trying, and perhaps rightly failing, to do so.

Making Them Believe: John Grady in *All the Pretty Horses*

McCarthy's *All the Pretty Horses* presents John Grady Cole as someone with an almost mystical connection to horses. For him, horses are creatures of both beauty and utility, and though he is passionate about many things, his passion for horses is primary. McCarthy writes that John Grady "sat a horse not only as if he'd been born to it which he was but as if were he begot by malice or mischance into some queer land where horses never were he would have found them anyway" (23). Lacey Rawlins and Jimmy Blevins speak more prosaically about John Grady's abilities with a horse, though they do agree that John Grady is an excellent horseman. Rawlins provokes Blevins somewhat when he claims that John Grady is "just flat out the best," and an even better rider than Booger Red (59). Rawlins enjoys needling Blevins on this and other points, and when Blevins fails to challenge his comparison of John Grady and Booger Red, Rawlins makes his contempt clear: "You dont know shit from applebutter, said Rawlins. Booger Red's been dead forever" (58).

The rider Booger Red—more formally known as Samuel Thomas Privett, Jr.—did indeed die in 1924, some twenty-five years before this scene is set. Booger, who was famous as a bronc rider and horsebreaker from an early age, earned his nickname at age 13, when a gunpowder explosion severely injured him and disfigured his face. A small boy reportedly remarked of his looks, "Gee, but Red is sure a booger now, ain't he?" Despite the injury, Booger later won 23 first prizes at rodeo competitions and performed at the 1904 World's Fair in St. Louis (Jones).

Like John Grady, Booger was known for his way with horses, especially difficult ones that had proved unrideable by others. In that sense Rawlins' comparison is an apt one. But as McCarthy indicates, John Grady is not a typical cowboy, and his ability to break and ride horses is not, in fact, based on the kind of bronc-busting skills made famous by people like Booger Red and celebrated in rodeos. Blevins' acceptance of their comparison may be further evidence, as Rawlins would have it, of his ignorance. Where horses are concerned, John Grady takes a different approach.

That approach is highlighted in a sequence in the second section of the novel, shortly after he and Rawlins have separated from Blevins and stumbled on work at Don Héctor's enormous ranch in Mexico, the Hacienda de Nuestra Señora de la Purísima Concepción. They perform routine tasks like branding, castrating, and dehorning, and on the third day of this work, a "small herd of wild three year old colts" is brought down from the mesa and into one of the pens. Rawlins calls them "as spooky a bunch of horses as I ever saw" (98). John Grady admires them, but Rawlins doubts his judgment because the roan he points out is "coonfooted" and "colored peculiar" (99). They count 16 horses altogether.

Then John Grady puts his cards on the table. "You think you and me could break all of em in four days?" he asks. "Just halfway decent greenbroke horses. Say six saddles. Double and stop and stand still to be saddled" (100). John Grady reasons that these horses are the horses that they will later be asked to ride and work on, and he thinks four days is enough to have them "greenbroke," or just broken enough to be used to a saddle and rider. (Breaking 16 horses in 4 days would be no easy task even for the best of horsemen, though McCarthy's original idea was even more impressive, perhaps even implausible. In the typescript first draft of the novel in the McCarthy papers at Texas State University, John Grady's proposition is that they will break 19 horses in 3 days.[1])

As they consider the idea, John Grady tells Rawlins more. Don Héctor, it seems, has some four hundred horses up on a nearby mountain, and is breeding "media sangres." Rawlins has to ask what that means, and

John Grady explains, "Quarterhorses, what we'd call em" (101). "That roan yonder," he goes on, "is a flat-out Billy horse if he does have bad feet." John Grady knows his horses, and pegs this one as one of the Steel Dust line. According to the American Quarter Horse Association, the "legendary Steel Dust came to Texas around 1844, and five years later the great horse Shiloh also arrived. Shiloh's son Billy, out of a daughter of Steel Dust, became the fountainhead of Texas Quarter Horses" (Hedgpeth ix). John Grady further adds that the horse is part of the breeding line of "Jose Chiquito," or Little Joe, a horse from the early twentieth century. Rawlins has heard of Little Joe, but John Grady goes on, imparting even more information:

> Both of them horses were sold in Mexico, said John Grady. One and Two. What he's got up yonder is a big yeguada of mares out of the old Traveler-Ronda line of horses of Sheeran's.
>   What else? said Rawlins. (101)

John Grady has a detailed understanding of horses' history and breeding, and is also well acquainted with the appropriate terminology both in English and Spanish. It is unclear whether Rawlins' response here denotes surprise at the quality of the horses or confusion at John Grady's specialized explanation, but either way, Rawlins' knowledge of horses is clearly inferior to John Grady's. (In the first draft, Rawlins' comment implies a similar capitulation to his friend's expertise, if a coarser one: "Aint that the shits, he said.")

Gail Moore Morrison has aptly noted that "in an ironic double entendre on his estate's name," Don Héctor has "conceived a breeding strategy to produce a superior cutting horse by crossing his quarter horse mares with a thoroughbred stallion" (180). Morrison observes that this echoes John Grady's memory of a painting that hung in his family's home:

> They had the long Andalusian nose and the bones of their faces showed Barb blood. You could see the hindquarters of the foremost few, good hindquarters and heavy enough to make a cuttinghorse. As if maybe they had Steeldust in their blood. But nothing else matched and no such horse ever was that he had seen and he'd once asked his grandfather what kind of horses they were and his grandfather looked up from his plate at the painting . . . and he said those are picturebook horses and went on eating. (16)

These "picturebook horses" could indeed be cutting horses, the result of breeding Billy horses—horses from the Steel Dust line—with a thoroughbred. And so the union of the horses John Grady and Rawlins intend to break with Don Héctor's prize stallion would produce a horse such as one has never seen, and John Grady is given a "miraculous opportunity" to do just that (Morrison 180). But first he has to break the horses.

On Sunday morning they begin, and McCarthy details the equipment they will use: 40-foot maguey catchropes, saddleblankets, a bosalea or riding hackamore with a metal noseband, 16 rope hackamores and coils of all kinds of rope, and John Grady has a pair of gunnysacks that he has slept in and a Hamley saddle. Rawlins asks if John Grady is "dead set of sackin these varmints out," or rubbing them with the gunnysacks to familiarize the horses with the smell and feel of a blanket and also of people (103). This is a common procedure, but John Grady adds his own touch when he uses sacks that smell of him in particular. He takes great care with the action, absorbed in the task at hand and dedicated to what he believes to be necessary attention to detail. Rawlins advocates a more straightforward method: "My old daddy always said that the purpose of breakin a horse was to ride it and if you got one to break you just as well to saddle up and climb aboard and get on with it" (103). John Grady grins and asks if his daddy was "a certified peeler" and Rawlins answers that although he never claimed to be, he had sure seen him "hang and rattle a time or two." Rawlins appreciates the show put on by a good bronc-peeler, or bronc-buster, who simply gets on a horse (often with the help of other cowboys) and attempts to stay on until the horse is exhausted, in a contest of will between man and horse. John Grady has different ideas—he declares that there is "no such thing as a mean colt," and that he will "make them believe."

Then he gets started. First he ropes the forefeet of one of the horses, drops it to the ground, and talks to it while holding its head in his lap. He allows it to rise and he and Rawlins begin fitting several of the horses with hackamores and tying up one of each horse's hind legs. This hobbling, or "sidelining," makes it impossible for the horses to kick or move about freely. When the boys have three horses arranged in such a way, the other vaqueros of La Purísima take notice, and a few wander over to watch. It's unclear if they are unfamiliar with the approach— which, though different from bronc-busting, is still a common method of horsebreaking—or if John Grady's facility with it is simply a sight to see. On the evening of that first day, "the vaqueros seemed to treat them with a certain deference but whether it was the deference accorded the accomplished or that accorded to mental defectives they were unsure" (105).

Soon eight horses are sidelined and all of the vaqueros have come to watch. McCarthy describes the horses' increasing dread at this loss of autonomy: they are "coming to reckon slowly with the remorselessness of this rendering of their fluid and collective selves into that condition of separate and helpless paralysis which seemed to be among them like the creeping plague" (105). After each of the 16 horses has been arranged in such a way, John Grady begins the sacking out, rubbing the sack that he has slept in all over the horse's body while talking to it. "What good do you think it does to waller all over a horse that way?" Rawlins asks skeptically. "I dont know," John Grady answers, "I aint a horse" (106). Finally John Grady places a blanket and saddle on the horse, which doesn't move, replaces the hackamore with the bosalea, unhobbles the horse, and climbs up in the saddle. The horse briefly starts, and then responds, following his lead with the reins. Rawlins "spat in disgust" and complains, "What the hell kind of bronc is that? . . . You think that's what these people paid good money to see?" (107). Rawlins wants a rodeo, and he has gotten nothing of the sort. By nightfall John Grady has ridden all of the horses, and the crowd has grown to "something like a hundred people" who are picnicking and watching the show (107). In the following days he rides them all again, and then Rawlins does as well.

More than any other sequence in the novel, these scenes demonstrate John Grady's deep affiliation with horses as well as his practical skills with them. Though he and Rawlins "dont have no leaders" and are just buddies, as he tells Don Héctor, it is very clear that John Grady is the primary horsebreaker and Rawlins does little more than assist him. Something about John Grady's method and talent is enough to draw a substantial crowd, though most of what happens here is relatively standard horsebreaking: restraining the horse, getting it used to the touch and smell of people, sacking it out, saddling and eventually beginning to ride it.

Phillip Snyder has noted that John Grady's attitude, if not his method, is similar to "horse whispering," or natural horsemanship, as popularized by Monty Roberts and represented in Nicholas Evans' novel *The Horse Whisperer* (1995), as well as the 1998 film adaptation of the same name. In his book *The Man Who Listens to Horses* (1996), Roberts explains his own technique of horsebreaking, in which the breaker learns to mimic the body language of a dominant mare in a herd, and thus creates a partnership with the horse. Roberts calls this method of communication between person and horse "Equus," and identifies the moment when the partnership is created as "join up." When this happens, the horse will move voluntarily toward the breaker rather than away, and reach out with his nose (234). Other than the enclosed area of the pen, no restrictions are placed on the horse—and the pen itself may not be necessary, Roberts notes (233). He emphasizes cooperation and earning the trust of the horse, so much so that he stops calling what he does "breaking," which connotes violence and domination. "I called my method 'starting' horses," he says. "A significant moment for me came when I realized I could cause trust in a horse without pain or restraint" (14). A nonviolent approach has become relatively standard in contemporary approaches to horsemanship, and has found other advocates in trainers like Tom and Bill Dorrance and Pat Parelli.

John Grady uses more traditional horsebreaking methods than someone like Monty Roberts—he does restrain the horses, for instance, and approaches them on his terms rather than theirs—though he does so in a way that largely divests these processes of the brutality that Roberts claims they often entail. He doesn't use the non-contact body language of "Equus," but he does communicate with the horses, talking to them softly and at length. He doesn't "bust" these broncs, and no one—person or horse—has to hang and rattle.

John Grady dominates these horses with skill and care, and does not enforce his domination with violence, yet his relationship with them is still characterized by the imposition of control that is quite different from the partnership that Roberts and others would advocate. The horses, after all, are restricted from free movement, a "helpless paralysis" that frightens them, like a "creeping plague." They are subjected to the application of force—if not physically violent or abusive force—which operates as a kind of mental colonization: "They looked like animals trussed up by children for fun and they stood waiting for they knew not what with the voice of the breaker still running in their brains like the voice of some god come to inhabit them" (105). John Grady clearly loves horses, but here that love is expressed as a desire to master them.

This love and mastery is seen most notably a few pages later in the book, when he rides Don Héctor's prize stallion and speaks to him in Spanish. The passage is remarkable for its use of language as well as what John Grady actually says to the horse:

> He'd ride sometimes clear to the upper end of the laguna before the horse would even stop trembling and he spoke constantly to it in spanish in phrases almost biblical repeating again and again the strictures of a yet untabled law. Soy comandante de las yeguas, he would say, yo y yo sólo. Sin la caridad de estas manos no tengas nada. Ni comida ni agua ni hijos. Soy yo que traigo las yeguas de las montañas, las yeguas jóvenes, las yeguas salvajes y ardientes. While inside the vaulting of the ribs between his knees the darkly meated heart pumped of who's will . . . all sheathed and muffled in the flesh . . . and the hot globes of his eyes where the world burned. (128)

The Spanish sentences John Grady speaks indicate an assumption of complete control, mastery, even enslavement: I am the commander of the mares, he says, I and I alone. Without the charity of these hands you don't have anything. Not food or water or children. It is I who bring the mares from the mountains, the young mares, the wild and passionate mares. John Grady claims control over the stallion's sustenance and his breeding, all the aspects of his survival. If the "world burns" in the stallion's eyes, then John Grady likewise claims mastery over the world itself. At this point in the story, that mastery seems plausible—John Grady, after all, has successfully ridden from the United States into Mexico, demonstrated his skill with horses to great acclaim, and risen to prominent employment for a wealthy landowner. And, of course, he has met and danced with Alejandra, that landowner's spirited and beautiful daughter, with whom he will soon begin an intense and intimate relationship. That relationship, of course, begins and develops around the horses each appreciates and rides so well. "What he loved in horses," McCarthy writes of John Grady,

> was what he loved in men, the blood and the heat of the blood that ran them. All his reverence and all his fondness and all the leanings of his life were for the ardenthearted and they would always be so and never be otherwise. (6)

Alejandra, hot-blooded and passionate, certainly qualifies. In consummating his love for her, it seems—at least initially—that John Grady has mastered yet another remarkable challenge.

Georg Guillemin has argued that, whispering aside, John Grady's relationship with horses in these earlier scenes is indeed characterized by dominance, or "the master-subject relationship of traditional animal husbandry" (The Pastoral Vision, 133). Later in the book, however, this changes. After John Grady is arrested and jailed for his previous involvement with Blevins—now known as an assassin for killing three men—his expectations of mastery begin to falter. While in jail, he dreams of running with horses over a high plain, and the fact that he runs *with* them rather than rides or commands them signals a shift. As Guillemin notes, the "dream image makes for a parable of an eco-pastoral, rather than just pastoral, utopia because John Grady runs among the horses as their equal and not their master" (137–38). Certainly we do see evidence of more equality between boy and horse in the dream:

> and they flowed and changed and ran and their manes and tails blew off of them like spume and there was nothing else at all in

that high world and they moved all of them in a resonance that was like a music among them and they were none of them afraid nor colt nor mare and they ran in that resonance which is the world itself and which cannot be spoken but only praised. (161–62)

Here, their partnership is a resonance, like music, and none are afraid— there is no creeping plague of fear or mental colonization by the voice of "some god," and no creature withholds anything from any other. Their partnership *is* the world, which is not controlled, or even spoken of, but rather praised.

Much later, after John Grady has been released from prison and unsuccessfully attempted to reclaim Alejandra, he seeks revenge on the Encantada captain who arranged to have Blevins executed and who conveyed Rawlins and John Grady to the prison in Saltillo. Immediately before "men of the country" appear to take the captain from John Grady and, presumably, punish him appropriately, John Grady dreams of horses again. McCarthy writes that "what he saw in his dream was that the order in the horse's heart was more durable for it was written in a place where no rain could erase it" (280). Men's ordering of the world, John Grady seems to think, pales in comparison to the order in a horse's heart—and this is clearly not the order that John Grady previously sought to impose with his own voice and control. This order is durable and eternal, and John Grady's love for horses has here matured into a corresponding respect. The novel ends with the image of John Grady riding off from Rawlins' home and into the sunset, appearing to be literally at one with the horses who travel with him: ". . . and horse and rider and horse passed on and their long shadows passed in tandem like the shadow of a single being. Passed and paled into the darkening land, the world to come" (302).

The John Grady of *All the Pretty Horses* is a character whose skills with and relationship to horses undergoes a subtle shift, deepening into true partnership, though his facility with these animals is remarkable both before and after this change. Unfortunately his relationships with other people haven't fared as well. He loses his grandfather, father, and Blevins to death, and his mother, former girlfriend Mary Catherine, and Alejandra to what might generally be called a failure to communicate. Even Rawlins now seems to live in a different world than he does. But he and the horses end the novel together, poised on the cusp of "the world to come," whatever that may bring. The phrase implies potential and the possibilities for further development—and is more optimistically inflected, perhaps, than the original ending as seen in the first draft: ". . . and that was all."

"I can ride the son of a bitch": John Grady the Coonfoot

McCarthy's revision of that last line is apt, since *All the Pretty Horses* is hardly the end of John Grady Cole—or, as it turns out, his beginning. *Pretty Horses* is the first novel in McCarthy's Border Trilogy, which continues with *The Crossing*, a novel that focuses on the protagonist Billy Parham, and finishes with *Cities of the Plain*, in which Billy and John Grady are working together on a ranch near El Paso in 1952. *Cities* was originally conceived as a screenplay in the late 1970s, well before the other two novels, and an early treatment of the film is titled "El Paso/Juarez."[2] In an incomplete typescript of the screenplay titled "Cities of the Plain" and labeled by McCarthy as an "early draft," John Grady's character is established in an opening scene in which he attempts to break a horse that he has recently acquired.[3] Another cowboy holds the horse, and John Grady climbs on, only to be immediately bucked off. He tries again and again, hurting a foot that he had already injured while trying to ride a bull at a recent rodeo. Billy and the other cowboys have to stop him from trying again and injuring himself more seriously. John Grady objects: "I can ride the son of a bitch," he insists. "Not today you caint," replies his friend Oren. That night, John Grady implores Billy to help him break the horse, and when Billy refuses, John Grady goes straight back to the barn to try again on his own. "You are a goddamned idjit, aint ye?" Billy says in frustration. "What the hell is wrong with you?" When John Grady keeps accosting the horse, Billy says, "Will you leave that thing alone?" The conflict results in a fistfight between the two young men, during which Billy knocks John Grady down repeatedly. Despite onlookers telling John Grady to "stay down," he keeps coming back for more. When the fight finally ends, he tells Billy, "Goddamn you."

As originally conceived, John Grady's character was defined by stubbornness, grit, and an inability to take no for an answer. His approach to animals is literally rodeo-style, though that approach seems to fail both in the barn as well as in the actual rodeo in which he competes. Billy objects to John Grady apparently tormenting the horse, and John Grady speaks harshly both about the horse—"I can ride the son of a bitch"—and to Billy, whom he curses. His way of dealing with the Mexican prostitute Magdalena (in the film treatment, she is called, less evocatively, Elvira) is more tender, though equally unsuccessful in the end. John Grady here is literally and figuratively coonfooted. His footing is neither solid nor steady, and like Oedipus—another man with bad feet and bad footing—he is fated to experience love, loss, and tragedy.

When he crafts *Cities of the Plain* into a novel, McCarthy keeps this scene with the horse, though he changes the emphasis dramatically.

In the book, the horse, rather than the young man, is the difficult one, described in the narration as "shrieking" and "crazed" (17). As Billy, Troy, and Joachín watch John Grady "work the colt" in the corral—rather than merely chase it around, as he does in the earlier versions—Billy remarks that "I got a suspicion that whatever it is [John Grady] aims to do he'll most likely get it done" (14). Troy asks if John Grady "is supposed to be some sort of specialist in spoiled horses," and Billy refers the question to Joachín, asking him if the cowboy knows horses. Joachín just shakes his head. Billy clarifies to Troy, "Joachín thinks his methods is unorthodox" (15).

Here, John Grady is not reckless or unskilled, but simply willing to take the time—and the licks—to break the horse he considers his responsibility. Joachín's designation of "unorthodox" refers to the same considered and gentle horsebreaking method we see in so much detail in *Pretty Horses*. John Grady hasn't injured his foot being rowdy and trying to ride a bull as in the original screenplay, but while working with this same difficult horse. Finally, when Billy discovers John Grady in the barn, late at night, continuing to work with the horse, he and the other cowboys convince him to cease and desist without the added persuasion of a bloody fistfight. In the end, John Grady's only comment to Billy about this is that it "wasnt any of your business" (19). He's clearly irked, but well in control of his emotions—a notable difference from the way the character was originally written. Though the film adaptation of *All the Pretty Horses* does not portray John Grady as coarse or ineffective, it returns in some ways to the young man of the *Cities* screenplay, who is more of a tough cookie than a smooth-talking mystic.

"Whoa": John Grady on Film

Seemingly everyone involved with adapting *All the Pretty Horses* for the screen had a deep respect for what they saw as a remarkable novel. For a documentary called *Acting McCarthy: The Making of Billy Bob Thornton's "All the Pretty Horses,"* Peter Josyph and Raymond Todd interviewed most of the principles involved in the making of the adaptation, and were consistently impressed by everyone's respect for McCarthy's work. "Most of them had read the novel," Josyph notes,

> and some, such as Henry Thomas (who played Lacy [sic] Rawlins) and Julio Oscar Mechoso (who played the Captain), had wanted to be involved in the filming even before they were cast . . . Several of the actors referred to the novel as their bible, which they relied on for guidance in shaping their performances. (Josyph, "Losing Home" 132)

Though the actors, screenwriter Ted Tally, and director Thornton all express a desire to reflect the novel as closely as possible in the film, no one comments on the considerable changes made to John Grady's relationship with horses, perhaps the most significant element of the book. Whereas McCarthy's novel depicts that relationship as one that shifts from non-abusive dominance to deeply committed partnership, the film portrays it very differently. This is most evident in the horse-breaking scene, one of the most striking sequences of the film. In the novel, John Grady may break horses with a dominant voice and presence, but he never has to force his body onto a horse's back. In the film—well, if the Rawlins of the novel thinks a horsebreaker should "hang and rattle a time or two," then the Rawlins of the film gets that wish, and more.

After John Grady and Rawlins have been signed on as cowhands at La Purísima, they linger outside the bunkhouse, smoking and watching the 16 wild horses in the pen. As they watch, the camera cuts briefly and repeatedly to close-up shots of the horses' flanks, punctuated by the sound of their agitated whinnies. John Grady proposes breaking them all, and Rawlins reluctantly agrees. As they carry equipment toward the pen, Rawlins emphasizes the importance of succeeding at their task, and thus establishes the horsebreaking as a high-stakes effort rather than a lark: "We mess this up, bud, it's going to be a long ride back to Texas."

The horsebreaking sequence, which is presented in montage, begins with a slow-motion shot of a lasso swinging against the sky. A quick cut puts the viewer right in the middle of the action, as John Grady ropes one of the horses and loops the rope around a pole. The horse resists, bucking and moving away, and when John Grady approaches it with a saddle he is forced to drop it. A slow-motion shot of a saddle swinging through the air toward a horse's back is repeated three times during the montage, and we see wide shots of John Grady being bucked off the horse followed by other shots of him staying on successfully. Another repeated shot reveals John Grady approaching a horse with a saddle, intoning "whoa, whoa."

A crowd gathers, first the vaqueros and then others—families, a band—who cheer and applaud as the boys attempt to ride the bucking horses. Both John Grady and Rawlins are shown flying through the air in slow motion and taking hard falls. At one point Rawlins nods after rising to acknowledge the approval of the crowd. Finally night falls, and the audience watches, rapt, as the boys ride around the pen. Their task completed, the two boys exit the pen and walk toward the bunkhouse, accepting sips of tequila from one observer and their forgotten jackets from a small child who chases after them.

Though the film sequence features a great deal of slow-motion shots that linger on the lasso and saddle, it reveals few details about the variety of equipment used or the entirety of the process. Here, no real philosophy or special technique is explicated or demonstrated—both John Grady and Rawlins just get on until they can stay on, and more often than not, they are shown hitting the dirt. This is a sign, as Roberts might note, that the two are working for dominance rather than partnership.

Also in the film, the crowd that gathers comes more for the entertainment of a rodeo and the spectacle of two young Americans getting the stuffing beat out of them rather than to witness a form of horsebreaking so new or otherwise impressive that fathers would hold up babies to see it, as they do in the novel. As we see in the film, children laugh at the beat-up pair, and adults offer tequila to dull their aches and pains. John Grady does speak to the horses, but only very briefly; he says "whoa" and intones that he's "gonna put a saddle on you right now," but hardly maintains the ongoing and lengthy communication that he does in the novel. Finally, when their work is done, John Grady and Rawlins sit and eat a meal. As he does in the novel, Rawlins asks, "You tired?" The response is still definitely affirmative, but in the film it entails not only a hard day's work and mental exhaustion but a good bit of hanging and rattling as well.

The changes in the horsebreaking sequence dramatically alter the story of this young man as presented in the novel. The film, however, still conveys the importance of the scene, which is shot and edited beautifully, its striking composition second only to the scene leading up to Blevins' execution. Jim Kitses calls the horsebreaking sequence one of "three brilliant passages that effectively translate McCarthy's themes into film, relating the characters' inner life to history and myth." He goes on to note the ways the sequence succeeds:

> In what is at once a private experience and a spectacle, the boys assert their identity and establish their skill, commune with and master the animals, and contribute to their community. The effect is also one of timeless ritual—the play of light, the horses' defiance, the repeated falls and remounts. (15)

As Kitses implies here, the film makes Rawlins more of a key player. This is less John Grady's chance to show his mystical communion with horses than for *both* the boys, as Kitses says, to show their grit, determination, and masculinity. The two boys are figured as partners rather than as master and assistant.

If Rawlins is elevated in the film, then John Grady is also, in some sense, lowered. He never says, "Soy el comandante de las yeguas . . . yo y yo solo. Sin la caridad de estas manos no tengas nada. Ni comida ni agua ni hijos," or anything like it. He says "whoa." This film sequence demystifies John Grady as a character, and thus the story as well. It becomes tougher, less metaphysical. The John Grady of film is more like a real boy—he makes bad decisions, loses a friend, gets left by a girl and beat up all to hell, but manages to keep his best friend and recover their horses. And if he wants to break a horse, he gets on the thing until it kicks him off.

A Good Ride

Near the end of McCarthy's *All the Pretty Horses*, John Grady returns to Texas and to Rawlins, who urges him to stick around. "This is still good country," Rawlins insists. "I know it is," John Grady responds. "But it aint my country" (299). Then what is? Rawlins asks. "I dont know," John Grady responds. "I dont know where it is. I dont know what happens to country." John Grady, it seems, has largely given up claims to ownership and mastery, eventually abandoning the search for the owner of Blevins' horse as well. Of all these iterations—the screenplay typescripts and the novel of *Cities* as well as the novel and film of *Pretty Horses*—the end of McCarthy's *Pretty Horses* presents the most nuanced and sophisticated version of John Grady's character. Here, he has maintained an almost otherworldly attachment to and expertise with horses, and yet has moved beyond his claims of dominance or command. All the skill in the world, after all, doesn't guarantee the absolute assumption of control. In the language of the Dueña Alfonsa, he has learned that he doesn't always "get to say" (137).

As faithful as the film attempts to be to the novel, and as successful as it is in other ways, it loses this aspect of John Grady's character and development. Ironically, however, questions about the illusion and the elusiveness of mastery are raised in the story of the production of the film itself. Originally slated for release on December 25, 1999, the date was pushed back repeatedly until it was at last released a year later. Rumors surfaced of conflict between Thornton and the studio. Some 3 hours and 48 minutes of filmed material was cut and cut again, with Thornton working with then-chairman of Miramax, Harvey Weinstein. "During the trimming," Rick Lyman reports, "Columbia and Miramax decided that Miramax would handle the movie's domestic distribution and that Mr. Thornton had to deliver a version of around two hours."

When Peter Josyph and Raymond Todd interviewed those involved in making the film, many of them spoke in enthusiastic detail about the final scene, the farewell between John Grady and Rawlins that ends with the former riding off into the landscape and the sunset. "Thornton called it the most beautiful scene he ever shot," notes Josyph (146, n. 6). This scene, however, was cut from the final version of the film, and one gets the sense that, in many ways, these actors and filmmakers are commenting on a film that no longer exists.

The film that was finally released returned disappointing box office revenues and generally tepid reviews. "The material to which Mr. Thornton and [screenwriter Ted] Tally have been so ardently faithful has betrayed them," A. O. Scott noted in the *New York Times*. Jim Kitses calls the film "disappointingly uneven," but after reporting on the apparent conflict between director and studio, argues that Thornton is "no victim of the corporate enemy." His reach, Kitses writes, may simply have exceeded his grasp. Others disagree, and strongly. Josyph himself writes that those who would cut the film down solely for marketing purposes "disrespected the trained professionals who were paid to make the movie, and effectively abrogated their respect for the author" (Todd 203). In *Acting McCarthy*, Josyph and Todd ask Thornton what will constitute his contract with studios in the future. "Kiss my ass," he answers.

Film is a collaborative art. Even in the case of auteur directors, many pairs of hands contribute to the final product, often for better and occasionally for worse. As such, the stories behind such efforts—like this adaptation of *Pretty Horses*—often raise considerations of mastery, ownership, artistry, and skill similar to those McCarthy has written about in that novel and many others. His work reveals a fascination with craft and technique, especially that which is honed to such a level that we might call it art. McCarthy, however, is careful not to equate physical and metaphysical mastery. Art, after all, may ultimately be as much about knowing when to let go as when to hang on. Even writing itself is less of a one-man game than we might expect. The archive at Texas State includes correspondence with editors, translators, and others, all of whom contribute in some way to what we might call a "finished product" if these products were not such rich fodder for elaboration, revision, extension, adaptation—and, of course, interpretation. Rightly heard, all tales may indeed be one, but there are a few here (and perhaps more to come) that will keep us hanging and rattling for a while yet.

CHAPTER 3

McCarthy's Multitude(s): *All the Pretty Horses* and Los Hombres del País

Andrew Husband

Cormac McCarthy often writes about peoples many would characterize as members of the lower classes. Class—a significant cultural and literary topic of great conceptual and historical merit—features prominently in his oeuvre. McCarthy himself encountered the ups and downs of mid-twentieth century class, or at last income, stratification. His father, a lawyer, took a job with the Tennessee Valley Authority and moved the family to Knoxville in 1937. The move simultaneously augmented their status but displaced them to one of the poorest urban areas in the southern United States after the Great Depression. These transitions must have had an effect on McCarthy, as John Cant notes, he "declined the security of paid employment more or less throughout his entire career" (Cant 20). Nonetheless, only a handful of writers have devoted any concentrated attention to McCarthy's treatment of class. The scholarship of the past 30 years mainly focuses on expansive categorizations: Faulknerian, Southerner, regionalist, modernist, late modernist, postmodernist. As David Holloway remarks, "Some of the best critical writing on the fiction of Cormac McCarthy has unearthed a range of . . . positions at work in the novels" (3). However, despite the superfluity of these identifications and the diverse premises informing them, McCarthy criticism has yet to recognize significant trends in globalization theory responsible for drastic alterations to class as a critical and social subject. These developments are crucial for an adequate understanding of McCarthy's novels, all of which he produced during the post-World War II era that many correlate with the beginning of modern globalization. This chapter hopes to assuage this lack with an informed (re)reading of McCarthy's 1992 novel *All the Pretty Horses*.

One important aspect of this evolving discourse is class itself, which—in the presence of important discussions of gender, race, and postcoloniality of the last 50 years—has fallen to the wayside of critical attention. As the prominence of other analytical categories rose, many deemed class unimportant, especially in the realm of literary criticism. Yet globalization has generated a number of important questions about the presence of class in contemporaneity. Namely, we must reconsider the idea of class within the current framework of global capital, how the latter reconfigures it, and whether or not we can discern its literary and cultural emanations. In this chapter I will affirmatively argue for all three of these in the context of *All the Pretty Horses*, the first installment of McCarthy's "Border Trilogy." It reconceptualizes class with a series of relationships between John Grady Cole and Lacey Rawlins, the captain, the vaqueros at the Hacienda de Nuestra Señora de la Purísima Concepción, and los hombres del país, the men of the country, who reclaim the captain from John Grady's custody. McCarthy exhibits a progressive sense of cultural and economic acuity that observes the formation of and the complications with what political theorists Michael Hardt and Antonio Negri call the *multitude*. This new global formation of class describes the struggles between it and the worldwide sovereignty of *Empire*—Hardt and Negri's postulated political structure of networked capitalist power. After following this arc through McCarthy, I propose the adoption of Hardt and Negri's methods of analysis as a new post-Marxist literary criticism capable of reinstating class as a necessary category of analysis. This analysis will not only revitalize class as a critical subject in *All the Pretty Horses*, but it will also conjoin its discourse with the related identarian aspects of race and gender with which McCarthy scholarship has recently familiarized itself.

Class

Many, according to Wai Chee Dimock and Michael T. Gilmore, assume that "the imminent demise of Marxism, evidenced by the collapse of the Soviet Union and of Eurocommunism, would seem to mark the demise as well of 'class' as a category of analysis" (1). The editors express this sentiment in the introduction to a collection they published in 1994 concerned with rethinking class as an analytical category. While their intent to reinvigorate class is noteworthy, the arguments collected in their book are now somewhat dated. *Rethinking Class* was published five years after the physical collapse of the Berlin Wall and a string of anticommunist revolutions in 1989, a year considered a significant turning point in global politics. A turning point it was, but the Wall's collapse did not collapse class itself. Such distinctions continue to exist in social relations. Six years later *PMLA* published a topical issue concerned with "Rereading Class" in the twenty-first century. Troubled with the popular (mis)representations of the working class, Peter Hitchcock opines that "Most literary critics visibly wince at the mention of working-class representation as a significant component of cultural analysis" (20). While his own anxiety revolves around a particular facet of class, Hitchcock's affirmation confirms the suspicions of Dimock and Gilmore and reveals that class's problematic identification did not simply disappear during the 1990s. That the majority of scholars scoffed at the topic does not equate to the formation of a utopian classless society. Nor could anyone immediately assume that class was characteristic only of pre-globalization politics, lest we overlook the related subjects of race and gender. Critics have not forgotten what Eric Schocket ironically terms the "triumvirate of race, class, and gender," of which class became "the silent member" during the late twentieth century (11). Such silence is illusory.

The presence of class differences and struggles is easily distinguishable throughout McCarthy's Appalachian and Southwestern narratives. The relevant passages are especially remarkable for their attention to socio-economic detail. Christine Chollier confirms this in her article "The Questioning of Market Economics," which surveys eight of McCarthy's novels for his indisputable interest "in the interaction between different modes of exchange" (43). Her study spotlights a number of explicit economic transactions in the vein of the orthodox Marxist criticism of market economies. Chollier catalogues what she considers signi-ficant instances of exchange or barter-becoming-exchange that express exchange value and use value, Karl Marx's dichotomization of value. She is right to make these observations: "The issue of economics has rarely been addressed in McCarthy studies because his novels tend to be examined as reconfigurations of pre-existent literary myths, themes, or characters" (43). What Chollier's article radically implies is a significant gap in the scholarly appreciation of the socioeconomic aspects of McCarthy's works that pertains directly to their respective literary qualities. The myths, themes, and characters with which previous examinations tend to create dialog cannot exist in a vacuum separate from the complex subject of class.

Nowhere in *All the Pretty Horses* is this issue more apparent than in the relationship between John Grady Cole and Lacey Rawlins, two childhood friends who spend the first three parts of the novel traveling through and working in Mexico. A widely publicized and accepted aspect of their relationship is John Grady's dominance. Even the back cover of the first Vintage International paperback edition describes the narrative as telling "of young John Grady Cole, the last of a long line of Texas ranchers."[1] To be sure, the story primarily follows John Grady's movements. He catalyzes the trip to Mexico, garners much of the attention at the hacienda, and ultimately lands Lacey and himself in jail. Gail Moore Morrison argues for his centrality when she asserts that the

> novel is fundamentally a *Bildungsroman*, a coming of age story . . . that archetypal American genre in which a youthful protagonist turns his back on civilization and heads out—into the forest, down the river, across the sea or, as in John Grady's case, through the desert and mountains on horseback—into the wilderness where innocence experiences the evil of the universe and risks defeat by it. (178)

However, what Morrison neglects are the inherent racial, gendered, and socioeconomic qualities that empower the boys' ability to pack up and leave home. It would be naïve to assume that any one person, regardless of this triumvirate, could simply leave a place of significant sustenance with the appropriate means of continued general security and not question the origins of both. How is John Grady Cole capable of such flight, of the capacity to turn "his back on civilization" and head "out" toward better things? And what exactly are these better things? How would they benefit John Grady, and at what cost to others? This naivety plagues much of the accepted criticism, which tends to agree that he is a hero and "romantic dreamer who gradually awakens to reality" without questioning how he defines this reality (Luce 155). Is it the same for Lacey Rawlins or the other characters? Presupposing John Grady's characterization with the bildungsroman narrative structure negates such questions. Ultimately, it does not probe its subject's class nor its linkages to race and gender. After all, John Grady's status on the family ranch compliments his identification as a white male.

John Grady originates from a family of substantial status struggling with considerable debt. Set in 1949 after the end of the World War II and during the mid-twentieth-century boom in the industrial production of oil, the narrative opens with the diminishing economy of family-owned cattle ranching. The narrator presents the ranch's history after the opening funeral of the ranch's patriarch, John Grady's maternal grandfather:

> The original ranch was twenty-three hundred acres out of the old Meusebach survey of the Fisher-Miller grant, the original house a oneroom hovel of sticks and wattle . . . . Five years later his great-grandfather sent six hundred steers over [the] trail and

with the money he built the house and by then the ranch was already eighteen thousand acres. (McCarthy 6–7)

Despite the ranch's financial failure, John Grady aligns himself with his dead grandfather and the ranch as both current and future vehicles for stability. He broaches with his divorced parents the prospect of buying the land from his mother, who has inherited it from her now deceased father, and managing it. Yet, unlike everyone else, he cannot recognize the reality of the situation. His mother explains "This place has barely paid expenses for twenty years . . .. Anyway you're sixteen years old, you cant run a ranch" (15). Though John Grady questions her motivations and later goes so far as to stalk her in San Antonio, the validity of his mother's observations stands. He is four years shy of the ranch's supposed last year of economic sustainability and does not possess the level of maturity necessary to fully administer such a large property. Ultimately the family lawyer must remind him of his legal status as a minor (16). Nonetheless, the Grady family's commercial failure does not dissuade him from his aspirations. John Grady remains in his own estimation a member of a higher and more competent class. This characteristic rigidity influences his decision to leave Texas and find work in Mexico, driving the central narrative.

However, this summary is somewhat misleading. Accompanying John Grady is his older friend Lacey Rawlins. The relationship evident between them not only reveals much about John Grady's self-image, but also details Lacey's societal status in relation to his own. The class hierarchy that distinguishes between the lower, middle, and higher divisions evinces itself quite powerfully in their friendship. When extrapolating *class*, Raymond Williams remarks that from the early nineteenth century on, "the *upper* or *higher* part of the model virtually disappears, or, rather, awareness of a *higher* class is assigned to a different dimension, that of a residual and respected but essentially displaced aristocracy" (63). John Grady Cole falls succinctly within this definition of the higher class as a displaced socioeconomic group. Lacey, however, seems much closer to a bridged lower-middle class position that is "not very different from the COMMON *people*" (62). John Grady retains a position of dominance whereas his friend is generally compliant. By Williams' terminology, then, the former dictates the latter. But if "literature is a means to access the way class becomes part of subjectivity," or "how it forms . . . a discursive subject" (Dow 1), then one can assume that the fictional friendship tackles this subjectivity head on. When the boys debate about whether or not Lacey will also leave for Mexico, John Grady asserts his authority. Lacey willingly admits that John Grady "has more reason to leave" than he does, but the latter does not let it rest: "What the hell reason you got for stayin? *You think somebody's goin to die and leave you something?*" (McCarthy 27; my emphasis). Socioeconomics wield an imposing influence as John Grady indirectly commands his friend to accompany him. Without the promise of financial security, of a future free of instability, Lacey finds himself highly susceptible to the argument.

This relational animosity does not abate. Closer to the Texas-Mexico border, Lacey ponders aloud his family's status back home. John Grady's response mirrors the topic and tone of the previous outburst: "Well . . . probably they're havin the biggest time in the world. *Probably struck oil. I'd say they're in town about now pickin out their new cars and all*" (McCarthy 36–37; my emphasis). His chastisement of Lacey, though friendly, declares the latter's inferiority and obedience to monetary manipulation. Lacey's common status therefore limits him to socioeconomic dependence. Yet John Grady's interpretation remains biased. On multiple occasions the subordinate's status allows him to recognize certain peculiarities about their situations that John Grady cannot or will not see. After their arrest at the hacienda, Lacey expresses his irritation wholeheartedly while John Grady rebukes him, saying:

> Don't sull up on me. Let's get it aired.
> All right. When they arrested you what did you say?
> I didnt say nothin. What would of been the use?
> That's right. What would of been the use?
> What does that mean?
> It means you never asked em to go wake the patrón, did you?
> No. (155)

What Lacey points out to John Grady is that he seems unwilling to question the commands directed at him, almost as much as he unwaveringly commands others. So while Lacey, largely because of his status, possesses the ability to recognize authority and its intricacies, John Grady's location within such displaced forms of power prevents a similar recognition. Also, his knowledge of his own wrongdoing—of his sexual relationship (which Rawlins has earlier warned would lead to trouble) with Alejandra, the daughter of his employer and social equal, Don Héctor—further confounds John Grady's position with the police and the patrón. He is unable to counter their questions or protest his innocence.

These comparisons outline the class differences between John Grady and Lacey, a set of distinctions that McCarthy employs to divulge the discursive subjectivity of class in the narrative. However, this relationship does not denote the entirety of *All the Pretty Horses'* treatment of class. McCarthy advances these divisions to a degree that supersedes Raymond Williams' *Keywords*. In a sense, his development of class becomes post-Marxist.

Multitude

Such understanding has a parallel in critical theory: in their large philosophical polemic *Empire* (2000), Michael Hardt and Antonio Negri describe a set of new global formations of social, political, and economic powers of control and the means by which the exploited can harness these powers. Along with the developments of global production, Hardt and Negri determine that a new form of global sovereignty has emerged: "Empire is the political subject that effectively regulates [the new] global exchanges, the sovereign power that governs the whole world" (*Empire* xi). We no longer live in a strictly colonial, postcolonial, or imperialist era of sovereignty; the rule of globality is Empire, it is Imperial, and it subsumes all previous states.

The concept of Empire, however, is only significant for its identification of that which it exploits: the *multitude*. Hardt and Negri neglect to provide an unambiguous definition of the multitude, and for good reason. To do so would deflate its conceptual power and applicability. The two best explanations offered occur via oppositions: the first against Empire and the second against the modernist concept of *the people*. "The multitude," they argue in the former, "is the real productive force of our social world, whereas Empire is a mere apparatus of capture that lives only off the vitality of the multitude" (Hardt and Negri, *Empire* 62). In other words, Empire is the prison and the multitude the prisoner. Against the people, they describe the multitude as "a multiplicity, a plane of singularities, an open set of relations, which is not homogenous or identical with itself and bears an indistinct, inclusive relation to those outside of it" (103). The people, however, are created via means of homogenization and the exclusion of "what remains outside of it" (103). Hence the Declaration of Independence—Hardt and Negri's exemplar for this Enlightenment ideal—and its reliance for subjectivity on the phrase "We the People," a construction that implicitly excludes those considered as nonparticipants in political constitution. Even from the beginning the United States established itself by omission.

Ultimately, the multitude "is a class concept" of postmodernity that does not require one to "choose between unity and plurality," the old binarism between the merging of all labor into Marx's proletariat class and the indeterminate multiplicity of social classes exhibited by gender, race, and former colonial subjects (Hardt and Negri, *Multitude* 103–05). The superfluity of the multitude presents a highly malleable concept for analysis rather than a resolution to opt for one of two unproductive choices. One no longer must pick among highly specific class types (Hitchcock and the working class) or hypothesize class's conceptual destruction after Eurocommunism (Dimock and Gilmore). In reading *All the Pretty Horses* through this lens, we detect the multitude in both its becoming and actuality, and discover where in the novel McCarthy creates his multitudes and, subsequently, how they progress.

John Grady and Lacey's arrival at the hacienda and meeting with the vaqueros introduces the first instance of the multitude. They instantly take to one another, recognizing each other "by the way they sat their horses" and exchanging genialities: "[T]hey called them caballero [gentleman, but literally horseman] and exchanged smoking material with them and told them about the country" (McCarthy 93). They identify one another by their actions and bridge the social boundaries that dichotomize them. This is not to say that the boys become indistinguishable from the Mexicans or vice versa. Rather, both parties are willingly inclined to lessen their emphasis on such distinctions and focus instead on commonality. In short, the exchange establishes the multitude in its becoming. It achieves actualization after the work day when the boys and the ranch hands come together for the evening meal: "After dinner they sat at the table and smoked and drank coffee and the vaqueros asked them many questions about America and all the questions were about horses and cattle and none about them" (95). McCarthy's narrator admits the subjects of nation and nationality—in this case, John Grady and Lacey's association with the United States—but qualifies it further. Again, despite the presupposed racial and national identity markers, they unite on topics with which everyone can relate. They continue the process of becoming the multitude, realizing their differences and similarities simultaneously. Or, to adopt Hardt and Negri's phrasing, the cowboys and vaqueros install themselves on to the plain of singularities.

However, the class distinction between John Grady and Lacey does not readily dissipate. They eventually take two different paths at the hacienda based on their previous affiliations in the United States, morphing the boys into the ranch's class hierarchy. John Grady identifies himself with Don Héctor Rocha y Villareal, the owner of the hacienda and a figure not entirely unlike his deceased grandfather. The narrator renders this much apparent when outlining La Purísima as "one of very few ranches in that part of Mexico retaining the full complement of six square leagues of land allotted by the colonizing legislation of eighteen twenty-four," an enormous establishment whose "owner . . . was one of the few hacendados who actually lived on the land he claimed, land which had been in his family for one hundred and seventy years" (McCarthy 97). Comparing this passage to the one describing the Grady family ranch reveals shared constructions. Both describe large pieces of land claimed by white Europeans and designated for cattle ranching, lands whose original owners have either been relocated or pressed into service. While the Grady family held their ranch lands for a little over eighty years, almost a century less that Don Héctor's heritage, John Grady's grandfather and the Mexican cattle baron remain close in profession and age: "His grandfather was the oldest of eight boys and the only one to live past the age of twenty-five" (7). The parallels could not be any clearer. Yet Lacey, hailing from the lower rungs of Anglo ranching society in the southwestern United States, recognizes the hacendado before he's been introduced, and before John Grady does, telling his friend, "Yonder he is" (98). While John Grady's path at the hacienda easily melds itself to the higher rungs, Lacey's awareness of authority engenders his position.

Lacey's grouping with the vaqueros and the burgeoning multitude that results from their meeting directs his class-influenced path closer to their placement at the ranch. He is the first to recognize the worth of the new communal relationship during the boys' first night there, telling John Grady, "I believe these are some pretty good old boys" (McCarthy 96). The latter agrees, but Lacey remains vigilant. Much of his ability to notice peculiarities about their encounters begins with his background as a member of the lower to middle classes in the southwestern United States during the late 1940s. He is a worker, from a working class family, and although John Grady repeatedly reminds him of this, Lacey finds powers of detection in it when he situates himself with the vaqueros at the hacienda. After their initial separation at the ranch—John Grady to the horse breeders and Lacey to the bunkhouse—their meetings become infrequent. Even so, the latter retains his penchant for distributing advice from the underground to the former, educated suggestions that often go unheeded. Their arrest marks a dramatic example of this.

Earlier, during a trip out on the nearby mesa he interrogates John Grady about his relations with Alejandra and asks, "You got eyes for the spread?" (138), thereby equating her gendered body with the ranch lands. When John Grady responds circumstantially, "I dont know . . .. I aint thought about it," Lacey rebuts, "Sure you aint" (138). Sarcasm aside, Lacey's position as working class, or rather, as a new member of the hacienda's multitude, allows him the privilege of a subjective discursiveness that John Grady's immersion into the situation does not. Nor, more importantly, does John Grady's position permit him to see the severity of the consequences of his choices beyond himself and those who occupy a similar class status. Concluding his round of questions, Lacey surveys the scene with a claim that will partially come true with their later arrest: "What I see is you fixin to get us fired and run off the place" (138). Lacey's chief concern seems to be their jobs. Even so, John Grady ignores him. The latter's inherent stubbornness, which many attribute to a characteristic sense of heroism and fortitude, plants the seeds for the boys' arrest, imprisonment, and torture.

Their forced departure from the hacienda only reinforces these class distinctions, as well as providing additional credence to the budding multitude with which they are linked. Just as Hardt and Negri initially attempted to loosely define the multitude with a comparative discussion of Empire, so too does McCarthy oppose the boys to the figure of the captain and the authority he exerts. This new addendum to McCarthy's relationships finds a strong equivalent in *biopower* and *biopolitics*. The chief form of Imperial might is biopower, an idea adopted from Michel Foucault and Gilles Deleuze that Hardt and Negri modify extensively. "Biopower," they assert, "is a form of power that regulates social life from its interior" and "thus refers to a situation in which what is directly at stake in power is the production and reproduction of life itself" (Hardt and Negri, *Empire* 23–24). Biopower subsumes everything. The figure of the worker succumbs not only to Empire on the production line during working hours, but also off the line and outside of the working day. The distinctions "working hours" and "work days" no longer have any meaning. Biopower controls the entirety of life, and the multitude is its victim. Opposed to this is the biopolitical, an inversion of biopower harnessed by the multitude against Empire. "When we speak of the biopolitical," says Negri, "power and violence are considered, so to speak, 'from below', that is, from the point of view opposite to that of bio-power" (65). And because of the powerful ambiguity harnessed by the multitude, "no dialectical contradiction between living within the structures of biopower and the ability freely to transverse these structures in antagonistic ways, qua biopolitical subjects" troubles the multitude's insurgency (65). Therefore, the multitude resides in the Imperial structure of biopower while it rebels biopolitically from within it. These are the types of struggles that complicate the development of the literary multitude. And if we extend its application to *All the Pretty Horses*, we will find several instances of the biopolitical succumbing to and acting out against the forces of biopower.

A hint of the violence engendered by these confrontations challenges John Grady's own moral notions when he first meets the Dueña Alfonsa, the grandaunt and godmother of Alejandra. Concerned with the boy's unsupervised meetings with the girl and how the community at large may perceive them, the Dueña attempts to explain the situation to John Grady while advising no further contact. "Here," she says, "we live in a small world. A close world . . .. a world of men" (McCarthy 135). Social differences uncomfortably resurface from the periphery of John Grady's consciousness as she goes on to caution that Mexico "is another country. Here a woman's reputation is all she has" (136). When the boy expresses his discomfort, saying "that dont seem right," the Dueña corrects him: "It's not a matter of right. You must understand. *It is a matter of who must say*" (137; my emphasis). According to the elder's estimations, neither Alejandra nor John Grady can afford to disregard these contingencies to their own individual lives and vantages. Violent consequences remain for those who act out biopolitically against the forces of biopower. The Dueña Alfonsa knows of these consequences all too well. However, her warnings fall on deaf ears. John Grady secretly continues his sexual relationship with Alejandra. While he had protected the boys from earlier police inquiries regarding their involvement in Jimmy Blevins' killing of two men in his attempt to reclaim his lost horse, the patròn allows them to be taken into custody after learning of John Grady's actions with his daughter.

John Grady and Lacey's first major encounter with biopower happens in the jail with Jimmy Blevins and the captain. Blevins' incarceration has altogether debilitating effects on his person:

> I caint walk.
> You caint walk?
> That's what I said.
> How come you caint walk, said Rawlins.
> Cause they busted my feet all to hell is how come. (McCarthy 161)

The captain and his men not only imprison Blevins for his crimes in a hasty manner, but they also physically harm him. They exert a violent form of biopower. The bodily violence has the effect of rendering Blevins utterly immobile: he cannot escape, rejoin the multitude as a productive member, or speak to anyone who might possess the capability of biopolitically retaliating against the captain. He cannot even productively operate within the jail. Lacey, whose class affiliation marks a much stronger resemblance to Blevins than John Grady, subsequently receives similar treatment from the guards. When they return him to the cell, Lacey collapses to the floor in a heap of beaten bones and flesh and, in keeping with his character, dispenses advice to John Grady: "Tell em whatever they want to hear, bud . . .. It dont make a damn" (165). The torture of Lacey is severe enough that Jay Ellis suggests that it may have been rape (66–68). Considering the verity of Imperial power, its violence against the multitude, and its focus on the body, such a lurid act is feasible. John Grady, on the other hand, is spared such feminizing violence.

Though his responses to the captain's questions mirror Lacey's, John Grady escapes physically unscathed. He actually deduces much from the meeting and discovers what the police intend to do with Blevins: "I think they aim to kill him" (McCarthy 170). The captain and his posse eventually exert the final form of biopower: the cessation of the ability to (re)produce in biotic and abiotic manners, or the termination of life. During Blevins' execution, the boys react in their characteristic manner: John Grady is silent but Lacey biopolitically protests their actions, and though he remains confined by the literal shackles with which his wrists are bound, he speaks out: "They caint just walk him out there and shoot him . . .. Hell fire. Just walk him out there and shoot him" (178). As a member of the multitude, the grouping he first met with the vaqueros, Lacey acts in accordance with himself and with this counsel. He does not deny himself. John Grady, however, keeps silent.

The captain embodies Empire's expression of biopower against the members of the multitude in an exploitive manner. After shooting Blevins, he returns to the other prisoners and the guards and the narrator reflects on the scene:

[T]he captain inhabited another space and it was a space of his own election and outside the common world of men. A space privileged to men of the irreclaimable act which while it contained all lesser worlds within it contained no access to them. For the terms of election were of a piece with its office and once chosen that world could not be quit. (McCarthy 179)

McCarthy separates him from the others—not just John Grady, Lacey, and Blevins, but the guards and the brother of Blevins' victim who paid to accompany them and take part in the execution. The captain onto-logically exists and maneuvers in a fashion totally alien to everyone else. He is the decisive form of Imperial biopower, and though the guards and the accomplice act in accordance with his judgment, the captain's word remains final. He imprisons the boys, falsifies the evidence to torture Lacey and kill Blevins, and eventually moves the survivors on to other Imperial territories. During John Grady's interrogation, the captain confesses the complexity of his position when he says, "We can make the truth here. Or we can lose it" (168). He illustrates the horrific side of the violence inherent in class struggle, when patriarchal authority forcefully exerts itself onto the bodies of a gendered, lesser group. But it also provides a means of distinguishing the multitude in its formation and actualization.

Blevins' murder, Lacey's beating and possible rape, and John Grady's cross-examination admit their place in direct opposition to the captain, much like the multitude's meaning originates largely in its confrontation with Empire. Yet the narrative of these three boys does not fully realize the larger changes occurring to class and class struggle. This kind of portrait can only achieve near completion through a much deeper consideration of the vaqueros with whom John Grady and Lacey work, the various communities they encounter in and around the hacienda, and the men of the country who will eventually take the captain.

Los Hombres del País

If the meeting linking John Grady, Lacey, and the vaqueros at La Purísima parallels the creation of a multitude, then the people of the community surrounding the hacienda, the men whom John Grady encounters, and the vaqueros sans the Texans *are* the multitude as a living and breathing entity long after gestation. Yet the class affiliations of both characters, and the struggles they provoke between the two, render class formation as a seemingly new thing. That may be so from the boys' perspectives, but the majority of the novel's storyline follows their actions from Texas and back. Little narrative credence is allotted by McCarthy or the narrator to these communities which dwell outside the primary narrative. But this does not mean that we cannot accrue such credence from a reading of pertinent passages. The following section will address the ontological presence of the multitude in the novel through an examination of los hombres del país, the men of the country.

After the first day's work on the hacienda, two of the vaqueros take John Grady and Lacey to the gerente [ranch foreman] so that the boys might formally apply for work. In the process they are defended by the vaqueros, who second "their every claim" and volunteer "testimony . . . concerning the qualifications of the güeros [blondes or fair ones] of which they themselves were not even aware, dismissing doubt with a sweep of [the] hand as if to say these things were known to everyone" (McCarthy 95). Based on a single day's hard labor, the vaqueros develop a communal sense of confidence in the boys' abilities as ranch hand and are therefore comfortable enough to speak on their behalf. As before, social differences are ignored. A sense of separation between them and the boys does not develop until John Grady and Lacey follow the former's lead and decide to break a pen of horses in record time. John Grady aims to establish his credibility on the hacienda and set himself apart from the rest of the ranch hands, pulling Lacey along with him. Only then do the vaqueros detect a difference: "When they went down to the bunkhouse for dinner the vaqueros seemed to treat them with a certain indifference but whether it was the deference accorded to the accomplished or that accorded to mental defectives they were unsure" (105). Despite the individualist measures enacted by John Grady in breaking the horses without the aid of the other ranch hands, thus setting himself apart from them, the vaqueros remain what they were the day they met the boys: laborers of a lower, working class. Their sense of self, as members of the multitude, never compromises with other parties. Although the narrative depicts them only as a large and apparently indistinguishable community, their disparity for the boys' attempts at elevating themselves suggests that the vaqueros retain their individual identities as long as they do not break violently away from the larger group. Basically, they are the multitude of Hardt and Negri's definition, an undifferentiated plain of singularities who are both individual and the same.

An even larger group joins the jumble during the second day at the horse pen. "When they came back up to the trap in the afternoon there were some twenty people standing about looking at the horses—women, children, young girls and men—and all waiting for them to return" (McCarthy 105). The previous day's adventures with the horses quickly spread throughout the area, and those community members who are physically capable make the trip to witness the spectacle. Or, as Lacey astutely puts it, "Word gets around when the circus comes to town, dont it"? (105). Whereas the vaqueros represent the multitude's members of the working class in the traditional sense, the larger community McCarthy envisages expands the horizon beyond the linkage of labor. As indicated, these are not just men of the labor-ready age—they are women, children, young adults, and the elderly. They come to watch the horsebreaking in a communal gathering, creating a festive atmosphere with bonfires, music, and drink (107).

But like the semblances of the multitude witnessed thus far, the community surrounding the hacienda refrains from any intensive action that would allow them to become the target of Imperial oppression via biopower. Like the vaqueros—who despite their insistence on defending John Grady and Lacey when they apply for work, easily succumb to a kind of idleness when the boys are subject to arrest and removal—the people of the area recognize their class position for what it is and do not attempt to break its confines. In the town of

La Vega, where John Grady and Lacey race their horses for money and merriment, the locals react appropriately:

> the campesinos [country people; peasants] afoot in the road with baskets of gardenstuff or pails covered with cheesecloth would press to the edge of the road or climb through the roadside brush and cactus to watch wide eyed the horsemen on their horses passing. (McCarthy 119)

John Grady and Lacey are "alien" to them as Anglo-American cowboys from the southwestern United States, privileged by their gender and national affiliation, but in the eyes of the crowds they are lumped together into the local class system that pits pedestrians against riders (119). A similar distinction occurs when the police appear at the hacienda after the boys' arrival. As the five officers approach the ranch on horseback Lacey and the vaqueros "come to the door and [stand] looking out" at them (142). Like the citizens of La Vega, the vaqueros recognize the riders for what they are and stay back, observant but non-participatory. In both cases the possibility of class struggle is significantly reduced due to widespread inaction. The power of the oppressors, the figures of authority who either represent or work for the higher classes, serves as enough of a deterrent to discourage any action. Fundamentally, Empire's exertion of biopower can be enough to restrain the multitude and prevent biopolitical rebellion.

An example of the multitude's successful expression of biopolitical dissent, however, occurs in the fourth part of the novel, during which John Grady returns to the hacienda to reclaim his and Rawlins' horses and takes the captain with him as a hostage as he escapes into the desert. The appearance of a fully realized multitude is both sudden and brief: "When he woke there were three men standing over him. They wore serapes over their shoulders and one of them was holding the empty rifle and all of them wore pistols" (McCarthy 280). They confiscate the keys to the handcuffs and release the captain, whose hands John Grady has cuffed in front of him, only to resituate his bindings behind his back for better control. Noting John Grady's badly wounded leg, one of the men gives him his serape. After a brief exchange, the three men then take the terrified captain and prepare to leave the boy alone in camp. John Grady, however, stops them,

> Quiénes son ustedes? he called.
> The man who'd given him his serape turned at the outer edge of the light and touched the brim of his hat. Hombres del país, he said. Then all went on.

Men of the country. He sat listening as they rode up out of the
ravine and then they were gone. (281)

These men of the country, or los hombres del país, supply *All the Pretty
Horses* with its strongest example of the multitude yet. John Grady's
broken connection to the middle to higher classes of Texas and his
failed ambitions at La Purísima confine him uncomfortably to the
multitude-in-becoming with Lacey and the vaqueros. And though
Lacey's stronger identification with the vaqueros and his unique insight
into his class-influenced relationship with John Grady suggests his
betterment, McCarthy's finest illustration of the new seditious class
exists in the book for only a single page's worth of text. Their presence
is minor but their effect major. They take the captain away into their
custody and, like him, are never seen again by John Grady. As men of
the country they are readily equipped with the knowledge and the
power to defend and return to the country from which they came. Their
actions serve as a model for the others: the vaqueros, the community,
Lacey, John Grady. The latter witnesses their manner but does not
possess the necessary comprehension to process it in a way that would
benefit himself. As a result, John Grady leaves his camp without
further comment. His past affiliation with and eventual expulsion
from the Anglo, male land-owning classes of the Texas cattle industry,
a place in which figures like the captain were never able to exert
themselves enough to obtain a young boy's attention, negates the
actuality of what the men of the country stand for. John Grady cannot
compute them, and therefore forgets them.

When he finds Lacey back in Texas and returns his horse, his friend
offers an explanation of events in the local community in their absence
and during John Grady's return trip. As one who has had plenty of time
for recuperation, Lacey's account offers answers to his friend's countless
questions. Yet the emphasis of Lacey's information illustrates his
continued alliance with the lower classes and his new connection to the
multitude. When he tells John Grady that the woman he calls abuela
[grandmother]—an older Mexican woman who has been a domestic
worker on the Grady ranch for most of her life—is ill, he qualifies the
family's condition with work-related news concerning her relative
Arturo: "I seen Arturo over in town. Thatcher Cole got him a job at the
school. Cleanin up and stuff like that" (McCarthy 299). John Grady
expresses concern, but mostly about the older woman. I do not wish to
suggest that his disregard of Arturo's job experience marks John Grady
detrimentally, but it does admit more about his class status. Luisa,
abuela, and Arturo are former workers for the Grady family, people
whom John Grady has known his entire life. His care for abuela, who

was essentially his nanny and raised him after his parents separated and his mother left the ranch, is founded on a lifetime's worth of familiarity, but his former hierarchical position toward her biological family explains his disregard for Arturo's relocation to another job for another employer. Even after encountering the men of the country and their biopolitical action against the captain, John Grady remains imprisoned within the rigid boundaries of his former class status.

Class as critical subject abounds in McCarthy's fiction. The critical reading of Christine Chollier on the author's use of economics gathers enough peripheral evidence to support this assertion. Yet, as Chollier herself divulges, there remains much to be seen and said about McCarthy's grasp of class as a political subject. The unique and collective representations of different classes and class struggles throughout the Appalachian works, the Southwestern books, and the other creative media necessitate additional scrutiny. While this chapter is not the place for such a lengthy endeavor, *All the Pretty Horses* presents a fascinating case study for McCarthy's treatment of the subject and its parallels to contemporary post-Marxist theory on the topic of class as affected by globalization.

PART II

No Country for Old Men *(2005)*

Introduction

Part II begins with Stephen Tatum's chapter, "'Mercantile Ethics': *No Country for Old Men* and the Narcocorrido," arguing that Sheriff Ed Tom Bell's opening narration of the shooting of his patrol car by the passenger of a Mexican pickup truck that Bell attempts to stop one night along a small Texas highway

> reveals in condensed form McCarthy's novel's overall invest-
> ment . . . in exposing the contagious violence along the U.S.-
> Mexican border and in detailing the complicity of all involved
> in this country's *"strange kind of history and a damned bloody
> one too."*

Through Bell's narrative and his questioning of the nature of evil in the modern world, Tatum explains, "McCarthy both formally and them-atically produces an internal corrido or border ballad" recording the disruptive effects of drug smuggling and the violent "mercantile ethics" of late capitalism which enable its destruction of individuals and communities on both sides of the border. Tatum examins McCarthy's internal corrido through the history and form of the narcocorrido—the latest incarnation of what a character in McCarthy's earlier novel *The Crossing*, calls "the poor man's history."

In Chapter 5, "'Do you see?': Levels of Ellipsis in *No Country for Old Men*," Jay Ellis examines the "preponderance of visual tropes" in both the novel and film versions of *No Country for Old Men*, especially those associated with the character of Anton Chigurh, suggesting that the emphasis on the visual "might extend beyond mere scopophilic power, though it most certainly also derives from that especially male need to see, and to see more than to be seen . . . " Rather, he argues, Chigurh and his continuing insistence that other characters see what he sees, functions not just as an evil killer

> but also as a Socratic figure who . . . engages in extended dialogue intended to help his victims see what they could not before see, that their past actions, in conjunction with chance events, have determined their fated end at his hands.

Ellis explores the presentation of visual tropes by McCarthy in his novel (originally written as a screenplay) and the creative re-visualization of those tropes by filmmakers Joel and Ethan Coen in their award winning adaptation.

Dan Flory's "Evil, Mood, and Reflection in the Coen Brothers' *No Country for Old Men*," closes out Part II through a further philosophic analysis of the film, extending Tatum's examination of evil on the socioeconomic level and Ellis' discussion of Chigurh as a Socratic figure intent on forcing his notions of fate and free will by examining him as a manifestation of evil, arguing that viewers' "understanding of Chigurh as a morally evil individual is fundamental to the film" as well as the novel. Noting that critics have remarked on the generally philosophical nature of the novel, Flory points out that "In an analogous fashion, the Coen brothers' cinematic version of Sheriff Bell," as well as their portrayal of Chigurh, "poses the problem of evil and the question of properly grasping it." Many critics (and the character of Bell) seek a religious basis for engaging this question, particularly as it relates to Chigurh, a figure Flory suggests has excited more discussion than any villain since Hannibal Lecter in that other wildly successful filmic adaptation of the popular novel *The Silence of the Lambs*. Flory argues, however, that "the Coen brothers' film invites viewers to think reflectively about their limits for understanding evil individuals" by suggesting that traditional, theologically based explanations of them are inadequate. In Part 3 Donovan Gwinner will extend this investigation of the presentation of fate, free will and the existence of evil in his discussion of religion, theology, and morality in *The Road*, furthering a scholarly debate about these issues which has fascinated McCarthy scholars since the publication of his first novel.

CHAPTER 4

"Mercantile Ethics": *No Country for Old Men* and the Narcocorrido

Stephen Tatum

You take somebody that will actually throw down on a law enforcement officer and open fire you have got some very serious people. I never saw that truck again . . . Maybe I should have took out after it. Or tried to. I dont know. I drove back to Sanderson and pulled in at the café and I'll tell you they come from all over to see that cruiser. It was shot full of holes. Looked like the Bonnie and Clyde car. (39–40)

"Just Kindly Collectin My Thoughts"

At the outset of chapter two of Cormac McCarthy's *No Country for Old Men* Sheriff Ed Tom Bell describes what turns out to be a violent night-time encounter with a pickup truck bearing license plates from the north central Mexican state of Coahuila on a Terrell County, Texas, two-lane blacktop road. Trailing the truck and noticing two men sitting in its bed, he turns on his police cruiser's lights to signal the truck to pull over for inspection, and then an *"old boy settin in the bed of the truck"* (38) proceeds to fire three shotgun blasts at Bell's cruiser, which skids sideways into a bar ditch beside the road when he slams on its brakes. The cruiser's windows and windshield are shot out and its cab largely filled with dirt, and by the time Bell is able to return fire with his pistol the pickup truck has vanished in the night, prefiguring the leitmotif of the novel's main pursuit-and-escape plot involving Anton Chigurh and Llewelyn Moss. As Bell's retrospective account of this event then mentions three times in quick succession, he just sat there in the wrecked cruiser's cab, *"kindly collectin"* (39) his thoughts, before eventually driving back to Sanderson where he seeks out a cup of coffee at its one café. When his account turns from narration and description to commentary, Bell's thought is this: "*Point bein you dont know what all you're stopping when you do stop somebody. . . . and you dont know what you're liable to find*" (39) out on the highway, a judgment especially confirmed, as readers know, by Chigurh's two murders in the novel's opening chapter.

However, the larger question on Bell's mind is concerned not only with how one does not know for sure what one might face when patrolling the roads of Texas counties bordering Mexico. For this particular confrontation with the Mexican pickup truck "*from a few years ago and it wasnt that many neither*" underscores a key theme of his first-person accounts interspersed throughout the novel's length. "*I dont know if law enforcement work is more dangerous now than what it used to be or not*," Bell remarks, allowing that "*maybe you see worse now.*" However, as his monologue that opens chapter two ends, his notation of the increasing violence accompanying border drug trafficking and the news reports both of serial killing sprees and of a young woman putting her baby in a trash compactor provides a direct answer to his "*I dont know*" rhetoric. For such developments, in point of fact, confirm how nowadays law enforcement just "*keeps gettin harder*," with the result that his rhetorical circumlocution highlights his elision of "but that" ("I dont know *but that* law enforcement is more dangerous now. . . ."). So Bell confesses he reads the daily newspapers, hoping "*to try and figure out what might be headed this way. Not that I've done all that good a job at headin it off.*" In the end, the "*I dont know*" that opens Bell's monologue—and that becomes a refrain sounded throughout the novel's dialogue scenes—*evolves* into his summary comment "*Well, we dont know*" that concludes it (38–40).

Bell's retrospective, framing narration occurs here both after Chigurh has killed two men and after Moss has discovered the dead human and canine bodies and shot-up Mexican pickup trucks from an abortive drug deal—and after he has fled the scene with weapons and a document case containing $2.4 million. Bell's police cruiser's accident during this chance encounter with a Mexican pickup truck foreshadows the later car accident in Odessa, Texas, when Chigurh's Dodge Durango, also bought in Mexico, gets T-boned at an intersection by a ten-year-old Buick driven by a young Mexican man who runs a stop sign while passing a joint with his two companions. All told, then, Bell's narration of this event—its themes and imagery and rhetoric—reveals in condensed form McCarthy's novel's overall investment: (1) in exposing the contagious violence along the US-Mexican border, the effect of which is to destabilize bodies, material objects, and geopolitical boundaries; and

(2) in detailing the complicity of all involved in this country's "*strange kind of history and a damned bloody one too*" (284). Through Bell's narrative commentary on the traumatic events recorded in the novel's main plot, it is as if McCarthy both formally and thematically produces an internal *corrido* or border ballad, whose emergent sense of mourning indexes both directly and indirectly the political, financial, moral or ethical, and even linguistic crisis emerging along the US-Mexico border in the wake of the Vietnam War.

Sitting in his wrecked police cruiser, Bell describes himself as "kindly collectin" his thoughts (39). His "thoughts," which is to say his ability to comprehend and explain matters at hand—as well as perhaps their relation to some historical past signified here by the reference to the Bonnie and Clyde death car—are for the most part outstripped by the novel's events, both by their sudden penetration into the banality of everyday life and by the cumulative record of their unforeseen or unintended consequences. That he must "collect" his thoughts underlines how this accident has dispossessed him, fragmenting his subjectivity like the broken windshield whose fragments surround him, as if he is detached from or sitting beside himself, watching his composure return. That he relies here on his favorite adverb "*kindly*" also confirms the overall crisis of identity and faith and vocation he discloses throughout his narrative interludes. For in one direction, "*kindly*" implies an agreeable or obliging manner of action, a response or affect seemingly fitting or natural, given the circumstances at hand. Yet in another direction, Bell repeatedly speculates about a "*some new kind*" of criminal traveling the highway, especially that "*true and living prophet of destruction*" named Chirgurh, whose often-grotesque actions are anything but natural or native, are not "of a kind," but rather alien or, to use another of Bell's locutions, "*peculiar*" (4). With its connotation "of a kind" or native thus conjuring up its dialectical opposite "alien" during this recollected encounter with the Mexican pickup truck, Bell's adverb reveals how the flow of drugs, money, people, and guns across geopolitical borders has made him simultaneously both at home and "unhomely." He is a figure who presumably still loves this country that "will kill you in a heartbeat" but who remains haunted by a spectral figure whose movements and violent acts—like all the signifiers of the Mexican presence in the novel—force the uncanny return to consciousness ("thoughts") of Greater Mexico's repressed historical record since the Treaty of Guadalupe Hidalgo in 1848, ending the US-Mexican War and forcing Mexico to cede to the United States the northern third of its nation.

As registered by the "kindly collectin my thoughts" and the "I dont know" and "nothin" phrases that predominate in both Bell's narration and in the novel's other dialogue scenes, *No Country for Old Men* diagnoses a cognitive paralysis regarding the capacity for anyone living in the traumatic, "unhomely" present to apprehend his or her situation and grasp the truth(s) of history. Just as events like the encounter with the Mexican pickup truck conspire to put Bell's subjectivity in disarray—not of a "kind" with or native to himself—so too his narration often falters on the edge of comprehension, falling back on formulaic phrasing and clichés or simply recording the flow of sensation as his eyes scan the surfaces of what meets his increasingly troubled gaze. McCarthy formally *spatializes* the disjuncture between acting and thinking ("collectin thoughts"), between performing and narration, by dividing the novel's narrative structure between Bell's more interior or private confessional mode and the more external escape-pursuit narration that serves to hollow out all the characters' interior lives and presents them essentially as proper names who orbit around a leather document case that itself is overdetermined by commodity exchange relations operative in 1980 (the novel's present). And yet, as signaled by his allusion here to "the Bonnie and Clyde car," as well as by the long conversation about his and his family's history he has late in the novel with his wheelchair-bound Uncle Ellis, Bell's abiding narrative desire is to produce a narrative explanation that will make disjunctive things and events in time and space cohere—and in that coherence hopefully provide him some answers regarding all the assorted *"signs and wonders"* portending *"what is to come"* and *"what shape it [will] take"* along the border (295). To use a moment later in the novel when Bell once again sits in a vehicle, this time around unable to "name the feeling" besetting him on his last day as sheriff, perhaps all the remembering and repetition afforded by the narrative process will allow him to get over the numbing sense of "being beaten. More bitter to him than death" (306).

Toward that end, Bell later tells a young female reporter inquiring about the high crime rate in Terrell County, *"Any time you quit hearin Sir and Mam the end is pretty much in sight."* Alluding to the event that sets the novel's main plot in motion, Bell then remarks that when *"You finally get into the sort of breakdown in mercantile ethics that leaves people settin around out in the desert dead in their vehicles and by then it's just too late"* (304). As if experiencing post-traumatic stress disorder, Bell (and others) in the novel comment on the absence of ethics, or the loss of morals and religious faith (Moss' father's explanation for the Vietnam War defeat), the existence of Satan, or even the role of "this country" that in the end "has got a lot to answer for" (271). Still, such causal explanations to Bell's mind ultimately neither understand the past nor offer any *"idea of the world that is brewin out there"* (283).

For as we can see by his adjective "mercantile," amid all the "I dont know" and "I dont have no answer" expressions in his discourse, Bell begins to understand how his (and his family's) personal history is sutured together with the larger social world—with "*ever strata of society*."

Here we should consider how Bell's narration of his encounter with the Mexican pickup truck is structured by a binary of motion and stasis that, in turn, reveals a tension between two kinds of desire: on the one hand, a desire for the flow of peoples and commodities to proceed unimpeded, a process which destabilizes the spatial, economic, and political scales of city, county, state, and nation; on the other hand, a desire for the "collectin" or maintenance (policing) of established geopolitical boundaries and legal codes. This structural binary and its attendant tension supplements what Moss' discovery of the aborted drug deal on "an old wagonroad that bore eastward across Harkle's land" (25–26) more generally suggests: how the "*mercantile* ethics" associated with the endeavors of the Juárez or Sinaloa drug cartels, in league with corporate financial interests in the United States such as the Matecumbe Petroleum Company, produce a tension between terri-torialization (the space of places) and deterritorialization (the space of flows). The point here is that such illegal endeavors signify not so much how "*ethics*" or "*Satan*" (218), but rather how the "*signs and wonders*" Bell bears witness to are bound up with the contradictions of late capitalism in transition. Its expansionist energies into "*ever strata*" of society not only effect social relations—as we can see by the fortunes of Llewelyn and Carla Jean Moss—but also force Bell "*to look at it* [history] *again and I've been forced to look at myself*" (304; 296). For better or worse, Bell's gringo corrido discloses by stages that his emergent tasks—which are also those of the novel's readers—center both on recovering the repressed content of history and also on learn-ing how to mourn properly, how to re-imagine self and community on the basis of an ethic grounded on shared grief.

"The Poor Man's History"

There's days I'm in favor of givin the whole damn place back to 'em, the sheriff said.

I hear you, said Bell.

Dead bodies in the street. Citizens' businesses all shot up. People's cars.

Whoever heard of such a thing? (134)

I guess that's it. Were these Pablo's men?

Yes.

You're sure.

Not in the sense that you mean. But reasonably sure. They weren't ours. He killed two other men a couple of days before and those two did happen to be ours. Along with the three at the colossal goatfuck a few days before that. All right? (141)

Robbers of citizens' businesses and shooters of cars and people, Bonnie Parker and Clyde Barrow were shot and killed in their 1932 Ford V-8 car by Texas and Louisiana law enforcement officers in Bienville Parish, Louisiana, on May 23, 1934. The bullet-riddled car containing their blood-splattered bodies was then towed to Arcadia, Louisiana, whose population reportedly swelled from 2,000 to 12,000 people within a few hours of the news of the celebrity outlaw couple's death. Two of the four Texas officers involved in the ambush, which was made possible by the betrayal of a Barrow gang member, were former Texas Rangers. Their death car—referenced by Sheriff Ed Tom Bell when describing his own shot-up police cruiser at the beginning of chapter two—was to become a touring attraction at amusement parks, various state fairs, race tracks, car museums, and Nevada casinos in the decades between 1934 and 1980, the present moment of *No Country for Old Men*.

Five months after the killing of Bonnie and Clyde, on October 13, 1934, the corrido or Mexican border ballad "El Contrabandista" was recorded in a San Antonio, Texas studio. Featuring a persona singing of his illegal exploits while inside a jail cell, "El Contrabandista" describes the smuggling of various liquors into Texas during the Prohibition years—until, that is, its persona relates how he is at last captured and jailed by Texas Rangers acting on an informant's tip. Still, before this first ever recording of a smuggling corrido, ballads about the smuggling of liquor, textiles, candle wax, and various drugs had already become staples of the border culture's oral tradition both during Prohibition and the early years of the Great Depression. Whereas in Bell's encounter with the Mexican pickup truck the drug traffickers escape into the night, in the early smuggling corrido "Los Tres Tequileros," by contrast, three Mexican bootleggers cross the border only to end up being killed by the Texas Rangers. A decade later, in the 1940s corrido "Carga Blanca" Mexican smugglers travel to San Antonio with heroin and cocaine, sell the drugs, and then get hijacked and killed on their way home. With their cash in the end being returned to the anonymous man with whom the drug traffickers had initially arranged the deal, this corrido's plot trajectory anticipates the main escape-and-pursuit plot of *No Country for Old Men* set in motion by the "colossal goatfuck," to use the anonymous businessman's words to Carson Wells in the above epigraph.

In the wake of the shootout in Eagle Pass, Texas, involving Moss, Chigurh, and Mexican drug traffickers seeking either (or both) the return of the missing drugs and money, the sheriff of Eagle Pass tells Bell that he's all "in favor of givin the whole damn place back to 'em." His statement references the Treaty of Guadalupe Hidalgo which formally ended the Mexican-American War in 1848 by, among other things, redrawing the US-Mexico border so that "the whole damn place" described in *No Country for Old Men*—its landscape; its place names; its territorial divisions—became United States possessions. In the years following this treaty, as a mostly Anglo-settler culture expanded into and along the south and west Texas frontier, violent skirmishes regularly occurred between these newcomers, native tribes such as the Comanche, and Mexicans displaced of citizenship and, often, of property. The Texas Rangers, active as guides and guerilla fighters both during the years of the Texas Republic and also the recently concluded war with Mexico, were formally organized to protect these frontier settlements along the border. During Sam Houston's presidency of the Republic of Texas, John Coffee "Jack" Hays led the Rangers, training them to shoot and reload their Colt pistols while on horseback and himself becoming legendary for repelling an 1842 incursion by the Mexican army into south Texas. This is the 150-year border "history" condensed into Bell's Uncle Ellis' reference—when describing the 1879 murder of their Texas Ranger forefather on his front porch in Hudspeth County, east of El Paso—that their "Uncle Mac" never rode with "Coffee Jack" during his time as a Texas Ranger (269). An expressive cultural form with roots in the Spanish romance ballad tradition, the corrido developed along the US-Mexico border within this long history of violent conflict, social stratification, and economic subordination. To use the phrasing of the character Quijada in McCarthy's 1994 novel *The Crossing*, the corrido "is the poor man's history" (386), its tale celebrating a subaltern or local folk hero's resistance to authority figures, these ranging from local police to county sheriffs to the Texas Rangers to the military or judicial agencies of the US and Mexican governments. At the heart of the corrido, José Limón suggests, exists "an aestheticized and eroticized figure of strong masculinity confronting other men with the phallic power of his pistol in his hand" (106). As exemplified by the classic corrido from the turn of the twentieth century, "El Corrido de Gregorio Cortez," the themes of social injustice and the hero's defiant bravery emerge through a story about a Texas sheriff who falsely accuses Cortez's brother of stealing a horse and then shoots him when he resists arrest. Acting in self-defense, Gregorio Cortez shoots the sheriff and flees the scene, eventually surrendering after a lengthy chase that reveals his courage and skills in eluding capture.

Though arrested and jailed, his individual exploits speak to the resilience and the values of the corrido listening audience, and along with the Robin Hood or social bandit theme, this corrido dramatizes how a rural, agrarian community is, in the end, regenerated by the subaltern hero's resistance, their more communitarian values opposed to the nexus of property and economic exchange of the modernizing, dominant Anglo culture.

The corrido form flourished immediately before and during the years of the Mexican Revolution at the beginning of the twentieth century, and evolved during the Prohibition era to include the liquor and drug smuggling themes mentioned above. Their subject matter based on the local history of oppression along the border contact zone between the United States and Mexico, and their content augmented by the later smuggling corridos' additional themes of betrayal and tragic death, again typically at the hands of the Texas Rangers, these corridos prefigure the narcocorrido, a type of corrido centering on the exploits of drug traffickers or *narcotraficantes* that emerged during the 1970s and remains popular today on both sides of the border. The narcocorrido typically follows the rhyme scheme and stanzaic form of the traditional corrido, but its duration is shorter, often the same as a 3-minute popular song. And like the classic or traditional corrido, the narcocorrido opens with an introduction of the specific setting and names of the protagonists; features a core narrative centering on a violent encounter between its charismatic hero and the dominant culture's authorities; and ends with the singer's farewell, his closing commentary either celebrating the exploits of the narcotraficante, whether alive or dead at the end of the core narrative, or—as is the case in the early years of the narcocorrido— warning the listening community about the dangers involved with the illegal drug trade. Characterized by some observers as rap music capturing the street reality of the border's *barrios, colonias* and *maquilas*, the narcocorrido's core themes and imagery foster regional identification and ethnic pride, as well as celebrate the drug trafficker's upward social mobility. Indeed, although some narcocorridos relate the gifts made by *narcotraficantes* to their local communities in, say, Sinoloa or Juárez, the major difference between the narcocorrido and the traditional corrido centers on how the narcocorrido's focus on social mobility and material wealth dislodges the earlier corrido's thematic focus on the hero's social banditry, which epitomized the congruence felt then between the subaltern hero's activities and the corrido listening community's values.

In *No Country for Old Men*, when Carson Wells meets with an agent of the Matecumbe Petroleum Company, he asks if any of those involved in "the colossal goatfuck" were "Pablo's men." His allusion refers to the real life Pablo Acosta, drug lord from Ojinaga, south of Juárez, a man who once defeated a rival drug lord in a shoot out and who then sustained his legend by having his competitor's shot-up Ford Bronco— a *narcotraficante* death car à la Bonnie and Clyde—placed on blocks by the road entering Ojinaga. Acosta is the main protagonist in the narcocorrido "El Zorro de Ojinaga" (The Fox of Ojinaga). In this narcocorrido, Acosta initially is said to have "watched the border under Uncle Sam's orders," hunting down "terrorists, those who knew how to kill." But then "other orders were given," and "he brought down planes with cocaine to start." As a result,

> From the skies in Arizona, they tried to bring him down.
> They sent Vecias, it was said, with a Mirage motor,
> but the Fox with his Cessnas made the Devil look bad.
>
> They killed his brother, who was his right-hand man,
> And later at the ranch they charged the rent [killed more of his men]
> But because he's dead now, it's not like they can contradict him.
>   (Edburg, 61)

Here the narcotraficante's courage and tactical skills at eluding capture are qualified by his tragic flaw of overconfidence and his inability not to trust those closest to him. Here too, in this narcocorrido specific signifiers encode the layered history of violence on both sides of the Rio Grande. The reference to the killing of Acosta's brother conjures up memories of the deadly event that initiates the escape-and-pursuit narrative of "El Corrido de Gregorio Cortez." Moreover, the classic corrido tradition's common theme of death by betrayal joins with the relatively new narcocorrido theme of corruption, deceit, and hypocrisy by both "Uncle Sam" and the Mexican government that sends Vecias, "with a Mirage motor," after Acosta.

This partnership between federal authorities, here personified as "the Devil," and their supposed betrayal and dogged pursuit of Acosta likely signifies for the narcocorrido listening community both Acosta's publicized bribery of authorities and the Operation Condor program launched in the late 1970s in which US and Mexican governments colluded in the aerial spraying and the burning of marijuana and opium fields in rural northern Mexico, one effect of which was to displace farmers and their families north to the border *colonias* and *barrios,* and then into the United States as legal or illegal immigrants. For our purposes, the specific imagery here of cat and mouse aerial pursuits and escapes also resonates with Bell's recollection in the novel of a DC-4 airplane abandoned on a remote dirt airstrip in Presidio County after delivering its cargo of marijuana (217). Moreover, this imagery involving Cessna airplanes (in other narcocorridos the comparable signifier might be a Bell helicopter) trespassing national borders registers the specialized role of transport and security operations filled by the Mexican drug cartels during the period in which the novel is set.

"With his [Captive Bolt] Pistol in His Hand"

> You cant count on em to kill one another off like this on a regular basis. But I expect some cartel will take it over sooner or later and they'll wind up just dealin with the Mexican government. There's too much money in it. They'll freeze out these country boys. It wont be long, neither. (138)

For the elite and middle-class strata of the corrido listening community, a figure like "the fox of Ojinaga" most likely represents a declension of traditional moral values, a judgment Ed Tom Bell himself certainly puts forward with reference to the drug traffickers' corruption of law enforcement agents. Yet the narcocorrido representation of contemporary social life—as exemplified by Los Tigres del Norte's 1988 "Corridos Prohibidos" album—appeals to the greater demographic of the corrido listening community because it "provides a street-level view of all the surreal juxtapositions of modern Mexico: the extreme poverty and garish wealth, the elaborate courtesy and brutal violence, the corruption and craziness, sincerity and mythologizing, poetry and excitement and romance" (Wald 6). Moreover, for the specifically subaltern strata of the corrido listening community the narcocorrido apparently appeals because its representation of a hypermasculine, charismatic individual with power, status, and newfound material wealth represents a compensatory form of *symbolic* resistance to the dominant cultural and economic order. Thus, like the traditional corrido voicing the triumph of the local hero over a racially and culturally distinct, hostile and authoritative Anglo Other (such as *la migra* (the U.S. Border Patrol)or the Texas Rangers), the narcocorrido also "appears at a cultural-ideological level as a compensatory form of resistance for a lack of victory in the material realm" (Limón 106). Nevertheless, unlike the traditional corrido, the narcocorrido and its narcotraficante persona are clearly enmeshed with the very commodity form and its attendant social relations, which serve to sustain the corrido listening community's continuing subordinate economic, social, and political status. Indeed, while the narcocorrido's commercial success on both sides of the border speaks to the long history of drug cultivation and trafficking in Mexico, its extensive circulation via cassette tapes and CDs, radio show playlists, and live concerts illustrates an emergent transnational, rather than local or even regional, economic network. The same circuits of global capitalism that spawned the low-wage manufacturing and service economy jobs in the urban American West and in the *maquilas* (American-owned factories) along the US-Mexico border, and that served to bind the two countries closer together through the transport of legal and illegal commodities also delivers the narcocorrido sound to both sides of the border.

So when we regard the lyrics of "El Zorro de Ojinaga" from this perspective, the corridista's investment in local historical events and characters, as well as specific place names, not only registers the narcocorrido's compensatory symbolic resistance to ethnoracial subordination or its nostalgia for the Mexican homeland. Such lyrics also speak to the ongoing deracination of the corrido listening community as a result of the transnational industrial geography of cocaine. Consider this narcocorrido's juxtaposition of aerial transport and distribution with local narcotics cultivation and manufacturing, of the latest surveillance technology and automatic weapons with the rural family ranch setting. Whether imaged by this narcocorrido's reference to Cessna aircraft or by Sheriff Bell's reference to DC-4s, aerial transport dissolves the spatial scales demarcating the local or regional from the national and international, in the process registering the overlap of both agricultural and industrial modes of production and consumption in the post-Operation Condor narcotics economy. Along with the formal and thematic tension between mobility and stasis or containment that structures both the narcocorrido and McCarthy's novel, this dissolution of spatial scales and the overlap of modes of production and consumption disclose both the contradiction and the crisis accompanying the globalizing world system's transition to a flexible, more specialized mode of production during the time frame of McCarthy's novel. There is a contradiction with this system because, on the one hand, a neoliberal free market economy seeks to eliminate borders and barriers so as to accelerate the flows of peoples, drugs, capital, and commodities, whereas, on the other hand, a barricaded border or militarized regulatory framework needs to discipline this space of flows, supposedly to enable capital to broaden and deepen its markets through better coordination and stabilization of the labor force, technology, finances, and legal issues. There exists a crisis whose human toll Bell bears witness to in his serial accounting of the unsolved homicides in his and other Texas border counties in the wake of Operation Condor and of Acosta's bribery of and betrayal by public officials. And there is a crisis also because—as Bell notes when he speculates that "these country boys" will soon be taken over by some Mexican drug cartel—apparent small-scale production at this time uneasily coexists with the operations of Mexican drug cartels led by such *narcotraficantes* as "the fox of Ojinaga."

As Christian Allen notes in his *An Industrial Geography of Cocaine*, throughout the 1980s Mexican drug traffickers essentially were transport specialists, sub-contractors for the powerful Columbian drug cartels (26–29; 80–84). Eventually, however, the combination of increased US interdiction in the Caribbean and the market oriented reforms of the Salinas presidency, in part illustrated by the NAFTA trade agreement, led Mexican drug organizations to battle for greater prominence, a development Bell notes when mentioning his inability to buy *"half quart mason jars nowheres"* during *"them dope wars across the border"* (217). Successful organizations were those who specialized in flexible production or the specialization of tasks ranging from the growing of crops or refining of chemicals to money laundering and security, as well as those who developed strategic alliances with a dispersed set of international economic players. The emergent mercantile model defined through spatial diffusion and specialization of task meant that local, dispersed enterprises were networked by the up- and downstream flows of drugs, transport (e.g., Chigurh's Durango; Acosta's Cessna), and financial services. At the time of the events narrated in *No Country for Old Men*, this emergent flexible, and more cellular mode of production coexisted in tension with the mass production and more vertical integration of the larger Columbian drug cartels. And it is this emergent organization of anonymous, dispersed cells linked solely by flows of commodities (which is one way of describing a terrorist organization) that Chigurh's very presence and movements epitomize. Here we might recall that when he eventually locates the financial source for the abortive drug deal in the desert that sets the novel in motion, he is questioned by the surprised businessperson: "How did you find me?" (251).

So with the supplement provided by the narcocorrido's themes and imagery, one might generally conclude that the drug economy at the time of *No Country for Old Men* appears as the illegal mirror image of a globalizing world system in transition to a post-Fordist mode of production, a mode defined in part by the deregulation of industry and markets, by the outsourcing of labor and the rise of a service economy, and by a strategy of flexible accumulation, in which a hypermobile capital restlessly circulates across geopolitical boundaries or scales, this circulation enabled by advanced communication technologies, improved transportation networks, and multinational corporations and banking institutions. For Ed Tom Bell, *"if you were Satan and you were settin around tryin to think up something that would just bring the human race to its knees what you would probably come up with is narcotics"* (218).

In "El Zorro de Ojinaga," however, "the Devil" instead represents the US and Mexican governments efforts to capture Acosta. From the cross-border perspective of the narcocorrido, Chigurh could be regarded on one level as that aestheticized and perhaps even eroticized figure of strong masculinity prevalent in the corrido tradition, in this novel confronting and defeating other men (and women), both civilians and law enforcement officers, with the phallic power of his captive bolt pistol in his hand. And yet, on another level, he also appears as *"a ghost,"* as a mysterious spectral figure (299). As we can see with the first line that opens nearly all of the novel's sequences, Chirgurh never journeys, which is to say departs, travels, and then arrives somewhere. He—like the other characters in the novel—is always *arriving* somewhere, the temporal duration of the journey compressed or entirely elided in McCarthy's screenplay-like narration. Like the fox Acosta in his Cessna airplane escaping the clutches of "the Devil," Chigurh magically appears and disappears, a man about whom *"You wouldnt think it would be possible to just come and go thataway"* (248). His spectral, relentless movements and violent actions epitomize narcocorrido resistance to authority and, more generally, an utterly alien Otherness at the chaotic heart of existence McCarthy's novels explore. But to introduce the figure of Satan into this cellular network of commodity flows is to mystify what Chigurh also materially personifies or embodies: the very space-time compression and the spectral flows of global capital and bodies that put localities like Terrell County and subjectivities like Ed Tom Bell's in crisis.

"Some Sort of Promise in His Heart"

I had two dreams about him after he died. I dont remember the first one all that well but it was about meetin him in town somewheres and he give me some money and I think I lost it. But the second one . . . I was on horseback goin through the mountains of a night . . . It was cold and there was snow on the ground . . . He just rode on past and . . . when he rode past I seen he was carryin fire in a horn the way people used to do and I could see the horn from the light inside of it. About the color of the moon. I knew that . . . he was fixin to make a fire somewhere out there in all that dark and all that cold and I knew that whenever I got there he would be there. (308–09)

"I think I know where we're headed," Bell remarks toward novel's end, just before his last day in office and his recounting of the above dreams about his father: *"We're bein bought with our own money. And it aint just*

the drugs" (303). His summary comment recalls his earlier question to a county prosecutor about Mammon's identity in the Bible, and its prophetic mood discloses his narration's increasingly apocalyptic mood. But if he appears to *"know as certain as death that there aint nothing short of the second comin of Christ that can slow this train,"* just why or how the train got on this track seemingly remains as mysterious to him as are Chigurh's ghostly movements (159). Thus: *"I dont have no answers to take heart from"* (303). On the one hand, Chigurh's exploits could be said to disclose the narcocorrido's moral ambivalence toward its narcotraficante persona: admiration for his beating a system that marginalizes the subaltern narcocorrido audience; yet implied criticism of the narcotraficante's primary allegiance to money and—what we might call in Chigurh's case—his narcissistic personality disorder. On the other hand, within the novel's overall narrative structure, Bell could be regarded as its gringo *corridista*, telling anything but a tale of redemptive violence regenerative of family, community and nation and diagnosing his historical moment's tragic contours.

"*If I'm wiser in the ways of the world it come at a price*," Bell concludes, a *"[p]retty good price too"*: the loss of belief in his vocation and the rule of law; the loss of *"some sort of promise"* in the heart or faith about the future (296; 308). As if in prolonged mourning, Bell relates how his beliefs and faith are tested, *"held to the light,"* forcing him to reconsider—like the corrido form does in its distinctive way—the relation between historical events and transcendent values and truths, between the temporal and eternal (296). For Carson Wells, Bell represents simply a "redneck sheriff in a hick town in a hick county. In a hick state" (157). But what the novel displays is how the trajectory of Bell's corrido of mourning and abjection courses neither toward denial nor toward a sadistic fantasy of mastery like that informing Chigurh's character. Nor toward simply identifying an equivalent person or thing to substitute for his serial losses. So his characteristic pose: waking at night or sitting in his pickup or police cruiser trying to *"put things in perspective,"* hoping at last to achieve that cognitive distance necessary *"to see yourself for what you really are and even then you might be wrong"* (295). Even as the novel subtly registers the "mercantile" history informing its local crisis through its allusions and its formal tensions at the level both of narration and rhetoric, Bell's honesty, his very willingness to hold his actions and beliefs *"up to the light"* or truth of experience, amid his state of *un*knowingness, forces crucial ethical questions that contrast with the "mercantile ethics" associated with the narcotics economy: To what and whom, exactly, are we bound in relation? How should one conduct oneself, learn to mourn properly, amid grief, abandonment, and fear? That is, how to make a life founded on grief, which essentially defines what he calls the "price" paid for achieving partial wisdom in the ways of the world? (Butler, 19–44).

What he bears witness to along the border in 1980 and his eventual decision to retire rather than pursue Chigurh resurrect memories of his World War II military service, the pivotal event of which was his abandoning dead and wounded comrades rather than face certain death from advancing German troops. Reflecting on this event with his Uncle Ellis, Bell says, "*I didnt know you could steal your own life. . . . I think I done the best with it I knew how but it still wasnt mine. It never has been*" (278). Now Bell's emergent sense of dispossession and indebtedness underlines the enigmatic nature and transformative power of loss. *Enigmatic*: As if in the very recesses of loss—in Bell's case the failure to capture Chigurh or protect Llewelyn and Carla Jean Moss; the loss of a squad of men in World War II and, later, of an infant daughter— something also has gone missing inside Bell, something misplaced, unable to be grasped, always "losing shape" like his reflection he ponders in the shifting, dark liquid of a coffee cup (127). *Transformative*: for the power of narrative discourse to shape things and resist such entropy yet also produce results one cannot exactly know in advance or control in the aftermath. After all, during the conversation with Uncle Ellis his narration about abandoning his squad "*took a shape I would not have guessed it to have*" (282). The central point is that Bell's narrative recollections about how such values as honor and loyalty get tested in proximity to death reveal an ethics grounded on the idea of *obligation*, of mutuality and reciprocity. This ethics materializes through the leitmotif of gift exchange that organizes his dreamwork about his dead father that concludes the novel.

Bell's account of his first dream about his father centers on the failure of monetary exchange, on receiving and then losing a gift: "*he give me some money and I think I lost it*" (309). Within the charged family romance context of Bell's dreamwork, this theme recapitulates in short-hand form the novel's larger plot that tracks the shattering consequences of an abortive drug and money transaction. Although his dreamwork's syntax seemingly stresses an abiding sense of guilt over misplacing the father's gift, that should not distract us from noticing how this failure to reciprocate the gift, to keep it in circulation, is preceded by finding and connecting with the (lost) father who initiates the exchange. So in the first place, Bell's gift exchange metaphor underscores his mature sense that our individual lives are never properly and finally our own, but rather always already implicated with Others in ways that can't always be known, much less explained and understood. Successful gift exchanges, in short, reveal how at bottom reciprocal social relations constitute our beings. As a result, as Bell seems also to realize through his analogous "stealing a life" trope, misplacing the father's gift signifies not so much that the exact nature of the gift, in this case money, is being mourned, as does it project his desire not to be abandoned without either the fact or the promise of *relationality* itself.

In the second place, then, even as Bell's initial dream about meeting and then misplacing the father's gift underlines the entropic forces of personal, familial, and borderlands history recorded throughout the novel, and in the process validate his pose of abjection, it also discloses how missing and losing some one or thing prompts a consequent seeking for recognition in and reunion with the Other, at some future place and time. So although Bell confesses he can't *"remember that first one* [dream] *all that well,"* the regret and vulnerability saturating his one-sentence dreamwork not only registers his mourning the loss of relations (with a father and, by metonymic extension, with a daughter, a vocation, and a country) under the dominance of the commodity form. Bell's dreamwork here also manifests his desire to retrieve some kind of *"promise in the heart"* that he speculates motivated the anonymous person who committed to carving a stone water trough on his family's property over a century ago. I take his phrase to mean a commitment to and faith in the future that sustains one's labors in the present, amidst one's state of ignorance about the shape of things, and it is this utopian ideal that grounds his second dream's more expansive elaboration of an ethics of obligation through the metaphor of gift exchange.

By means of its archetypal motif of the night journey *"through this pass in the mountains"* and its juxtaposition of light and dark imagery, Bell's final dream about his dead father again centers on the idea of obligation or indebtedness. Earlier in the novel, Bell mentions his father's advice not to carry around a burden of guilt—*"Dont haul stuff around with you"* (249)—but here in the novel's final paragraph, by contrast, the father carries embers in a horn, on his dogged way *"fixin to make a fire somewhere out there in all that dark and all that cold"* (309). The light and heat from the remnant of fire inside the horn carry the promise of life amid all the darkness that exists outside its containing shape or protective chamber. And the processional journey itself, anticipated as reaching its end when a larger fire gets made out there in the dark and cold, projects Bell's dream of nonalienated labor and the promise of the hearth—of bodies reunited, both ringing a fire and related by its ring, of bodies restored by food cooked over it. Further underlined by his dreamwork's linkage of male and female symbols (the union of fire with a hollow container or sheltering womb; the sun and moon), the projected reunion around the hearth suggests also the promise of reproduction, the transmission of new life as well as light and heat.

All told, this imagery positions Bell's emergent *"promise in the heart"* in direct contrast to the novel's opening sequence, where under a solitary moon "swollen and pale and ill formed among the hills" Moss discovers the corpses of humans and dogs (26). As a hollow container harboring the promise of new life and light, the animal horn carried here by the father figure resonates too because it symbolically binds together two other important containing shapes that provide material evidence of Bell's ethic of obligation and his emergent "promise in the heart": the stone water trough he ponders at the beginning of this final monologue; the figure of the boat that he employs to identify his motivation for becoming a lawman: *"there was a part of me too that just wanted to pull everybody back in the boat"* (295).

Through Bell's narration and commentary, *No Country for Old Men* asks whether there is something valuable to be learned from living with grief, which is to say from recognizing one's vulnerability to loss and to remaining exposed, in a condition of unknowingness or cognitive paralysis, not seeking a resolution through fantasies of denial or of violence as redemptive. Certainly Bell feels passive and to a degree powerless, admits to being defeated, his failures testifying to the power of the *narcotraficante* with whom he wages war and of whom the *corridistas* sing, "But there is another view of the world out there and other eyes to see it and that's where this is goin" (4). The string of losses and failures Bell enumerates testifies in the end to how he is both done, and undone, by those he grieves for and by all those nameless and faceless deaths that form the background of his (and our) social world. So he comes to understand *"the dead have more claims on you than what you might want to admit . . ."* (124). Passed in the dark by his father on horseback, but fully confident that the father figure will wait for him to catch up, Bell's second dream renders both his sense of obligation to the dead and his seeking of recognition. Not so much a validation of where and what he already is or has been as much as toward a future becoming, an arrival whose *"promise in the heart"* counters the kind of catching "up with myself" Chigurh articulates (173). It is an arrival founded on that slow, at times excruciating process by which one develops a point of identification with suffering and then stakes one's being in the struggle for collective responsibility for the lives (and deaths) of others. This is the promise externalized in the second dream by the image of fire carried in the horn; this is the promise externalized by Bell's awarding of his heart to Loretta: "That's my heart yonder, he told the horse. It always was." (300).

CHAPTER 5

"Do you see?": Levels of Ellipsis in
No Country for Old Men

Jay Ellis

'It's a hard thing to understand [. . .]
I see people struggle with it.'

(*Chigurh in McCarthy, 257*)

Precepts

In Cormac McCarthy's ninth novel, Anton Chigurh kills his victims
with a variety of gruesome weapons: handcuffs, a cattle gun, a shotgun
with a beer can silencer, several pistols. He kills enough to divide his
victims into groups. Most are killed wordlessly, or near wordlessly, often
in the midst of action, and without ceremony; these victims are killed
quickly and in some cases purely to save Chigurh time. But they are
never killed carelessly, and never without reason, even if the surface
reason for their death shocks and repels us. After a shootout with a
gang, a scene notably passed over by Joel and Ethan Coen in their adaptation of *No Country for Old Men* (but whose sense is found elsewhere,
in the film's silence, its implicatures of doubling, missed connections,
and attention to tropes of sight), Chigurh finds time to deliver more
than the quickest execution. Having won the gunfight, he has time for
something more. A man lies wounded in the street, "watching him."
Chigurh "looked at the man." "Help me," he says to Chigurh.

> He looked into the man's eyes. The man looked away.
> Look at me, Chigurh said.
> The man looked and looked away again.
> [. . .]

Dont look away. I want you to look at me.

He looked at Chigurh. He looked at the new day paling all about. Chigurh shot him through the forehead and then stood watching. Watching the capillaries break up in his eyes, the light receding. Watching his own image degrade in that squandered world. (121–22)

Why does Chigurh insist on this looking? The preponderance of visual tropes might extend beyond mere scopophilic power, though it most certainly also derives from that especially male need to see, and to see more than to be seen; such is certainly the case at a surface reading. At this level, Chigurh realizes his autonomous power in part by seeing what he is not, or at least what he hopes he will not be: a victim. (He finds out otherwise, of course, in his wounding in a firefight and finally in the auto accident.) Jacques Lacan's concept of an observer obtaining a psychological level of maturity through his gaze—his projection of himself onto other people and objects—helps explain the Coens' shot of Chigurh staring into a television screen's reflection of himself in the Moss trailer (80).

By importing the concept of scopophilia ("taking other people as objects, subjecting them to a controlling and curious gaze") into cinema criticism, Laura Mulvey notably developed a more specifically gendered theory: films insist on a "male gaze" in part by projecting an image of women as seen through the camera's supposedly male eye. Thus men look, women are looked at. Not only in depictions of women, but also in films replete with male on male violence, looks can kill. Mulvey sought to kill the pleasure in looking as it was historically constructed: "It is said that analysing pleasure, or beauty, destroys it. That is the intention of [my] article" (3).

This scene from the novel, where we see Chigurh looking at a victim longer than at any other time, is of course elided in the film. But the inclusion of a television screen as mirror, especially as the Coens later show us Bell sitting in the same position, suggests that while sound, this reading remains only one level of interpretation. Indeed, I am arguing that understanding Chigurh merely as a scopophilic sadist misses an entire level of reading of both the novel and film. When we return to this scene, we will see how Bell, later looking into the same screen, suggests not only a male contest for power through seeing, but also less psychological suggestions of doubling and consequently suggestions that these characters need not be read merely as constructions of psychology (let alone only in terms of gender). Assuming Chigurh must kill the man he looks at, we must note that he helps him: the man dies with courage, in that he faces—he "looks" at—his death, and we may imagine that he therefore accepts it; Chigurh helps this victim by exercising the patience to teach, or more precisely, to reveal.

The Coens simply elide this man's killing altogether, while in the later killing of Carson Wells, and even more so at the killing of Carla Jean, they cut away. By practicing ellipsis at these points, however, they allow us the opportunity to fail to see, and fail to hear, what we must infer from a deeper level. Reading and viewing below the surface of these works, and attending to what the Coens do not show us, we find the greater complexity that is more obvious in the novel.

Anton Chigurh is more complex than just a figure of pure evil. He brings people to account in a hard cosmos of chance and choice that resolves itself only through entailment and responsibility; they live in a complex system whose indifferent demands on us might be called cosmocentric (Gayon 184), and so they complain about issues such as fairness in human terms. Chigurh functions not only as an executioner, but also as a Socratic figure who, when he has time, engages in extended dialogue intended to help his victims see what they could not before see, that their past actions, in conjunction with chance events, have determined their fated end at his hands. Whether their deaths are "just" is not the point, and Chigurh spends considerable time attempting to move them from their cave of ignorance, to release them from their all-too-human chains of an anthropocentric sense of injustice. Ironically, in their most powerless moment they may see at least this: that the unimagined lines running on from earlier actions entail their meeting with Chigurh, and that their death at his hands (or escape by chance) at least originated partly in moments of free will. Death or escape: either eventuality derived in part from the victims' own agency accomplishing what we might later call fate, even as both remain in part related to chance.

The Coen Brothers' adaptation understands him in this way, but by leaving some of the novel's critical dialogue between Chigurh and Carla Jean unspoken, as in their notably merciful movement away from depictions of graphic violence, they simply conceal from many audience members—but not all—this deeper level of understanding Chigurh, and by extension, *No Country for Old Men*. To appreciate the depths of meaning implicit in the film, viewers must have read the book, and read it carefully. The Coens thereby also instruct, but more in the manner of Zen tricksters than of lecturers. In interviews, the Coens regularly evince misanthropic cynicism: "Everything's a lesson for America," said Joel in one (Stone in Allen 89). Careful criticism should nonetheless assume the artist's work is ultimately serious (especially in comedy) and even genuine unless analysis of the work proves otherwise. That the Coens both speak and work as tricksters, however, goes a long way to explain the difficulty created by the final ellipsis I will examine.

Ironically, ellipsis in this film spares their viewers the shock of more graphic violence than we imagine when reading McCarthy's book. Simultaneously, the Coens convey the chiasmus McCarthy achieved of a simultaneous diminution of action and movement along with a growing sense of dread and, as Bell's voice takes over the book, an implosion of insupportable nostalgic reflection. Ultimately, the Coens frustrate only those viewers who, like many reviewers of McCarthy, need their artist's visions, emotional imagination, and intellectual curiosity congealed into the easily digestible form of a take-out idea.

To be fair, the valuable work of critics working in popular media requires them to see far too many films, or review far too many books, to make their profession viable without the occasional rushes to judgment. The marketplace therefore becomes cruelly inimical to subtlety. Art deriving any of its formalistic qualities from genres more regularly over-whelmed by examples of mediocrity (such as science fiction or detective fiction, or thrillers and Westerns in cinema) suffers more regularly in early reception. Artists meanwhile employing an implicit rather than explicit style while working with dark material can be misread as amoral or even nihilistic. Dostoevsky suffered from such misreadings. Finally, artists delving into ideas that do not obviously and always place human beings at the center of the cosmos can come across as misanthropic instead of simply anti-humanist. Robinson Jeffers presents an important example of a cosmocentric artist easily misread as a nihilist, and one whose work has surely influenced McCarthy.

As I have argued elsewhere, the novel *No Country for Old Men* only appears to operate under the rules of hard-boiled genre fiction (see chapters seven and eight in *No Place for Home* for more extended arguments on the cosmological, philosophical, psychological, and theological problems running beneath the surface of *No Country for Old Men*). So, too, the Coens' adaptation runs far beyond the obvious possibilities for excitement and shock, accomplishing instead one of the quietest violent films of recent cinema, with a story whose surface merely appears to fit the genre of film noir (the cinema's adaptation of the hard-boiled). Before Tommy Lee Jones' Sheriff Bell closes the film in sad confusion—not with a visual representation of his dream, but rather with a Bergmanesque close-up of Bell telling the dream to his wife—the Coens' film regularly implies the level of philosophical problems with which McCarthy has powered the undercurrents of his novel. (The dream closing *No Country for Old Men* also closes the Coens' film, but with an extreme close-up of Tommy Lee Jones's Ed Tom Bell telling it to Tess Harper's Loretta that strongly echoes Bergman's *Persona*—a film that would be known to any serious filmmakers such as the Coens.) Ultimately, both the novel and film are concerned with fate and courage in a world where the tether tying consequences to our actions and the power of chance events remains, to most of us, invisible.

Modus Operandi

To return to the dying drug soldier, we may recall the repetition of visual tropes. Variations of the verb to "look" occur 11 times in a mere 21 sentences (I elided only a phrase and five full sentences). By then breaking up standard grammatical subordination into discrete sentence fragments, he gives each instance of "watching" its temporal due, until Chigurh is "watching" the man's ability to see—"the capillaries break[ing] up" the man's vision "degrade[s]" Chigurh's "image [. . .] in that squandered world" (122). What, more specifically, do we see through Chigurh's witnessing of this vision of final sight giving way to blindness?

The word "squandered" presents us with a key to the most difficult truth of the lives of Chigurh's victims. Of unknown origin, the word in Shakespeare's and his contemporaries' usage meant, "To spend (money, goods, etc.) recklessly, prodigally, or lavishly; to expend extravagantly, profusely, or wastefully," but it also referred to spatial dissolution, to things being scattered or to scattering things or people. Certainly the first meaning fits the life of a drug dealer dying after a shootout. It also reflects, however, the scattered lives of other characters. Even Carla Jean, who met her husband in the Wal-Mart where she works (132), is forced to go on the run to Odessa (125), then to El Paso (214), and finally back to Odessa (248), where on the day she buries her mother she meets her own end. As Chigurh helps his victims see, their lives were "squandered" long before he came in to end them. Scattered spatially and spent recklessly, they were squandered in these senses, but ultimately in a deeper sense, because the characters insufficiently apprehended the potential import of every choice, every moment.

Humans have a difficult time with what Milan Kundera called "the unbearable lightness of being" because in the particular case, our lives seem to take good and bad turns regardless of our attitudes, and indeed, we know that any of our choices may be aided or compromised by chance. The best we usually do at understanding this is through our love of games. Luck, we call it. Thus, for Bell, poker analogies proliferate in his monologues: *Somewhere out there is a true and living prophet of destruction and I don't want to confront him. [. . .] I wont push my chips forward and stand up and go out to meet him*" (4). Bell is unwilling, as players of Texas Hold'em will recognize, to "go all in," risking everything on one hand. Poker tropes occur in the narration as well, however, such as when Chigurh is described as having "stacked the change" from the gas station man "before him the way a dealer places chips" (53).

A coin toss works as well as the flip in Texas Hold'em. Chigurh's first of two coin tosses is given to the titular owner of the gas station, a man he spares based on the outcome. Appropriately, in a novel that tempts readers at the surface with illogical, if easier, readings, the coin toss of course turns up heads the first time and tails the second (for Carla Jean). This tempts our human difficulty at apprehending the true laws of probability, as the novelist's flip of the coin need not land heads and tails in two tosses. Also typically human in the optimistic mode, both the gas station man and Carla Jean call "heads" (56, 258). All of this of course amounts to a method employed by Chigurh, a modus operandi: Chigurh takes time for talk and coin tosses. But it can be argued (and has been, particularly in popular reviews) that such fancy styles in a killer is merely the surface slickness hiding an ultimately lack of depth in a work of genre fiction. Are there deeper reasons for Chigurh's method?

Principia

Carson Wells will tell Llewelyn Moss that Chigurh is "a peculiar man. You could even say that he has principles. Principles that transcend money or drugs or anything like that" (153). Chigurh's "principles" may be inferred from his actions, his patient listening and his patient explanations to his victims. Inference suggests that Chigurh's principles for killing derive not merely from his own ego, let alone from some inchoate nature compelling him to evil deeds, but rather from the conscientious—if all the more chilling—willed settling of accounts in a system of cosmocentric causation. It is one thing to act on principle, however, and something more to explain your reasons to someone else. Why does Chigurh take the time to talk to his potential victims?

His principles include explanation. His commitment to explaining to others the nature of their situation with him could nonetheless be mistaken as a generically typical indulgence in rhetoric as sadism: beyond killing these victims, he rhetorically deprives them of their last potential position of moral authority, by convincing them that their understanding of morality never amounted to more than a comforting delusion. Although human, he undermines their anthropocentric sense of justice. (It helps to note that however much Chigurh may come from or be attuned to the cosmocentric, he certainly bleeds, and he makes human mistakes.) Confronted with this dramatic trick of villainous philosophizing in its generically typical formulation, a reader or viewer reacts with moral outrage; we feel justified in maintaining a simple sense of the villain as pure evil. It is precisely this possibility that Joel and Ethan Coen toy with in their adaptation, particularly by eliding most of Chigurh and Carla Jean's dialogue. Prior to the killing of Carla Jean, however, the film's elision of McCarthy's more extended dialogues for these scenes need not unduly tempt viewers to a notably different interpretation, particularly a comforting retreat to the delusions of humanism. Our difficulty merely begins there.

To overcome that difficulty, we must wonder why Chigurh spares the gas station man. If Chigurh is indeed bound by the chance landing of the coin, and the gas station man lives (instead of dies) merely by that moment's cosmic turn of chance, we may react with a sense that the coin toss amounts to no more than cruelty: it places another person's life on the fulcrum of a fifty-fifty chance event. We must still note, however, that although Chigurh does not, by his own explanation to Carla Jean, have any "say in the matter" (259), he does seem to have a say in whether a potential victim receives the coin toss at all. Indeed, Chigurh seems empowered by whatever connection he bears to the larger cosmos to introduce one final chance event in a person's life just when they might otherwise find themselves (as they are in the way of Anton Chigurh in one sense or another) certain—fated, at least by past events of choice and chance—to die. A fifty-fifty chance far outweighs 100 percent certainty. Is it, however, more cruel?

Considering this in the film, Douglas McFarland thinks so. In "*No Country for Old Men* as Moral Philosophy" McFarland makes the mistake of claiming the film has no soundtrack (163). He has missed the extremely quiet but audible fade in of a few tones from a keyboard beginning when Chigurh flips the coin for the gas station man. This ambient music (by long-time Coens collaborator Carter Burwell) grows imperceptibly in volume so that it is easily missed as an element of the mis-en-scene. But it is there, telling our unconscious that something different is occurring with the toss; this becomes certain when it ends as Chigurh uncovers the coin on the counter. The deepest danger has passed as soon as Chigurh finds (and Javier Bardem's acting confirms this) and reveals to the man that he has won. "Well done," he says. With the toss, McFarland thinks, "Chigurh has almost sadistically transferred responsibility from himself to chance. In an instant he has *created* a world with its own arbitrary and simple rules that exclude ethical categories" (my emphasis, 172).

McFarland's argument, however, continually makes an anthropocentric a priori assumption we can see in his word, "created." He therefore sees Chigurh's coin toss as cruel:

[I]n the space of a few minutes Chigurh has shattered complacency, dispatched categories of ethical and religious belief, and catapulted the proprietor into a realm of contingent circumstances, random eruptions of violence, the dehumanized face of chance, the grim necessity of luck, and the quirkiness and perversity of life. It is a sudden and succinct tutorial in that world which Bell fears will put his "soul at risk." (172)

McFarland's description of the emotional terror inflicted on the man is quite good, but it conveys not only Chigurh's worldview (as intended), but also that of the novel (as McFarland seems not to see it). Is it impossible to imagine that our "categories of ethical and religious belief" are perhaps our own collective creations? If so, we would do well not to take them for granted; recognizing these as perhaps evolved but not cosmically necessary eventualities might be frightening but all the more heartening.

We should also remember, however, that well before the coin toss, Chigurh had already disrupted the man's worldview through dialogue. What he offers the man by choosing to toss the coin amounts to a gift, if a hard one to take. If ethics and morality (let alone religion) are indeed human creations in a cosmos that cannot recognize us as its center, Chigurh is teaching the man that fact. We need not dismiss the value of those creations simply because they have no ultimate foundational origin. That all of life, including our values for how one should live it and respect it in others, may be the result not only of our collective choices, but also of myriad chance events, leads some of us to celebrate and value it all the more so. To live without knowledge of this, however, to substitute for our own limits of knowledge a created certainty that our little lives have necessary, inevitable, meaning, however, squanders life. Such is precisely "the unexamined life [. . .] not worth living"; Chigurh's dialogue with the man makes this as clear as Socrates (*Apology* 38a). Of course, the philosophy behind Chigurh in no way follows that of Socrates (though it would be a mistake to see it in pure opposition), but that merely adds to the irony of Chigurh's method.

He increasingly acts out his part in Socratic dialogue through *No Country for Old Men*. The words "understand" or "understood" occur at least 23 times in this novel and at least 5 times in the film. As we will note when he kills Wells, Chigurh does not always adopt the method of the coin toss, however. Method applied differently for different situations further suggests Chigurh's "principles," and indeed we may derive these from a close reading of the three dialogues, in Carla Jean's bedroom, in Well's hotel room, and in the gas station. The coin toss may reinforce the knowledge Chigurh is attempting to convey, but it also alters the situation by introducing the fifty-fifty possibility of escape from it. The gas station man seems to gain nothing from Chigurh's prods and questions until the coin toss. Afterwards, we can only guess to what extent this man may now question the life he has led.

First Dialogue: The Gas Station Man

The Coens remain remarkably accurate to their source text as far as they go with this first extended scene of Socratic dialogue, but we should pause to note that accuracy has its limits in successful adaptations; over-valued, it becomes what film criticism has come to call the "fidelity fallacy." Writing about teaching film in literature classes, Thomas Leitch notes the ease with which we may make this critical error in classrooms:

> Whenever we teach a film adaptation—[. . .] as an adaptation— we treat it as an intertext designed to be looked through, like a window on the source text. Although it is certainly true that adaptations are intertexts that depend in a special way on their source texts, [. . .], every text [. . .] is an intertext that incorporates, refracts, refutes, and alludes to many other texts, whether literary, cinematic, or more broadly cultural. Taking fidelity as the decisive criterion of an adaptation's value is tantamount to insisting that it do the same job as its source text without going outside the lines that text has established, even though adaptations normally carry heavier burdens and labor under tighter restrictions than we would ever impose on any novel. (17)

A film adaptation of a novel remains its own accomplishment, apart from the degree to which we might say it was "faithful" to its source text. This chapter's examination of departures from the novel in the Coen Brothers' film assumes those departures not only to be deliberate, but to accomplish a third text, as it were: viewers who are also readers have access to meaning that mere viewers do not; in this sense, the Coens leave viewers unfamiliar with the source text to make serious interpretive errors. Where the film differs from the novel therefore matters in a different way.

Where McCarthy gives us Chigurh's question as, "What's the most you ever saw lost on a coin toss?" (55) the film elides the word "saw," but the Coens of course tend to the visual. Where the book describes the setting as "almost dark" (52), the film clearly depicts high noon: no shadows are notable in the establishing shot of the gas station, and the sunlight is bright even if behind cloud cover. The light through two windows and a door comes evenly through three walls in the interior shots. But this difference increases our sense of the man's desperation later, when he claims he needs to close and he closes at "near dark"; it is darker, as it were, in the cave of this man's ignorance than it is outside in the bright light of truth. The scene is a two-shot, and when we see the man from either Chigurh's point of view or from near Chigurh's shoulder, three details in the set provide further visual evidence the man has not examined his life. These partially fill in for dialogue elided from the end of McCarthy's novel. Two are images of impending death and one a satirical joke on optimism.

First, a card of air fresheners hangs beside the window behind the man. Most are gone, but two smiley faces remain with a space between them. These belie the false friendliness behind the man's inquiry, "Y'all gettin any rain up your way?" Neither of the men in this scene is smiling. Second, all along the window behind the man are hanging the lower loops of fan belts (for auto repair); whatever binds them and the points from which they hang remain invisible, so the loops cut into the window like nooses. Third, we can see through the window a backhoe, exactly the tool used to dig graves in ground as hard as that in West Texas; it sits inert, unused but menacing. The intentions behind these three items, their purposes and positions, suggest the man lives a paltry existence not far from a living death, with uncorrected gaps between the turning parts of things and more threat of death than life even in what would repair those gaps, the fan belts.

Bardem's acting with Gene Jones as the proprietor, the scene's pace and its quiet, all convey a dialogic disaster between these two men. We might be in a Beckett play, as regularly as Chigurh repeats himself but the man seems to understand nothing of what is implied in his questions. Chigurh is first of all attempting to determine whether the man poses a threat to him: by asking about the weather "up your way" and adding, "I seen you was from Dallas" (presumably by something on the car), the man makes Chigurh think he might later identify him to the police, who could realize that the killer of the traveling salesman had stopped at this gas station. (Interestingly, Texas license plates have never borne the names of their owners' cities or counties, but those in Tennessee—where McCarthy grew up—have long displayed their county of origin.) The gas station man attempts to relieve the tension with a direct question:

Is there somethin wrong?
With what?
With anything.
Is that what you're asking me? Is there something wrong with
    anything?

Attempting to end the conversation, the man says he must "see about closin," with no sense of the potential import of that quotidian act sharing a trope with death. The man's retreat from a realization that, at bottom, his life has no meaning keeps Chigurh thinking that he may also be attempting to avoid further conversation so as to sooner alert the police. The film clarifies, with its bright light, the absurdity of the man's claim that he needs to close. Chigurh observes at this point, "You dont know what you're talking about, do you?"

Chigurh therefore continues, soon probing deeper to determine the extent of the man's ignorance: he still needs to know if he is a threat, but he also needs to know in his capacity as a Socratic figure. When the man tells him the gas station "was my wife's father's place," Bardem adds a comic note by nearly choking on a peanut, before observing, "You married into it." We will see a similar focus on marriage as an act of will with unforeseen consequences in Carla Jean's case. For now, we should note that to this man, the fact that so much of his existence now depends on his marriage has remained totally unexamined by him, as he replies, "If that's the way you want to put it." Chigurh makes clear the truth heretofore unexamined: "I dont have some way to put it. That's the way it is."

Rather than simply play with the man's thinking (as in the film Bardem's Chigurh might be interpreted as doing), the novel's Chigurh attempts to extend the man's sense of the coin's provenance: "Anything can be an instrument," he tells him.

> Small things. Things you wouldnt even notice. They pass from hand to hand. People dont pay attention. And then one day there's an accounting. And after that nothing is the same. Well, you say. It's just a coin. [. . .] What could that be an instrument of? You see the problem. To separate the act from the thing. (57)

Things, acts, words—all are inseparable; we cannot merely choose parts of life to consider important and disregard the connection of smaller things to larger events. For want of a nail, the shoe was lost; for want of a shoe, the horse was lost; for want of a rider, the battle was lost and for want of the battle, the war. We regularly know that small things may carry large consequences. Chigurh is telling the man the coin toss itself is as entailed as his death would have been had the coin landed tails, precisely because he married into his position and stayed there, unquestioningly. The coin, like a vehicle running a red light, would have missed him had he made different choices, just as much as it misses killing him only by chance. The man has long ago placed his life on the fulcrum of chance more often than on that of choice, and he has just survived a fifty-fifty chance of dying.

When Bardem's Chigurh teases the man with the idea that, despite having told him it's his "lucky quarter," "it's just a coin" after all, he echoes the book's ending of the scene. The novel makes it clear that Chigurh is not obviating what he has just claimed for the coin's importance, however, as he follows "That's true" with "Is it?" We will see evidence in the film's depiction of Chigurh in Odessa that the Coens' film also understands him to be more than a mere trickster—although he is also that. He has remained in the gas station longer than necessary (as with the toss's revelation we know he will not stay or return to kill the man); the only reason is to attempt to lead the man to some truth about his unexamined life, not merely to torture him. Although he does that too.

Second Dialogue: Wells

Proof that Chigurh has given the gas station man a Socratic gift—however terrifying—follows when we see him kill Wells. The film elides Chigurh's explanation to Wells of why he must kill him instead of taking a bribe, but we will see other, again visual, evidence that in this case, the two works agree on Chigurh's methods and principles. Referring to his injuries from his gun battle with Moss, Chigurh admits, "Getting hurt changed" him, "I've sort of caught up with myself" (173). He then tells Wells what leads to his arrest by the deputy whom we see killed with the handcuffs: essentially, he killed for purely personal reasons, taking a verbal insult in a cafe so seriously as to kill the man who insulted him. He then "let" the deputy take him into custody. "I'm not sure why I did this but I think I wanted to see if I could extricate myself *by an act of will.* Because I believe that one can. [. . .] But it was a foolish thing to do. A *vain* thing to do. Do you understand?" (my emphasis, 174–75). Here the question, "Do you understand?" makes it clear that even in confession, Chigurh intends to persuade.

By characterizing the murder as "vain," Chigurh means that to test the limits of free will and personal agency for no reason other than to conduct the test is to tempt fate too much. "Hubris" to the classical Greeks meant not only pride, but also an excessive inclination toward violence. Furthermore, "Hubris means believing that you are a god, i.e., that you cannot suffer; pride means a defiant attempt to become a god" (*Horizon Aug. 87* usage in O.E.D.). Being wounded would remind Chigurh that, although no normal human, he is not quite a god, and the killing of the deputy certainly requires prolonged and horrifying violence far beyond a gunshot or even cattle gun bolt; it is outrageously violent. Why does Chigurh attempt to persuade Wells of anything here?

He does so because before he kills Wells (he will provide him no coin toss, no chance for escape) he wants to convince Wells that he has been guilty of that which tempted Chigurh: foolish vanity—hubris. Chigurh so easily captures Wells that this fact alone proves Wells has failed to take seriously his own vulnerability. The Coens play with the notion of these two as dark figures at odds on higher than human ground, as they film Woody Harrelson as Wells in a chair so wing-backed as to make him a comic angel. When Chigurh kills him we are spared the sight of it, but the shotgun blast we hear sends upholstery-stuffing flying out from the chair, like feathers. In their diminution of graphic violence, the sound and our guess at the sight of this killing cannot be said to go very easy on the audience. But it allows us to apprehend something more than we would were they to display this killing in all its gruesome visual detail. They also set up the certainty of what they do not show us when Chigurh meets Carla Jean, by having Chigurh lift his boots away from the spreading pool of Wells's blood.

The novel's dialogue between Chigurh and Wells includes several hints at a common station somehow separate from normal human concerns (beyond their profession). The dark angel tropes include Wells telling Chigurh to "go to hell" twice in the novel, calling him "god-damned crazy" and at last telling him, in his final words, "Do it and goddamn you to hell" (175–78). In a play on his own name, the novel even has him say, "Well the hell with it," suggesting, if subconsciously, that Wells expects to be the first one of them there. This comes as Wells admits, "I think I saw all this coming a long time ago. Almost like a dream. Déja vu" (178). Even here, however, in his admission that he has had some premonition of his fate, Wells fails to summon the courage to own that fate. Chigurh has told him he thought Wells "might want to explain" himself, not to Chigurh but to himself (175). This would mean self-examination perhaps by first facing the truth that he failed to respect Chigurh's abilities and thereby failed to respect himself (177). Although the film naturally elides some of this dialogue, the key words remain, and the visual additions deepen our sense of Chigurh as a Socratic figure. He now knows he cannot become a god, and he admits his mortality, but as he tells Wells, the inevitable act of dying "doesn't mean to me what it means to you" (177).

The reason Chigurh gives Wells no chance and yet takes the time for a dialogue with him is that he sees Wells as having already had the position and time to know better than he admits. Their common past experience in human terms was that they "used to work with" each other (152), perhaps when Wells served in "special forces" during the Vietnam war (156). In the Coens film, however, we as easily imagine them together just after their fall from a Miltonic heaven. (The novel mentions one of Satan's lieutenants from *Paradise Lost* when Bell recalls asking the Walker County Prosecutor "if he knew who Mammon was" (298).) Given the hints of a dark angelic allegiance turned to conflict,

Well's lack of self-examination can be seen as an error of omission, a willful ignorance. His failure is thus more severe than that of the gas station man, as he previously "worked with" Chigurh and has now been bested by him not merely tactically, but philosophically. Rather than failing to see anything below the surfaces of life, Wells indeed also possessed "things" that amount to more than merely money, material possessions, and so on, rather more like qualities and abilities; unlike Chigurh, however, he has squandered these. Chigurh tells him, "You've been giving up things for years to get here." The moment is yet educative for Chigurh, as he admits, "I dont think I even understood that." He then wonders, "How does a man decide in what order to abandon his life?" (178).

Tropes of falling and loss recur in the novel, even when things fall together rather than apart. "Some things have fallen into place," says Chigurh after self-examination (173). Foreknowledge further suggests consciousness reaching beyond the quotidian by its connection to unconscious awareness. Before *No Country for Old Men*, Edwin Arnold had already provided the best treatment of dreams in McCarthy. Moss and Bell come to realizations after dreams or in half-dream states. Here, however, the suggestion runs deeper than merely unconscious suggestion. Wells' realization of déja vu is nonetheless exceeded by Chigurh's abilities of foreknowledge. The Coens include this, as Chigurh tells Wells that he knows what will happen to the money, that, "It will be brought to me and placed at my feet." Indeed, in a way it is in the film more than in the novel: the Coens move the air duct in Moss's last motel room, as it were, from high up in the novel to Chigurh's feet as he enters near the end of the film. Things will fall to that level, Chigurh knows, for both Moss and Wells.

His dialogue with Wells encounters nothing but resistance, even though he tells him, "You should admit your situation. There would be more dignity in it," and in the novel says, "I'm trying to help you" (176). Chigurh regularly shoots his victims in the face, and often more particularly in the forehead—a rough form of wisdom's third eye, to be sure. This horrific delivery of knowledge with death, however, is lost on Wells. In the film, we see only a hand fluttering out beyond the back of the chair, along with those feathers of upholstery. In the book, he turns away from the shot and even holds up his hand, as if he could deflect it (178).

Flannery O'Connor's *Wise Blood* (1952) includes one of the most striking images echoing Oedipus's loss of sight just as he fully sees the truth of his situation. For O'Connor, the blindness of Hazel Motes removes whatever truth or grace he finds (or does not) from the reader's sight as well. Grace remains in O'Connor a mystery, but its reception is most strongly hinted at in moments of astonishing violence. O'Connor remains an important influence on McCarthy's work. Unlike O'Connor's Motes, Wells dies still unable to see the truth of his "situation" (176).

Doubling and Missed Connections

This last line could of course double for Moss, and we can imagine that if chance events had fated him to meet Chigurh face to face, he too would resist the opportunity for self-examination, let alone to face truth. Moss's hubris leads him to think he can pick things up without giving away other things. It seems to not even occur to him that he might not be able to protect his wife; he even seems surprised (if not more seriously concerned) with the loss of his truck. When he comes close to truly realizing his situation, it only has to do with himself. As he sees the figures on the ridge with the truck he says, "There is no description of a fool [. . .] that you fail to satisfy. Now you're goin to die" (27). Yet Moss's choices will lead to Carla Jean's accountability, to her death as well as his; everything is connected, and as his picking up of the hitchhiker also proves, he takes his marriage less seriously than he might (211). The woman joined to him in marriage will also die because of his actions, even if hundreds of miles away and by different hands.

The film helps us see how very many times we are in the same location but with different characters: Moss, then Chigurh, then Bell—Bell before Chigurh only in Carla Jean's case, and still that does her no good. Of these three men, no two are ever seen in the same frame. Where McCarthy has Chigurh take a milk bottle from Llewelyn and Carla Jean's refrigerator, sniff it and drink from it, the Coens extend the doubling. Rather than returning the bottle, Chigurh leaves it on a table between the sofa and the television set. When Bell and his deputy enter the trailer, the Coens provide great fun with the deputy's astonishment that because the bottle is still sweating in the heat of the trailer (and therefore still cold), they have arrived not long after Chigurh.

Rat, cat and dog are all on each other's tails, but never quite within reach. Tommy Lee Jones's Bell, however, takes this seriously. He sits and drinks from the bottle, seeing in the dark television screen his own reflection precisely where earlier we have seen Chigurh's. None of these characters touch each other even when they manage to be in the same frame. Moss sits close against Carla Jean on the sofa, but both have their arms crossed against the sensation, and the dialogue, whether interpreted as funny and sexy or as crude and disrespectful, suggests that sex is less about contact than conquest. Missed connections, rather, haunt *No Country for Old Men* book and film; the film medium simply makes these easier to see.

The novel and film reverberate with doublings. Even one notable change—having Bell in Moss's last motel room looking for Chigurh, rather than showing us McCarthy's Bell avoiding the encounter (essentially retreating)—adds an iteration of the book's implicatures of ideas. Only by watching the scene on DVD at extreme slow motion can one see that as Bell pulls up to the motel in the film, *two* deadbolt locks have been shot out by Chigurh. Through editing, the Coens have their audience struggling with what seems an imminent encounter between the last remaining hero, Bell and the evil Chigurh. Students in several of my classes have thought Chigurh must be a ghost after all, able to disappear when Bell enters the room in which he is hiding, perhaps behind the door. Others thought he does successfully hides behind the door and leaves as Bell goes into the bathroom.

The Coens (in the guise of Roderick Jaynes, credited as editor but actually a widely known pseudonym for Joel and Ethan), place the men in two different room, each space of course a mirror of the other—as in most hotels. A phantom reflection even seems to fall into the polished brass of the lock cylinder as Bell pauses at Moss's door; with editing we mistake it for Chigurh, who is actually standing beside the mirror door (next door), with light pouring through that emptied lock cylinder as well. Two doors, two men; Bell sees only his own reflection, just as he sees only his own shadow when he opens the door.

The possibility certainly exists that in this scene we are not seeing the world we are able to see in daily life. Even if we can account for the missed connections and doublings as mere coincidences (and missed timing), too many suggestions of doubled spaces and people proliferate not to wonder. Physicists have proven the severe limitations in our apprehension of the world through our immediate senses. Our experience of time, our inability to perceive most of the matter in the universe even as it exists among us (in the form of dark matter)—these epistemological limits stand witness against an anthropocentric valuation of perception as we usually understand it. Debate continues in the scientific literature on free will as to whether it exists at all; experiments in the laboratory find evidence running the gamut of possibilities. (A quick non-specialists tour of experiments in neuroscience and free will might begin with Benjamin Libet, followed by Daniel Wegner and V. S. Ramachandran.) One experiment finds a puzzling delay after an action (such as wiggling one's finger) before the conscious feeling of choosing to undertake that action—or even being asked to do so (Mele).

It is enough to try and catch oneself undertaking a routine action and noting how frequently some part of your unconscious brain drives your car, for instance, more than you think. Experiments in neuroscience not only suggest that many of the actions we take to be conscious are probably closer to autonomic (think of any argument you've had more than once), but also suggest that even the most deliberate actions may not arise from our will—in any meaningful sense of that word. Farther afield, not only string theory but also less theoretical ideas in quantum mechanics deeply problematize our comforting sense that we are where we are, when we think we are.

On one level, of course we can eventually locate Bell and Chigurh in that scene in a plausible manner. But we should assume that the editors have deliberately retained and yet kept to a minimum the moment when the headlights of Bell's prowler reflect back from the metal hardware of both motel room doors but with holes, as it were two blind spots, where the deadbolt cylinders should be for both doors. Bell sees what he expects to see: the door of Moss's last room, with police tape still protecting the crime scene. He therefore does not see what he also simultaneously expects but dreads seeing: Chigurh. For his part, Chigurh has no reason to kill Bell as long as he is bent on holding accounts, collecting the money, keeping his word, but no longer tempted to the type of hubristic killing he confessed to Wells was "foolish" (175).

McCarthy's doublings and missed connections at least reflect the influence of his friends and acquaintances at the Santa Fe Institute; more interesting possibilities of interpretation might occur to us than often do in professional reactions to McCarthy's work. I am not claiming that McCarthy intends that readers should unravel his fiction until they can see the ideas of his friend, the Nobel Prize-winning physicist Murray Gell-Mann. (The novelist and physicist met after McCarthy had read Gell-Mann's work.) But McCarthy keeps an office at the institute Gell-Mann founded, and McCarthy remains the only artist among the physicists, neurologists, population biologists, climate scientists, entomologists, and economists, etc., who work there.

In neither of the two works entitled *No Country for Old Men* do we arrive at a full philosophical system (nor should we), but we do get a sense of unseen forces, dreams and visions of a world governed by laws of probability, causality, chance, and a probably frighteningly small dollop of free will. These hints amount to a dramatic problem more than a philosophical answer. The frequent complaint of determinism against McCarthy could as easily have been be leveled at Sophocles, but no more successfully, as in both the forces of fate are not ultimately the focus so much as is the weight of choices where we find them. In *Oedipus Rex*, a man assumed to be destined by the gods to kill his father and marry his mother hears of this possibility and so skips town to avoid it; however, his limited knowledge means that he has just left his adopted home and avoided killing and marrying his adoptive parents; he will soon kill his unrecognized biological father and marry his unrecognized biological mother. Nonetheless, he assumes responsibility for the only thing he can: by catching himself and facing the truth of his situation, he claims some agency in the world beyond the dictates of fate.

Blind Oedipus sees the truth and accepts it in order to find a modicum of freedom. Bernard Knox has argued that fate is not as important as free will in the play, and the action of the play therefore elides everything I just described up to Oedipus hunting himself down. So, too, the entailments of myriad choices that, along with luck good or bad, create fated moments with Chigurh, are not usually shown to us but rather described in *No Country for Old Men*. (Moss of course gets the novel going through exceptional choices.) McCarthy furthermore externalizes the act of self-discovery, and like Flannery O'Connor's Misfit in 'A Good Man is Hard to Find,' Chigurh visits truth upon his interlocutors with horrific violence. None of his victims is as brave as Oedipus, but they do reach the same difficult choice: will they own their situation? If the dialogues reveal that Chigurh's mission includes helping his victims do this, then the Coens' choice to elide much of that work in Carla Jean's case stands as the most notable difference between the novel and the film.

Third Dialogue: Carla Jean

The Coens's shooting script notably omitted the coin toss from Carla Jean's killing. With no published version of the script available, no version of the script "leaked" online as of this writing included the second coin toss. Unofficial copies of the script (one given to me as the "shooting script") instead end Carla Jean's last scene with the following:

Carla Jean: I knowed you was crazy when I saw you settin there.
    I knowed exactly what was in store for me.
Chigurh: Yes. Things fall into place.

The script then continues where the finished film eventually does, with Chigurh outside.

In its final version, the film restores, as it were, the second toss. But the Coens still elide the majority of Chigurh's dialogue with her in the book. What remains not only makes sense, but arguably achieves with perfect economy the same tone—and ultimately, meaning—as the book. But not without difficulty. Indeed, the absence of so much of this final dialogue creates a trap. The trap catches out those who have not read or have misread the novel, particularly anyone too ready to assume that nothing complex goes on beneath its hard surface. Such viewers (though not all, of course) might assume that we hear Carla Jean's last words. What we do hear is defiant, and this allows us to forget the other philosophical points we have encountered in the previous dialogues.

Kelly Macdonald's performance elicits our sympathy on several levels: first, her note-perfect West Texas accent conveys the vulnerability varnished with hardness that would be required of a young woman living in a trailer in Sanderson, Texas; second, we have seen her put up with verbal abuse from her husband—though much of this works as believable trailer park romantic banter, he treats her concern for him with near disdain; third, unlike Wells and even the gas station man, she poses no threat to Chigurh. Even a rather cold-blooded analysis of the film would have to concede that she raises a serious possibility when she tells Chigurh he does not have to kill her.

Indeed, Javier Bardem's performance in this scene suggests none of the irritation, let alone anger, that simmer beneath the previous dialogues. He sits back in an armchair across from Carla Jean, calm, his hands at rest, and in response to most of her protests, he simply smiles and waits, as if he knows that with more time, she will understand what others might not. The smile is not sadistic. (One could not begin to compare it with the hubristic bliss on his face as he kills the deputy.) This Chigurh must kill her, because he promised he would—but more deeply, as in the novel, because she, too, has made choices that brought her to her end at his hands. Despite the last words we hear from her being protest, his last audible words suggest even to careful viewers who have not read the book that something is indeed inevitable, if not what we would call just, in this killing. The outrage at this, however, leads many viewers to prefer leaving the theater remembering selectively, particularly her words echoing Wells's, that Chigurh is merely "crazy." How might he not be?

This scene is preceded by a brief one in a cemetery and, before that, the ending of the Coens' version of Bell meeting with his uncle. After the uncle tells of Bell's great-uncle dying in a confrontation with outlaws, he corrects Bell's sense of injustice, particularly his frequently voiced sense that life is deteriorating: "What you got ain't nothin new. This country's hard on people. [. . .] It ain't all waitin on you. That's vanity." From this scene the Coens cut to a close-up of the headstone of Agnes Kracik, Carla Jean's mother. The jump cut is accompanied by the sound of an electric winch lowering the casket and revealing the text on the stone. It might as well say to Carla Jean, and to us, memento mori. The winch creates a clicking sound that will be echoed soon again.

We then find, with Carla Jean, Chigurh in her bedroom. Vanity has been proven repeatedly to be the greatest crime in the film (as I noted in the book, even for Chigurh). And as I have argued, it is not merely some nihilistic determinism trapping these characters, but rather the unforeseen consequences of their prior choices in life, along with chance. One choice in particular has sealed Carla Jean's fate: marriage to Llewelyn Moss. The gas station man, as we saw, made the most unexamined move of his life when he "married into" it. Here is Carla Jean in the novel, describing to Bell how she met Llewelyn:

> it come to me in this dream or whatever it was that if I went down there that he would find me. At the Wal-Mart. I didnt know who he was or what his name was or what he looked like. I just knew that I'd know him when I seen him. I kept a calendar and marked the days. Like when you're in jail. [. . .] And on the ninety-ninth day he walked in [. . .] and he looked at me and he said: What time do you get off? And that was all she wrote. There was no question in my mind. Not then, not now, not ever. (132)

Moss's pick up line is echoed by Wells, talking to the hotel clerk in Eagle Pass, and by Chigurh, to the gas station man. However resolute the Carla Jean we see confronting Chigurh in the film, here she seems to yield to a fate so unknown in its particulars that it runs beyond Hollywood romantic sentimentality. She is not, I am arguing, guilty at this moment. But it is a moment in which we have to think hard before calling her actions—really reactions to Moss—a choice. It is almost as if before she chose, some part of her had already chosen. And we should question the sense she conveys of delusional human optimism: people fated to marry may not be fated to a good end in that marriage. Whom, after all, do we now know she has married?

Moss is a man who chooses to take a risky shot at an antelope. Even with his special equipment and experience as a sniper in Vietnam (293), the shot is unethical; he indeed misses and therefore has to track an antelope he wounds to try and kill it. For this reason only, we may think, he finds the drug deal gone wrong. But then he chooses to take the drug money. Of every choice in the novel, this one stands out easily as the biggest gamble. Unlike Oedipus, whose actions seem so fated as to be invisible to the audience, merely recounted so we can see the main action as his own self-discovery, Moss's critical actions put at risk not only himself but also his wife. When he chooses to return to the dying man and take him water, his sympathy becomes foolish: he further places Carla Jean in danger as the money is now back in the trailer with her. Finally, in the one moment when he might "turn all this around," his hubris instead leads him to reject Chigurh's offer: "You bring me the money and I'll let her walk. Otherwise, she's *accountable*. The same as you" (my emphasis, 184). In the film Moss even slams the phone down on Chigurh; his emotions fail him again and his macho posturing will indeed lead to Carla Jean's death.

The last words we hear her speak in the film object to this, although in Macdonald's acting one can see a begrudging recognition of something alluded to in her husband's character when Chigurh tells her, "Your husband had the opportunity to save you. Instead, he used you to try to save himself." Her objection is not that it isn't true, but that it isn't "like that. Not like you say." This echoes even for the viewer unacquainted with the novel the gas station man's reaction to Chigurh's, "You married into it." While Carla Jean objects to the way Chigurh "say[s]" it, the gas station man tries harder to avoid disagreement. But here nonetheless, "There isn't any way to put it. There's just the way it is." Carla Jean married into her situation.

But does that make her as passive and unreflective as the gas station man? No, because of her resilience in the face of everything Moss puts her through. As she tells Bell in the novel, she never second-guessed her choice (or whatever we should call it) with Moss, "Not then, not now, not ever." Even her trope for the moment suggests that she recognizes some force outside the will of her or Moss, when she says to Bell, "And that was all she wrote" (132). The "she" here is not Carla Jean, but some personified writer beyond her. The evidence the film gives for this comes through the banter: she gives as good as she gets, and meeting with Bell, she also resists suggestions that her allegiance to Moss might not be in her best interest. But even though she characterizes her marriage to Moss as one of more than mere choice, she has owned it.

The tethers of accountability in her case, however, remain tenuous. This is why, when she appeals to Chigurh's agency, Bardem's Chigurh clearly decides to provide her with a chance: "OK. This is the best I can do." He flips the coin. "Call it." Her last words refuse this: "No. I ain't gonna call it. The coin dont have no say. It's just you." But it has already been established that it isn't up to how Chigurh "say[s]" anything. There is only the way it is. Bardem's last line here is delivered with an interesting turn of the head and glance upward away from her and then back, as if in appeal to another audience. "I got here the same way the coin did." We must note that this line is followed by silence, not protest, as a beat follows and we still see Chigurh sitting, waiting.

> My copy of the screenplay begins the porch scene with,
> HOUSE EXTERIOR
> Minutes later.
> A beat.
> The front door swings open and Chigurh emerges.

Clearly, an important interval of time has passed. We next see him check his boots on the porch. Simultaneously, we see two teenagers ride bikes past the house—close enough that they would have heard a shot on the otherwise quiet street had there been one at all recently (even with a silencer). The scene also immediately recalls the clicking sound from the lowering casket, although now it is the flipping of playing cards in the spokes of the boys' bicycles—a sound also like a roulette wheel. We of course infer from Chigurh checking his boots that he is checking for blood, and here the structure of the film helps us see it is no stretch to imagine much more dialogue in the film than we hear—extradiegetic dialogue, as it were.

We have progressed from seeing and hearing the murder of the deputy in all its prolonged horror and graphic violence, to only hearing the shotgun and seeing the blood of Wells spread under Chigurh's upraised boots, to now not hearing the shooting of Carla Jean or even seeing her blood. It is no less reasonable an inference to make that we missed also much of this final dialogue. Furthermore, the details of what the film does not elide support our inference of this elision. What, then, do we miss of the novel's dialogue with Carla Jean?

Chigurh slowly and patiently talks with her until she accepts her death. She tells him, "I dont know what I ever done [. . .] I truly don't" (256). But he makes clear to her, "None of this was your fault. [. . .] You didnt do anything. It was bad luck" (257). She nods at this, and it is with this acceptance of the importance of chance's effect on a series of choices that in the novel he tosses the coin. She resists here, too, but by the end of the dialogue, he has convinced her that the conjunction of chance and choice could end in no other way.

> You can say that things [. . .] could have been some other way. But what does that mean? They are not some other way. They are this way. You're asking that I second say the world. Do you see?
>
> Yes, she said, sobbing. I do. I truly do.
>
> Good, he said. That's good. Then he shot her. (260)

This final dialogue ends with her enlightenment; there's no reason to have the character change and acknowledge that she does now "see" after all her resistance, unless she indeed does. The silence before the Coens' ellipsis suggests as much, as does what follows. And again, the likely influence of O'Connor on the novel strengthens this interpretation. At the end of "A Good Man is Hard to Find," The Misfit kills the grandmother and says, "She would have been a good woman [. . .] if it had been somebody there to shoot her every minute of her life" (23). Though presented with less grim irony, Carla Jean's death echoes this, particularly if we change "good" to "enlightened".

Chigurh's severe injury in the car crash proves that he, too, can be prisoner to "bad luck". But his own choice plays a part in the collision, as, had he not stayed to talk to Carla Jean at all, he would have been through the intersection safely in time. The film shows him driving toward it and, hearing the clicking of the cards on the boys' bikes, he checks the rearview mirror. Literally, he seems to be paying attention to their location relative to his car, just as any normal person takes extra care when children are riding bikes nearby. But figuratively, the roulette wheel of chance is spinning for him, and he will come out the worse when it stops.

The Coens play a game of their own with their viewers: if accepting their perception that Carla Jean refuses the coin toss, they accept a delusional belief of their own, that she is right when she tells Chigurh that he does not have to kill her. Carla Jean must die, however, as surely as Oedipus must find himself guilty of that which he actively tried to avoid. Like Oedipus, she must *see* truth beneath everyday life even as she will soon be unable to see in life. Unlike Oedipus, she will not be allowed to live as a reminder of the constraints of fate on free will, but she will be allowed a realization of her situation in a cosmocentric universe. In the film, as in the book, she will accept that situation, even though the Coens don't let us see her "call it." By eliding her true dignity, they tempt us to see her dignified in a simpler way, a simpler world, where good is good and evil is evil, and none of our choices should come back on us with such a serious turn of fate.

Almost all the popular reviews of the novel (with one especially notable exception: Rodger Hodge's "Blood and Time: Cormac McCarthy and the Twilight of the West") grossly underestimated the underlying subtlety and depth of McCarthy's *No Country for Old Men*. The deeper implications of McCarthy's ninth novel, especially concerning philosophy, cosmology, and the nature of good and evil, had already slipped by most readers before the Coens adapted it to their form. McCarthy has woven a complex tapestry of dream-informed fiction from which hints, echoes and glimpses of philosophical problems emerge. Ethan Coen studied philosophy at Princeton (Allen xxiv), but whether the ideas explored here were consciously intended by any of these three artists (or for that matter, other artists who helped make the Coens' film) is beside the point. Without background knowledge of the full dialogue between Chigurh and Carla Jean, we may follow the red herring presented by the film's ellipsis and miss much of the richness available to both readers and viewers of *No Country for Old Men*. Both the novel and film present Chigurh as a man of "principles" indeed.

CHAPTER 6

Evil, Mood, and Reflection in the Coen Brothers' *No Country for Old Men*

Dan Flory

Reviews of Joel and Ethan Coen's 2007 film *No Country for Old Men* regularly mention its striking depiction of evil. Roger Ebert writes, for instance, that the movie "is essentially a character study, an examination of how . . . people meet and deal with a man so bad, cruel and unfeeling that there is simply no comprehending him;" it "regards a completely evil man with wonderment, as if astonished that such a merciless creature could exist." Reporting for *Multicultural Perspectives*, Bernard Beck links *No Country for Old Men* to the problem of evil itself and describes antagonist Anton Chigurh (Javier Bardem) as a "profoundly frightening, depressing, and inscrutable figure" (214, 216). Some commentators join Andrew Sarris in complaining about the film's nihilistic portrayal of evil. As both popular and academic critics observe, Bardem's character excites as much interest or horror as any malevolent figure since Anthony Hopkins' turn as Hannibal Lecter in *The Silence of the Lambs* (Jonathan Demme, 1991).

Despite numerous comments about the importance of evil in the film, the *kind* of evil depicted and its various meanings remain very much in dispute. From across a wide political and ideological spectrum, reviewers have characterized *No Country for Old Men* as offering an example of Satanic, "theological," or "demonic" evil, while others understand it more secularly as the study of a stone-cold killer. Joan Mellen, writing for the *Film Quarterly*, additionally notes that the movie's allusions to Vietnam and its 1980s setting are crucial elements for properly understanding its meaning, which she argues is decidedly political (24–26, 30–31). Likewise, *Sight and Sound* critics Ben Walters and J. M. Tyree claim that through its focus on "radical evil" the film suggests a negative appraisal of American masculinity, particularly "the frontier ethos of the Reaganite Cowboy Man," whose "most successful incarnation might be a serial killer" (48, 49).

This diversity of response, I would argue, stems in part from our own rather confused intuitions concerning evil itself. Here I part company with Richard Gilmore (among others), who argues that, "[i]t makes as little sense to speak of [Chigurh] as evil as it does to say that raw nature, a blizzard or a flood, is evil" (59–60). Gilmore implicitly invokes the traditional distinction between natural evil and moral evil and, like many thinkers, dismisses the former as not really evil at all. However one views such an argumentative move, I aim to make my case for a different conclusion. While I find much that is thoughtful and illuminating in Gilmore's analysis, what I hope to show is that our understanding of Chigurh as a morally evil individual is fundamental to the film. Ultimately, the Coen brothers' film invites viewers to think reflectively about their limits for understanding evil individuals by suggesting that traditional, theologically based explanations of them are inadequate. The film portrays its chief interpreter, Sheriff Ed Tom Bell (Tommy Lee Jones), as an unreliable guide to the problems he must face in the film by showing his understanding of evil to be unsatisfactory. The film also encourages viewers to contemplate the kind of evil Chigurh represents, even if not all viewers fully recognize or accept this invitation, by suggesting that this narrative figure is conceivably within their capacities of comprehension. It achieves these aims by subtly influencing their overall mood as well as their thinking, thus closely following Cormac McCarthy's novel itself. While I would agree that Chigurh exists at the edges of our capacity to grasp malevolence, the film pushes viewers toward the realization that adopting a perspective such as Bell's, that construes this villain as ultimately incomprehensible, mysterious, or demonic, is unsatisfactory, disadvantageous, and puts us at risk in ways that should be avoided.

Mood and the Coen Brothers' Presentation of Evil

One of the more remarkable features of McCarthy's novel is the number of times he describes characters thinking about and contemplating their lives. The protagonist Llewelyn Moss does so in connection with how the $2.4 million that he has stumbled upon changes his life (18, 107–09, 175–78, 210, 227), while Sheriff Bell's frequent philosophical ruminations frame and offer interpretations of the novel's action. His opening monologue, for example, is a meditation on the nature of evil (3–4), a topic to which he returns again and again (e.g., 216–18, 248–49, 298–99, 303–05, 307–09). One of Bell's most troubling failures is what he conveys in a soul-searching conversation about courage in war, his father's character, and life's meaning with his Uncle Ellis (263–80). In a similar way, Chigurh discusses the more abstract points of his senses of fate, chance, and justice with three different characters—the nameless filling station proprietor, Carson Wells, and Carla Jean (55–57, 175–78, 254–60). In part because of these reflections, critics have remarked on the generally philosophical nature of the novel. It seems safe to say that McCarthy seeks to evoke in his readers a reflective mood—a ruminative frame of mind regarding topics such as money and its effects on human lives, war and its consequences on those who fight in it, determinism, choice, tradition, criminality, violence, and evil. By focusing repeatedly on thoughts or events where his characters reflect on these matters, McCarthy invites his readers to do so as well.

In an analogous fashion, the Coen brothers' cinematic version of Sheriff Bell poses the problem of evil and the question of properly grasping it in his opening voiceover. Even before the film provides its first establishing shots, viewers hear him describing his accomplishments and those of the sheriffs of yesteryear, "the old-timers," with whom he cannot help but compare himself. He marvels at their frequent refusal to even carry guns in implicit contrast to the practice nowadays and notes, "You can't help but wonder, how they would've operated these times." He relates the story of a boy who "killed a fourteen-year-old girl," was subsequently arrested by Bell, and went to the electric chair based on his testimony. Rather than being a "crime of passion" as the newspapers claimed, the boy told Bell

> that there wasn't any passion to it. Told me he'd been planning to kill somebody for about as long as he could remember. Said if they turned him out he'd do it again. Said he knew he was going to Hell. Be there in about fifteen minutes. I don't know what to make of that; I surely don't.

Bell understands neither why nor how someone could knowingly choose to act so evilly. For him, such a decision is incomprehensible. From his traditionalist Christian perspective, to do so would be "to put your soul at hazard." It would be, in short, to commit a mortal sin knowingly and consciously, something no one would rationally elect to do according to his way of thinking. Bell's understanding echoes a dominant position in the history of Western philosophy. Figures such as Augustine, Aquinas, and Kant similarly viewed sin and evil as impossible to choose rationally, a position that reaches back to Socrates and was incorporated into Christian theology, where it later contributed to shaping a major strain of modern ethics called "moral rationalism." Bell's musings at the outset of the film thus evoke a well-known philosophical position as well as a familiar sense of wonder at the mysterious inexplicability of this kind of evil, its apparently breathtaking, fear-inspiring inscrutability.

As Bell finishes narrating his story about the young murderer, the camera pans for the first time slowly to the left, drawing our attention with it, and offers us our initial glimpse of Bardem's character, Anton Chigurh, who has just been arrested for some unknown offense. As we watch him being escorted into the back seat of a police cruiser, Bell explains, "The crime you see now, it's hard to even take its measure." In this way the Coen brothers link Bell's description of this new, seemingly inexplicable evil to Chigurh and propose that we see him as its representative—as something that neither Bell nor the old-time sheriffs he admires apparently had to face until now. In addition, the magnitude of such evil provides a further challenge to sensibilities like Bell's, which have no answer for the scale of iniquity that these crimes involve. The Sheriff continues his commentary on these perplexing new evils by noting, "I don't want to push my chips forward and go out and meet something that I don't understand." In this way the film raises its reservations concerning how to confront such evils because they seem to be, from a long-established, time-honored perspective, not only fundamentally irrational but also radically dangerous. In his opening remarks Bell is already reflecting on evil, and the ways in which many people ordinarily think about it fail to address some of our deepest questions. As the film shortly makes clear, viewers are invited to reflect as well.

The film reinforces its connection between Chigurh and this "new" problem of evil through the criminal's horrific murder of the deputy who had just taken him into custody as well as by his use of an unusual weapon to kill a second victim in the following sequence. Chigurh's tool is a cattle gun he employs in the same way it is utilized in a slaughterhouse. This singular piece of equipment punches a steel rod by means of compressed air through the skull and deep into the brain of those to whom it is applied: once this act is accomplished, the rod quickly retracts into its cylinder. Using such a weapon on people, of course, reduces them metaphorically to the level of cattle, an allusion that further enhances this character's confounding the supposedly natural separation between humans and animals. By depicting Chigurh as a wanton, insensitive killer, the film presents him as incomprehensible to us as he is to Bell. In these early moments of the film, viewers do not understand, any more than does our narrator or the hapless deputy this villain quickly dispatches, why he carries a tank of compressed air with a hose that runs down his sleeve; nor do we understand why he murders two people in less than three minutes of screen time. Likewise, viewers are further alienated from him because he seems to derive pleasure from his arduous and intimate strangling of the deputy. In the novel, Chigurh has just murdered someone and allowed himself to be taken into custody as a sort of crude Nietzschean test of will (174–75), but the viewers of the Coens' film are not initially aware of this. The moment after we hear Bell pondering what he sees as a "new" kind of crime, the film presents us with a villain performing shocking and unexplained violence that seems to mirror just the kind of evil that Bell describes. He concludes by telling us:

> It's not that I'm afraid of it. I always knew that you had to be willing to die to even do this job. But I don't want to push my chips forward and go out and meet something that I don't understand. A man would have to put his soul at hazard. He'd have to say: OK. I'll be part of this world.

Bell's apprehension over this new kind of crime is compounded by the fact that not only has it no place in his overall understanding, it does not even have a place in what he sees as "his" universe of experience. The motivations of individuals such as the boy he sent to the electric chair or Chigurh are not merely beyond his comprehension; he wants them to have no place in his life. And viewers in turn are initially invited to follow his lead. "Who *are* these people?" he exclaims in outrage at one point later in the film. Why would they *choose* to be evil—and so horrendously evil at that? How could they believe that they are making sound moral decisions? What benefit do they imagine they derive from acting on them? As his admiration of the old-time sheriffs makes clear, Bell yearns for a simplicity he believes existed in times past, when such evils apparently did not occur. The crimes he now faces seem to come from another world, not the one he sees himself inhabiting. His ponderings as well as the events depicted in these first few sequences of the film invite us to enter into an anxious, perplexed, and nostalgic state of contemplation regarding the topics he raises: this "new" problem of evil, how the individuals who commit such acts are possible, and how we might go about confronting them.

Over two decades ago film scholar David Bordwell pointed out that the openings of movies can have a "primacy effect" that sets up a whole web of expectations and anticipations regarding the narrative to be presented, a claim that has been seconded and augmented by other critics including Noël Carroll (Bordwell 38; Carroll, "Art and Mood," 542–43). In *No Country for Old Men*, the Coen brothers set the mood for their film not only by means of Bell's initial voiceover, but also by their other aesthetic choices—for example, the black screen against which Bell's monologue begins, so that viewers will focus on his voice and what he says rather than on any images presented. In addition, the filmmakers have Tommy Lee Jones enact Bell's delivery with a palpable sense of sadness, fear, resignation, and loss. The directors supplement these affective tones with establishing shots of barren, southwestern Texas landscapes that follow the initial black screen, as well as by means of accompanying sounds of wind howling that begin on the soundtrack even before Bell's voiceover. Dark and obscure landscapes, such as the predawn, sunrise, and deeply shadowed morning shots offered here "provoke trepidation" (Carroll 543), a misgiving that the wind's low howling throughout reinforces. Moreover, as Chigurh appears on-screen the Coens add a droning minor chord from Carter Burwell's music to emphasize this villain's ominous threat. These features provide a sense of foreboding and uncertainty, and collectively enhance the doubts that Bell expresses verbally as well as affectively about this "new" kind of evil. The first few images and sounds of the film, then, carefully augment Bell's soliloquy on evil and its subsequent pairing with an example of what he is talking about by encouraging viewers to let themselves experience the troubled, contemplative mood exemplified by this aging Sheriff.

According to Peter Goldie, the concept of mood may be understood as typically less specific, more global, and of longer duration than what Carroll calls the "emotions proper," such as anger, hatred, or fear (Goldie 143–50; Carroll, "Film, Emotion, and Genre," 25–26). In contrast, moods like irritability, rancor, or anxiety are not usually focused on specific objects, but influence us generally and tend to outlast particular expressions through action. Moods broadly shape how we perceive and what we do: they predispose us, for example, to see in certain ways and express other emotions that can serve as motivations for our deeds. Depression can lead us to see everyday, ordinary events as unbearably sad and bring us to tears over the most trifling of matters; irritability can lead us to become angry with people or things even when they do not deserve it (Goldie 147–48).

Greg M. Smith and Carl Plantinga have taken up the importance of mood in their recent books on affect and cinema. As they note, music, lighting, set design, editing, star persona, and other narrational as well as non-narrational cues can profoundly affect mood (Smith 38–64; Plantinga 60–61, 70–72, 130–32, 142). While I agree with Plantinga that Smith's definition lacks some desirable precision, the latter's detailed analyses and emphasis on interactions between mood and emotion underscore several points made by Goldie—namely, that moods and emotions intimately interweave with one another, that moods may predispose us to perceive, think, and act in particular ways, and that combined the two kinds of affective states greatly multiply the complexity of human experience.

Carroll fleshes out these and other claims about the importance of mood to cinema by describing how moods "predispose the subject in the direction of certain appraisals rather than others" ("Art and Mood," 528). Although such links to cognition through representational arts like film are typically indirect (530), these artforms may display moods "componentially" (533)—that is, in readily recognizable pieces—and thereby encourage the creation of "cognitive biases" that incline viewers to experience and thereby judge the narrative in particular ways. Films may accomplish this task by providing instances of the biases they aim to arouse and inviting viewers to take them up (535): their narratives can present certain "emotional episodes" that may, if entered into by the viewer, bring on particular mood states by means of "emotional spillover" (532, 540). As Carroll explains, being "immersed in the central components of the presiding mood state" (536) via exemplary emotional episodes can offer viewers ways to get "in the mood" for what will follow. Thus, the aesthetic decisions involved in constructing a narrative sequence can "prestructure in terms of cognitive biases" the judgments and appraisals that filmmakers wish to induce in their audiences (537).

Carroll argues that one mood which art may arouse is introspection, an overlapping term for the affective state that I argued above is encouraged by the beginning of *No Country for Old Men* (532–33). He also identifies techniques that films and other artforms may use to induce moods, including editing and monologue, which play crucial roles in the Coen brothers' opening sequence (534, 537). Bell's thoughtful, nostalgic monologue instantiates an "emotional episode" that urges viewers to experience and thereby take up his overarching mood, which the filmmakers augment by pairing his words with carefully selected images and sounds that seek to enhance their affective enticement. The emotional experience encouraged by the opening scenes, then, aims to bring viewers into an introspective mood state by self-consciously exemplifying *how* they should approach the problem depicted in the narrative: reflectively, thoughtfully, as well as with a sense of anxious loss regarding simpler times. Artists can reliably expect their audiences to already know such feelings, as they are not uncommon, so the cinematic features described here could easily serve as reminders of similar emotional episodes—the cinematic equivalent of Proustian madeleine cakes, if you will—that might readily "spill over" in the form of creating the moods they instantiate by making available major elements of how these affective states feel. As Carroll notes, "mood states can be engendered by emotional episodes" such as many arts provide

(540), so the experience as well as the taking up of a nostalgic, contemplative mood regarding evil by many viewers should be a dependable result of considerations such as those just outlined. By instantiating feelings and events that are recognizably similar to those viewers have commonly had themselves, the film presents components of human affective and intellectual experience that might easily lead, if the viewer is willing, to the creation of a similar mood while watching and listening to *No Country for Old Men.*

Of course, invitations to reflect or enter into other mood states exist for viewers to accept or reject (Smith 12)—and the invitation to reflect in this film is further complicated by the fact that it is interwoven with senses of nostalgia and defeat that may discourage going on to find new answers. However, *No Country for Old Men* ultimately rejects these moods and suggests alternative understandings of evil, even as these rejections have apparently been missed or rebuffed by many critics.

As Smith notes, efforts to arouse and sustain mood tend to be recursive in popular Hollywood narrative (40–42), and *No Country for Old Men* is no exception in this regard. Many early scenes, such as those of Llewelyn Moss (Josh Brolin) hunting and discovering the aftermath of the failed drug deal are accompanied by sounds of the lonely, howling wind that begin the film, and cracks of thunder occasionally add to a general sense of ominousness and uncertainty, thereby reinforcing those affective states. Moreover, Bell underscores the initial invitation to contemplate evil by returning to its puzzling nature time and again. He thoughtfully notes the impression that the men pursuing Moss have made on him once he tracks the ex-welder to his and Carla Jean's (Kelly MacDonald) mobile home just after the couple have gone into hiding; and when Bell's Deputy, Wendell (Garret Dillahunt), reports back to him about still another Chigurh-related crime scene, the Sheriff teases his subordinate about the ontological status of the murder victims (does death change who they are?), muses about the sorry state of the world, and here asks the question I noted earlier, "Who *are* these people?" before underlining his perplexity by describing a newspaper account of a couple who tortured senior citizens, then murdered and buried them in the back yard in order to cash their victims' social security checks. What is most outrageous of all, as Bell sees it, is that these killers were caught only after neighbors saw a man running from the premises naked except for a dog collar. Digging graves in the back yard, he remarks, was apparently insufficiently out of the ordinary to draw their attention.

Even more tellingly, later in the film, once Moss has been killed by the Mexican drug-runners who have pursued him throughout the film in parallel with Chigurh, Bell has a conversation with his fellow Sheriff from El Paso (Rodger Boyce). Clearly sharing a similar outlook (due largely to the fact that many of the thoughts expressed by the El Paso Sheriff are, in the novel, actually Bell's; see, for example, *No Country for Old Men*, 295), the other lawman complains:

> It's all the goddamn money, Ed Tom. Money and the drugs. It's just goddamned beyond everything. What's it mean? What's it leading to? . . . You know, if you'd told me twenty years ago that I'd see children walking the streets of our Texas towns with green hair and bones in their noses, I just flat out wouldn't have believed you.

Ed Tom, quoting Deuteronomy 26:8, replies in agreement, "'Signs and wonders.' But I think once you quit hearing 'sir' and 'ma'am,' the rest is soon to follow." Bell's biblical reference to the Hebrew Exodus from Egypt has, associated with it, God's terrifying power from the verse's previous phrase, and by implication, God's wrath. "Signs and wonders," then, have often signified the onset of the Apocalypse, an implication underscored by the other Sheriff's reference to "the dismal tide" in his response to Ed Tom. These two veteran police officers see the crimes they are investigating, the early punk movement's fashion tendencies, and the decay of old-fashioned formality as all of a piece with the "new" kind of evil they face, as well as precursors to the End of Days, a symbolism made even more explicit in the novel (e.g., 304–05).

In continuing their conversation as they head toward Bell's patrol car, the two return to the problem of Chigurh. The El Paso Sheriff notes that "none of that explains your man," and they go on to consider different possible explanations for this elusive criminal. After rejecting several clichés based on their mismatch with Chigurh's actions, particularly his strolling back into a previous day's crime scene and murdering still another victim, Ed Tom's colleague exclaims, "Who would do such a thing? How do you defend against it?" In doing so, he brings us back to Bell's recurring perplexity and the question of what to do in order to face such evil. How does one understand an individual who has so much indifference to right and wrong that he would brazenly re-enter a crime scene to commit another murder? And how does one pro-actively guard against such a person? The two aging Sheriffs have no satisfactory answers for these perplexities, and their conversation leaves the questions unresolved. Yet these characters' melancholy, reflective remarks serve to reiterate many of the thoughts and feelings that have troubled Bell since his opening monologue and that viewers have repeatedly been invited to experience moodily along with him. They recap the "new" problem of evil as symbolized by Chigurh, its apparent inexplicability—particularly in terms of established conceptions—the seeming other-worldly nature of Chigurh's ways, and the question of what to do to confront such difficulties, thus refreshing these matters affectively as well as narratively for the audience.

Moving Beyond Nostalgia

Crucially, the film comes to reject its earlier evocation of nostalgia as a fitting attitude toward these "new" problems of evil and even hints at alternatives. Later in the film, the soon-to-retire Sheriff Bell visits his Uncle Ellis, a disabled ex-lawman who lives alone with his feral cats in a cluttered, isolated ranch house. (The novel makes their filial relationship clear, although the film leaves it more ambiguous; see *No Country for Old Men*, 263–80.) Ellis is clearly someone Bell esteems; thus when the older man compels him to state his reasons for "quitting" Bell does so with a mixture of remorse, shame, and defeat: "I feel over-matched," he tells his uncle, and goes on to lament, "I always figured when I got older, God would sort of come into my life somehow. And he didn't. And I don't blame him. If I was Him, I'd have the same opinion of me as He does." In a significant change from the novel, the Coens give this speech to Bell, but it is Ellis's in McCarthy's novel (267, 283).

Narratively speaking, one point of Ed Tom's confession is to reiterate his fear-tinged incomprehension of the "new" kinds of crime and evil he faces. But just as crucially he reveals that he cannot even honestly profess the faith that he elsewhere claims (such as in the opening sequence or in his conversation with the El Paso Sheriff). In becoming disillusioned with his old values, Bell feels confused and defeated. He has lost faith in what had formerly given meaning and value to his life. Such a collapse of belief in previously held values is what Nietzsche describes as passive nihilism (17–18). Of course, Nietzsche also argues that this state of meaninglessness could be counteracted by an active nihilism that worked to transform old, rejected values into new, meaningful ones, but Bell is nowhere near that stage.

Bell's passively nihilistic defeatism, however, is not meant to be a sensibility that viewers should take on in sympathy with him, as critics like Sarris, Rosenbaum, and Braudy have assumed. It is true that the film makes explicit that Bell can see no way out of his predicament and is in a kind of existential crisis. But this crisis, I would suggest, is due to Bell's inability to imagine a moral perspective different from his traditionalist, theologically influenced conception of life's meaning and value that he has rejected. As Bell tells us in his opening monologue, he does not know what to make of views that lie outside his own. That incomprehension remains consistent throughout the narrative and plays a major role in the lawman's decision to retire. But in a perhaps surprising way his incomprehension also makes Bell similar to famous Nazi bureaucrat, Adolf Eichmann—only from the perspective of trying to prevent evil rather than commit it—because his "lack of imagination," as Hannah Arendt might put it, impairs his ability to grasp the forms of evil that Chigurh and his ilk represent (287).

Yet the film does not encourage viewers to follow Bell, either affectively or intellectually, in his imaginative shortcomings because Ellis immediately rejects Ed Tom's self-pitying nihilism. Presented as a more thoughtful, authoritative peer who has forgiven the man who put him in a wheelchair and as a representative of the "old-timers" Bell so reveres, Ellis dismisses Ed Tom's divine self-condemnation with an impatient wave of his hand and the declaration, "You don't know what He thinks." But more significantly, Ellis then takes the occasion to advise Ed Tom by means of a story about another old-timer, Uncle Mac, a lawman who died over seventy years before. The Coens move up the date of Uncle Mac's death by 30 years from McCarthy's novel (270), presumably to stress its contemporary relevance. As Ellis describes the incident in the film, seven or eight outlaws shot Uncle Mac as he stood unarmed in the doorway of his own home and calmly sat on their horses as he bled to death, from a bullet wound through the left lung, in front of his wife. Ellis' comment to Ed Tom that follows critically links this crime with those the retiring Sheriff has been investigating: "What you got ain't nothing new. This country's hard on people. You can't stop what's coming. It ain't all waiting on you. That's vanity."

In other words, these "new" kinds of crime, these "new" kinds of evil, as Ed Tom has been conceiving them, are not new at all. Even the old-timers that Ed Tom so admires had to deal with the sorts of individuals Chigurh represents. The rosy nostalgia in which Ed Tom has found comfort is rejected by his older, wiser peer, for to think in the way that Ed Tom does is, according to Ellis, to self-centeredly think that the whole world revolves around one's self, rather than having its own agenda. The film here urges viewers to side with Ellis both affectively and intellectually, because he is presented as a more thoughtful and emotionally mature figure than his rather self-pitying, unimaginative nephew. The old-timer reveals Bell's conception of a "new" kind of evil to be a comforting illusion rather than an effective way of facing the world. Ellis implies that even the Old West sheriffs understood better and acted as best they could on that knowledge. Uncle Mac could see the outlaws visiting his home for what they were; he just wasn't quick enough to get his shotgun, as Ellis observes. At this point in the film, then, the narrative aims to break the defeated mood of nostalgia that Bell has cast over the proceedings since the beginning through Ellis's rejection of it as false and delusional, and replace it with a more clear-eyed sense of the past regarding this kind of long-standing evil.

The film's conclusion further underscores the negative dimensions of Bell's nihilistic defeatism. Clearly at loose ends and unable to figure out what to do with himself after retiring, Bell tells his wife Loretta (Tess Harper) over breakfast about two dreams he had the previous night. Both involved his father. The first betrays a sense of shame. In it, Bell remembers hazily that his father gave him some money and "I think I lost it." The second, more significantly, places them both in "the older times," riding of a night on horseback through a cold, snowy mountain pass. Bell's father rides past him carrying fire in a horn,

> the way people used to do. . . . In the dream I knew that he was going on ahead, and he was fixing to make a fire somewhere in all that dark and all that cold. And I knew that whenever I got there he'd be there. And then I woke up.

The film then briefly holds the shot on Bell after he finishes, cuts to Loretta listening noncommittally, then back to Bell, who is unsettled by his confession. He sits quietly trembling and casts his eyes downward, unable to hold his wife's gaze. There is again a sense of defeat on his face, as with his confession to Ellis, and in the foreground of the soundtrack a kitchen clock ticks loudly, which continues over the black screen to which the filmmakers then cut and that they blend into the percussion of Burwell's solemn, ominous music over the closing credits, reminding us that time steadily marches on, even if we might prefer like Ed Tom for it to stand still or go backwards.

The dream is a false hope, as Ed Tom realizes, which is why his statement "And then I woke up," his sense of shame, and his final look of defeat constitute essential cues for the audience. He does not live in a dream, where his steady, reliable father will be there to lean on and help him out. Nor does he live in those imagined simpler, "older times," but rather in a reality where crimes like Chigurh's happen with depressing regularity. Ed Tom's crisis—of faith, of belief in the old-timers, of belief in a way of life that he had convinced himself possessed deep roots in his beloved old West—remains, and he does not know what to do about it any more than he knows what to do once he finishes breakfast.

This troubling, open-ended finale exemplifies the pressing need for continued consideration of the problems Chigurh represents, even if Ed Tom is not up to the task. The film implies it falls instead to viewers to take up reflecting on these problems, for they are no more resolved in our lives than they are in the retired sheriff's life. By presenting us with a story of evil deeds and the individuals who do them that respected, long-established conceptions cannot adequately accommodate and indicating that neither these deeds nor their perpetrators can be avoided except through delusion, the film invites—even urges—its viewers to thoughtfully and thoroughly consider how such difficulties might be better comprehended.

For the filmmakers and for McCarthy as well, the mood of nostalgia here becomes a trap. It prevents us from facing up to evil in the same way that it prevents Bell from facing up to the events involving Llewelyn Moss, Anton Chigurh, and the drug deal gone bad that plagues his rural Texas county. The narrative implies that nostalgia leaves us where Bell is at the end of the film as well as the novel: dreaming of finding a better way within what he knows, but knowing at the same time that it won't fit the harsh reality of evils that exist around him. Such a failure is, of course, passively nihilistic, and the film's conclusion drives home the point that such an unimaginative perspective regarding evil can even assist in its continuance and proliferation by providing at best lackluster, misdirected responses to it.

Alternatives to Incomprehensible Evil

So how should viewers think about evil, and especially evil individuals like Chigurh, if we are not to face them with Bell's wistful despair? The Coen brothers' film does not flesh out its answer in detail, but it does offer some suggestive possibilities that come straight from McCarthy's novel. Consistent with Mellen's argument, one crucial narrative detail worth considering is that many of the violent men in the story (Moss, Carson Wells (Woody Harrelson), and Chigurh) are Vietnam veterans—former soldiers who, in ways consistent with recent cognitivist theories of evil, psychopathy, and the effects of violence on the human mind, were explicitly trained to overcome barriers against harming others. They were trained to become killers.

The theme of military service and its consequences is certainly an important one in McCarthy's novel. Bell, for example, is a decorated World War II veteran who confesses a sense of shame in not protecting his fellow infantrymen better during an attack; Moss is referenced repeatedly through his Vietnam service; Wells is identified as a Vietnam veteran as well; and Chigurh as someone who "used to work with him" (152; see also 30, 75, 130, 156, 188, 272–79). Several of these references survive in the film narrative. Moss twice identifies himself as a Vietnam veteran in response to questions by Wells and a suspicious border guard; Wells tries to bond with Moss through their shared military service in Vietnam and is later identified as a retired Army Colonel; and he brags of knowing Chigurh "every which way," which I take to link him to this villain by means of shared military experience. Mellen notes as well that "Chigurh is a paragon of military discipline, who seems to have extinguished all compassion" (26). And, of course, all three men are the appropriate age to have served in Vietnam five to roughly twenty years before.

In his book *On Evil* Adam Morton explains his topic as "a property of actions" and thus most appropriately attributable to people rather than events (136). Accordingly he outlines how "[t]he average reader of [his] book is not unimaginably different from many of the perpetrators of evil deeds" (4). Rather than stemming from mysterious, irrational, incomprehensible, or diabolical motivations, "*[a] person's act is evil when it results from a strategy or learned procedure which allows that person's deliberations over the choice of actions not to be inhibited by barriers against considering harming or humiliating others that ought to have been in place*" (57; italics in original). Morton goes on to explain that "[e]vil acts arise from a specific failure of the way we choose our actions, in which the barriers against atrocity are overcome or eroded" (62). Closely following empirically based studies of violent individuals such as Jonathan Shay's *Achilles in Vietnam: Combat Trauma and the Undoing of Character*, Morton's analysis focuses on how certain ways of making moral decisions can be flawed and how these flaws may lead to the performance of evil deeds that would otherwise have been prevented by internal mental impediments to harming others, such as psychologist Robert Blair's "violence-inhibiting mechanism," which Morton describes as a "piece of mental machinery" that "is sensitive to signs of distress in others and in their presence inhibits aggressive behavior" (42). Evil acts, according to this theory, result from the systematic overcoming of psychological barriers to significantly harming others, which can be "fundamental features of [some] people's personalities," such as those of psychopaths (Morton 65–66).

One of the more fascinating and horrifying dimensions of Morton's theory of evil is how it may plausibly account for not only "born" psychopaths, but also those made by society as well as other "violentized" individuals. Morton notes that combat soldiers, for example, are typically forced to become violent due to a combination of military training and experience, long after they have developed a sound sense of morality. They are, in essence, trained to overcome an established sense not to harm others in order to become good combatants (35–38). Although a recognizable problem since at least the Trojan War, as Shay points out in both *Achilles in Vietnam* and *Odysseus in America: Combat Trauma and the Trials of Homecoming*, more efficient methods for training soldiers in the US military have exacerbated this phenomenon considerably during the last half-century. Military psychologist

Dave Grossman reports in his book, *On Killing: The Psychological Cost of Learning to Kill in War and Society,* that upon discovering that only 15–20 percent of all American riflemen in combat during World War II had actually fired their guns, military training was explicitly changed to increase the efficiency of conditioning personnel to shoot their weapons at the enemy. By the Korean War, firing efficiency had increased to about 55 percent. By the Vietnam War, internal Army estimates were that 90–95 percent of soldiers in combat were shooting at the enemy—a result that also helps to explain why attention to post-traumatic stress disorder in US war veterans increased dramatically after World War II as well as why it remains an acute problem in the wake of more recent conflicts (Grossman 3–4, 36, 251ff.). Of course, as Morton notes, soldiers are not generally psychopaths (38). Their training and experiences in war, however, can encourage them to overcome inhibitions against harming others that psychopaths also lack. Thus theories that explain how such transitions are possible will be of use in explaining both kinds of violentized individuals, as well as their intersection.

Morton's theory helps to clarify some of the problems involved in contemplating evil as presented by *No Country for Old Men*. Vietnam veteran Llewelyn Moss, for example, has more or less adjusted to peacetime situations that do not call for violent responses, so he falls into the category of "violentized" individual, as Morton describes it, someone who is capable of harmful action toward others but nonetheless possesses significant resistance to it (35). Incidentally, perhaps this is why the film and McCarthy's novel introduce him hunting: he has channeled his "violentization" into that pastime. On the other hand, when required to do so, Moss can summon the ability to seriously harm others that he presumably learned during his two tours in Vietnam. The retired Army Colonel Wells similarly seems able to turn this ability on or off depending on the situation, although his willingness to harm others appears to be much more ready to hand: he quite happily, for example, puts it out for hire, making him sociopathic (Morton 47–53). In contrast, Chigurh faces the world with the attitude that violence is one option as good as any other when considering how to act in relation to human beings. Rather than thinking that causing serious injury or death should not be considered in most situations except—perhaps in extremis—as a last resort, Chigurh acts in ways that presume its immediate and easy availability. In this sense McCarthy's character fits the accounts provided by Morton, Shaun Nichols, and others in explaining the evil committed by psychopathic serial killers. Chigurh acts in ways that show he has reliable strategies around the norm against significantly harming others (Morton 70–78; Nichols, "How Psychopaths Threaten Moral Rationalism," 299–301; Blair 12–13, 20–25). And of course, Wells implies the aptness of such an explanation with his unsettling wisecrack, "He's a psychopathic killer, but so what? There's plenty of them around." Later, when explaining to Moss why he should deal with him rather than Chigurh, Wells supplements his view of the villain by noting, "You don't understand. . . . He's a peculiar man. You might even say that he has principles—principles that transcend money or drugs or anything like that. He's not like you. He's not even like me." These descriptions are the only ones of Chigurh delivered by someone who knows him well, and they are not contradicted by other characters in the film or for that matter, the novel. These details also agree with the peculiar logic of Chigurh's actions, such as his killing of Carla Jean long after Moss has died because he promised Moss he would do so, or the revenge he extracts from his employer for foolishly employing the wrong "tool" in attempting to find Moss.

I would argue that Wells' sketch of Chigurh as well as Chigurh's own actions help us to see how the film invites viewers to not only contemplate the problem of evil, but to do so philosophically. If our understanding of Chigurh remains unsatisfactory through traditional conceptions like Bell's, the film—as well as the novel—encourage us to nevertheless find ways to improve on that understanding by incorporating this antagonist into the realm of humanity. Wells' suggestion that such evil individuals be understood as psychopathic killers who at the same time have principles (that is, use reason) thus presents itself as a ready possibility. It is an encouragement, I would argue, to become what Nietzsche describes as actively nihilistic by reimagining and transvaluating our old, rejected values into new, viable ones (3–4, 9, 17–18), and applying such efforts to evil individuals. Moreover, given Bardem's largely impassive performance as Chigurh, the idea that he lacks crucial emotional capacities regarding others presents itself fairly explicitly, a point that again agrees with arguments about the personalities of psychopaths advanced by Morton, Blair, and Nichols. These points, combined with Bell's failure to grasp Chigurh's evil character and the implied need for serious and sustained continuing reflection on the problem, invite viewers to take up that task in the most thoroughgoing way possible.

When we enter into a mood of philosophical reflection or contemplation, we generally seek to put distractions aside in order to prepare for an extended, focused, but at the same time open-minded consideration of some thing, idea, or set of relations. We use our best intellectual capacities to aim at achieving some truth, knowledge, or understanding of what we contemplate, so ideally our reflections will yield a conclusion of sorts, although such a result is by no means necessary, even if it is the most desirable outcome. Our intellectual concentration on some topic, like the problem of evil or how evil individuals are possible, thus achieves the level of philosophy if our considerations are sufficiently theoretical, abstract, or general, even if a resolution does not immediately result.

Our susceptibility to enter into philosophical reflection may depend on various background assumptions, knowledge, affective states, or other factors, such as a predisposition to concentrate intellectually, an ability to block out distractions, a sense of calm—whether momentary or ongoing—or quite simply the time in which we might allow contemplation to occur. Evil is additionally a philosophically fascinating topic, even if or perhaps because our intuitions and presumptions about it vary widely. In terms of general human experience, such thoughts and characteristics are hardly unusual or out of the ordinary. On the contrary, many viewers of a film like *No Country for Old Men* might be reasonably expected to have them, so bringing these features to bear on the evil represented by Chigurh might be readily advanced by configuring the affective and narrative elements of an artwork to "cognitively bias" the viewer to reflect philosophically, even if only for a short time. Of course, how much someone reflects will vary, depending on personal inclination, ability, mood, pre-existing intuitions and assumptions, circumstances, and so on. This variation, however, helps to explain the diversity of responses that *No Country for Old Men*, both as a fiction and a film, has generated. Different background assumptions and affective configurations, for instance, will incline different viewers to contemplate in different ways, whether religiously or secularly, politically or nonpolitically, philosophically or nonphilosophically—or even not at all. But given the carefully detailed aesthetic structure that the Coens have given their film and McCarthy his novel as well as their likely consequences, the preferred response would seem to be secular, political, and philosophical.

Cynthia Freeland argues that depictions of evil in film often stimulate our intellectual responses—our thoughts—about "its many varieties and degrees" (3). My argument agrees with her assertion, even if *No Country for Old Men* is not what she would term an "artful horror" film. I would suggest that it borrows from "realist horror" films in the way it portrays Chigurh as a moral monster along the lines of one of her favorite examples, *Henry: Portrait of a Serial Killer* (John McNaughton, 1990), but like many Coen brothers' films it freely mixes and reformulates genre influences in ways that make it difficult to categorize as simply a horror film or a Western. Moreover, in rejecting understandings of evil that rely primarily on the theological or the Satanic, both the film and McCarthy's novel make a political point as well as a philosophical one that will not be lost on many post-9/11 viewers—especially concerning the importance of secular understandings of evil individuals. Ellis's ambiguous reference to "this country" being hard on people, for example, makes the point for viewers to notice and implicitly invites them to take it up in their own considerations. Knowledge of theories such as those of Morton, Blair, or Nichols may further augment such insights by complimenting this and other suggestions made by the artworks themselves, but I do not think such knowledge is necessary. The character Wells, for instance, lacks it in spite of having a more accurate sense of Chigurh than anyone else in the story.

One complicating factor of the film is that Tommy Lee Jones' version of Sheriff Bell remains such a sympathetic character throughout that many viewers overlook or forgive him his fundamental lack of imagination when it comes to evil individuals and their implications. In this sense, the cinematic version of Sheriff Bell is not unlike the character Sal (Danny Aiello) in Spike Lee's *Do the Right Thing* (1989), whose racism many viewers forgive or miss because he is otherwise so sympathetic (for a fuller argument regarding such characters, see Flory, esp. 39–64.) For this reason I do not think that critics who saw the film's emphasis on evil's incomprehensibility or inexorability are entirely wrong. They simply fail to appreciate how *No Country for Old Men* places a burden on viewers to reject Bell as an interpretive guide and take up the task themselves of resolving the problems of evil so impressively presented, thereby moving beyond the passive nihilism embodied by this character. Chigurh is, after all, human. He bleeds when shot, and in some ways his efforts to "fit in," symbolized in the film by his awful haircut and slightly out-of-style clothing, are pathetic, so narratively as well as formally the film depicts him to be at least in some respects imaginably a human being like us. Our responsibility, which both McCarthy's novel and the Coen brothers' film consistently raise, is to try to resolve *how* that might be so in the most thorough-going way possible—a way that involves, in its most subtle expression, philosophical reflection.

PART III

The Road *(2006)*

Introduction

In the first chapter of Part III, " 'Everything uncoupled from its shoring':
Quandaries of Epistemology and Ethics in *The Road*," Donovan Gwinner
continues Part II's engagement with philosophic ways of knowing
by questioning the ethical implications of characters' behavior and
choices in *The Road* based on their perceptions of the nature of the
world around them. Like Dan Flory, he argues McCarthy problematizes
a simple religious reading or theologically based answer. "As the
main characters deploy their survivalist semiotics," Gwinner writes,
"the postapocalyptic pragmatism ironically yields an abstract ethical
dimension . . . which maintains that determining 'whether an act is
morally right depends only on the *actual* consequences (as opposed
to foreseen, foreseeable, intended, or likely consequences)'." This
indication of moral ambiguity extends, Gwinner adds, to other parts
of the novel, suggesting that the conceptual barrier between good
and bad is indistinct or permeable, in contradiction to more simplistic
readings of the novel's characters as "good guys" or "bad guys". "There
is at least a modicum of tension between the good of the heroes and an
act such as running away from the trapped people kept as livestock,"
Gwinner argues, pointing out that "Insofar as it makes perfect sense to
ignore the appeals of the doomed people in the cellar or risk sharing
their fate, the father's reaction conforms to his survivalist consequentialism," confirming the complexity of the novel's presentations of good,
evil, and the ethics of epistemology. Similarly, Jay Ellis pointed out the
complexity of evaluating the character of Anton Chigurh or reducing
him to simple craziness or insanity in Part II.

Susan Kollin insists in Chapter 8, "'Barren, silent, godless': Ecodisaster and the Post-abundant Landscape in *The Road*," that the ethical concerns examined by Gwinner in Chapter 7 extend beyond the two main characters of the novel to encompass "a larger social order in crisis." The father and son, she says, "face what is clearly a natural as well as a human disaster, or . . . a crisis of 'nature-culture.'" Rather than thinking of these things separately, Kollin explores the ethical dimension of their linked and overlapping characters. Like John Steinbeck's 1939 road novel, *The Grapes of Wrath* (which also won a Pulitzer Prize)

> McCarthy's book is a novel of disaster, a horrifying account of environmental decline in the context of larger social failings . . . an allegory of a hyperabundant America, [that] calls into question various master narratives of national identity, particularly notions of U.S. exceptionalism.

She extends here as well Steven Tatum's reading of hyperabundancy and late capitalism as driving forces in violent social disruption and decline on both sides of the border in his examination of *No Country for Old Men* in Part II.

Kollin's challenging reading of *The Road* is followed by Dana Phillips' equally contentious chapter, "'He Ought Not Have Done It': McCarthy and Apocalypse." In fact, Phillips argues, McCarthy hasn't "done it"—*The Road* is not about apocalypse at all. While "the world may have come to an end" in McCarthy's book, "the world is also the same as it ever was: filled with mortal peril, because it is shaped by causes the advent of which is pure chance, while the effects of these causes seem more or less deterministic." Rather than struggling to place McCarthy's work in some historic continuum of dystopian, post-apocalyptic, or post-nuclear traditions, Phillips posits that critics should instead recognize the startling singularity of *The Road* and its constant defiance of the strictures of genres and other classificatory systems. "Minimalism, pragmatism, or naturalism" Phillips writes,

> these labels may come close to identifying McCarthy's stock in trade in *The Road*, but none is likely to stick for long. For in the latest work of this writer, the labeling impulse itself is called into question, and naming has become a quaint activity.

CHAPTER 7

"Everything uncoupled from its shoring": Quandaries of Epistemology and Ethics in *The Road*

Donovan Gwinner

He rose and stood tottering . . . with his arms outheld for balance while the vestibular calculations in his skull cranked out their reckonings. An old chronicle. To seek out the upright . . . .. Eyes closed, arms oaring. Upright to what? Something nameless in the night, lode or matrix. To which he and the stars were common satellite. Like the great pendulum in its rotunda scribing through the long day movements of the universe of which you may say it knows nothing and yet know it must. (15)[1]

To know *and* not to know—that is a central quandary for the two main characters, a father and a son who live like "two hunted animals" (130) in "the wasted country" (6) of "post-apocalyptic" America, a terra damnata in which their very existence is threatened constantly by the elements, made harsher by a global cataclysm, and by the relatively few other survivors, most of whom are predatory. While Shakespeare's philosophical Dane, whose soliloquizing I echoed, ponders (not) being, Cormac McCarthy's heroes continually confront the ways in which their survival in a fundamentally unsafe environment hinges on (not) knowing. The epigraph above crystallizes powerfully the ways in which the novel stages routine acts of their survivalism as matters of "knowing," and the quotation alerts us as to how those mundane matters relate to broader, if elusive, questions about the bases of knowledge: the mechanisms and precepts that sometimes facilitate, as with the father and the son, navigating and remaining "upright" in "the nothingness."

Moreover, as the epigraph stresses, their knowledge informs various forms of counting, calculating, and reckoning—a continual reading of what remains of the natural environment, civilization, and humanity—on which their survival depends. The centrality of drawing interpretive conclusions from what is sensible coheres with what John Rothfork regards as characteristic of some of McCarthy's later novels, a philosophical "shifting [of] focus from metaphysics to epistemology" (202). Further, in Rothfork's analysis of McCarthy's work, which extends to *Cities of the Plain*, the epistemological emphasis is specifically pragmatic, a position the critic associates with "recurrent . . . caution in response to claims of revelation or of a breakthrough to a perfect or total understanding" (204). For a pragmatist, Rothfork observes, "Knowledge . . . [comes] . . . only through experience" (206), and pragmatic epistemology persistently raises this basic question: "How do you know?" (204). *The Road* makes evident its pragmatism by highlighting the protagonists' application of their experiential knowledge to the work of interpreting their surroundings to exist in them, a "survivalist semiotics." As the main characters deploy their knowledge, however, the post-apocalyptic pragmatism ironically yields an abstract ethical dimension, a type of "actual consequentialism," which maintains that determining "whether an act is morally right depends only on the *actual* consequences (as opposed to foreseen, foreseeable, intended, or likely consequences)" (Sinnott-Armstrong). In maintaining their well-being, they uphold the fundamental "good" of survival. In particular, from the father's perspective, that which is right depends only on the *actual* survival of his son. Taking into consideration both the earlier stress on survivalist semiotics and their adherence to pragmatic "goodness," we can see that the novel somewhat surprisingly couples questions and assertions of knowing with questions and applications of values and ethics. In this way, the phrase "To seek out the upright" takes on a second meaning because the father and the son seek "goodness" in various manifestations and see themselves as embodying goodness, or "carrying the fire." As they aspire to goodness in carrying the fire, they also travel the path of the pendulum insofar as father and son struggle, as readers do, with knowing and not knowing. Indeed, the ambiguities and obscurities associated with (not) knowing and marching into nothingness produce an interpretive quandary: by the conclusion of the text, the revelation of triumphant goodness, ostensibly symbolized by the survival of the son and his adoption into a "good" family after the father dies, follows awkwardly from a narrative that persistently denies or casts doubt on epistemological and ethical certainties. The novel thus places readers in the position of knowing *and* not knowing what to make of an apparently hopeful resolution that cannot fully overcome the pervasive images and declarations of dissolution and hellish desolation.

Knowledge and Survivalist Semiotics

In the first few pages of *The Road*, McCarthy introduces the overlapping of epistemological and ethical concerns by establishing the bond between the man and his son, which constitutes a nucleus of goodness, and their reliance on survivalist semiotics, the interpretation of physical evidence and (or *as*) signs. The fundamental nature and the commingling of these concerns are immediately depicted by the act of the man "reach[ing] out to touch the child sleeping beside him," to confirm that his son is still there, alive: the father's "hand rose and fell softly with each precious breath" (3). Beginning from that center of meaning—his son's life—the man rises to take his bearings, "stud[ying] the country to the south" (4), after which two simple declarations follow up on the certainty of the boy's breathing. "They were moving south. There'd be no surviving another winter here" (4). Virtually every other piece of information is an ambiguous product of sight and inference: "he glassed the valley," "He studied what he could see," "Looking for anything of color . . . [or] movement . . . [or] trace of standing smoke" (4). What does the man see? "Everything paling away into the murk" (4). From this murky, inconclusive vantage, he recalls the source of his claims for truth, his son: the father "knew only" that the boy "was his warrant," and he declares (conditionally) to the "ashen daylight" that the boy is "the word of God" (5). The father's "worship" of his son, who is the reference point against which everything else is considered, compels every move, measurement, glassing, surveying, and act of scavenging. Readers of McCarthy might recognize this mode of "reading" the signs that still signify in the wasteland as an intensified version of interpreting the text of the world evident in his other works. In his previous novel *No Country for Old Men*, for example, early passages involving a main character, Llewellyn Moss, foreground an interpretive methodology that can be categorized by a tracking term McCarthy uses, "cut for sign" (15). Also of interest for *The Road*, there is in the preceding novel an emphasis on the hunter being hunted. Just as Moss survives only as long as he succeeds in keeping track of and eluding those who hunt him, so too do the principals of the later novel stay alive by "cutting for sign" to find what they need and to avoid falling prey to hunters of humans.

As the leading survivalist reader of signs, what does the father know? The overall impression he leaves on the reader is that he is equal to just about every task or problem other than curing his unnamed terminal sickness. Unlike many of McCarthy's heroes and anti-heroes, such as Llewellyn Moss, whose most significant schooling surely occurs outside a classroom, the man of *The Road* possesses an abundance of both practical knowhow and formal education, which the narrator shows and implies mainly through the character's actions, though something of what the man knows becomes evident as he reflects on his past or talks to his son and others. Regarding his more formal education, several passages reflect medical training: he uses such specialized anatomical terms as "colliculus and temporal gyrus" (64); he performs minor surgery on himself (266); and he recalls that antibiotics have "a short shelflife" (248). While patching oneself up and avoiding spoiled antibiotics have pragmatic implications, much of the man's knowledge is clearly based on less formal sources of practical education. For instance, the man knows how literally to "carry the fire" by making use of such found items as an oil can (136–137), a camp stove (145), and even a pair of pliers (129) to produce flames for heat and cooking. Evidence of the foundation on which the man's practical knowledge is based emerges in an early passage that flashes back to when the father, as a youth, accompanied his uncle on firewood gathering trips: they "used to go in the fall" by "rowboat" not far "from his uncle's farm" (12). Therefore, we learn that this "perfect day of his childhood" (13) was an annual outing, part of the warp and woof of a rural life that still required basic hands-on practices and skills. The pastoral simplicity and integrity of the firewood trips are also signaled by the workers' humble methods and materials. To get under way, "his uncle bent to the oars," the only exhaust coming from a "cob pipe" (12), a perfect emblem for the old world this perfect day encapsulates. As if foreshadowing the material scarcity with which the nephew will later contend, they do not even seem to employ tools to extract the stump from the ground: they "us[ed] the roots for leverage, until they got it half floating in the water" (13). The simplicity of the work extends to how the two interact with each other, which the narrator remarks upon at the end of the passage, underscoring a key source of the perfection. As they labored, "Neither of them had spoken a word" (13). The perfection is largely based on the fundamental harmony of their collaboration experienced as pure physical activity: they went; his uncle rowed; they got the stump; neither needed to speak; as if the mediation of signs should not interfere with the essential work. At the same time, however, the young nephew would seem to have absorbed such practical lessons as the navigational method of "dead reckoning" the uncle uses when he "[took] a sight on the far shore" (12), another way of reading the world. Further, it seems a notable coincidence that the father's perfect day is powered by "oaring," the term this chapter's epigraph mentions as a method the man later uses to remain "upright." The man's application of oaring, a practice he observes in the old world, underscores the most salient feature of the man's knowledge: it bridges the pre- and post-apocalyptic worlds in a way that his son's does not.

As the less experienced of the two born during the period of cataclysmic change, what does the boy know? Certainly, his father has taught him virtually everything the boy has learned, even if the elder has not the desire or the opportunity to impart all of the knowledge he could. The boy himself seems like a somewhat reticent apprentice to the man—observing, asking, absorbing—but perhaps reluctant to know too much, too soon. Much like the wordless learning that takes place during the remembered perfect day, the son presumably ascertains much by studying his father, an example of which closely follows the firewood gathering passage. The man silently repairs a wheel on their cart, and the boy "watch[es] everything" (17). Underlying the more practical elements of his knowledge, however, much as the man knows the boy to be "godly," the son knows his father is simply *there*. When the boy first awakes in the novel, he responds to the man's assurance of presence ("I'm right here") by declaring, "I know" (5). As with many of their exchanges, this spare dialogue suggests a daily ritual of confirmation and comfort. They are together: the man protects them; leads the boy; the boy follows; is protected. Otherwise, the man has inculcated some conventionally "boyish" behaviors, such as when the boy suggests that his father "read [him] a story" (7), "paint[s] his facemask with fangs" (14), and plays with a toy truck (60) and a whistle (77). Clearly, the man has also taught the boy basic literacy. Later in the novel, for instance, the man observes that they no longer work on the boy's lessons, yet the boy is able to read roadside messages (131) and canned food labels (139). Overall, the man has taught the boy two main lessons: the father and the son are interdependent and must apply knowledge, including the interpretation of signs, to survive.

Not only do the constant pressures of survivalism cut into the boy's study time, but they also limit inquiry into stable notions of being, specifically a distinct post-apocalyptic identity. The closest the man comes to ontological speculation is in this rare moment of philosophizing. "Query: How does the never to be differ from what never was?" (32). This seems a bit like asking if an old sum of zero is different from a future sum of zero. As a reflection on "being," this query certainly suggests a negative proposition, one that prepares us for the hard line the man's wife takes in announcing her intention to commit the act that ensures she is "never to be" anymore: ". . . my only hope is for eternal nothingness and I hope it with all my heart" (57). Although the man tries to convince his wife that they are "survivors" (55), she dismisses such an identity as groundless. She says, "You talk about taking a stand but there is no stand to take" (57). In hindsight, he actually concurs with her:

> And she was right. There was no argument. The hundred nights they'd sat up debating the pros and cons of self destruction with the earnestness of philosophers chained to a madhouse wall [did not dissuade her]. (58)

The man acknowledges the "madness" of such philosophizing, especially of arguing the "pros," presumably, and so the woman's suicide effectively denies the need for more of such debates. With her death, the novel dismisses explicit philosophical inquiry into notions of being as a "dead end." If "she was right," then the man and the boy are survivors without the benefit of secure self-identification as such.

If they are not survivors, who are they? Because the man and the boy proceed after the woman's suicide, the man evidently believes in some type of stand, but specific answers to the question of identity, which is put to the protagonists at certain points, are unedifying. In general, the sense that basic identities are uncoupled from referents is established when they see evidence of or interact with others. When they see the first person they encounter in the novel, an apparent victim of a lightening strike, the boy wonders, "Who is it?" (49). The man replies, "I don't know. Who is anybody?" (49). Although the man is somewhat more confident in attributing basic identities or intentions to people elsewhere in the novel, this early exchange highlights how little can typically be known of people's "being." More importantly, uncertainty about identity applies to the protagonists themselves. When a hostile "roadrat" asks if the man is a doctor, the man asserts that he is "not anything" (64). Later, when another man, Ely, asks "What are you?" they are at a loss to tender self-identification: "They'd no way to answer the question" (162). The response to the roadrat conveys defensiveness more than confusion, perhaps, but the formulation following Ely's query, a reply to someone who is not threatening to them, suggests genuine uncertainty rather than a posture. In both cases, of course, surviving their encounters with strangers would be uppermost in their minds, not exchanging particular biographical information. To a great degree, then, father and son appear so burdened by survivalism that the energy and thought they can invest in notions of identity are minimal, even insofar as they might claim to be "survivors."

Goodness and Carrying the Fire

In the absence of lucid self-images, as they travel the road, the father and the son use their experiences, knowledge, and survivalist sense of themselves as "good guys" to bear up under the monumental burden of merely carrying on in a world where stable meaning, along with everything else, has been "uncoupled from its shoring" (11). Just as the narrative undermines systematic inquiry into being, so too does it powerfully stage a largely completed process of signs becoming irrevocably divorced from the things they represent, a dying state of signification and meaning to match corporeal death. In particular, the following passage crucially "centers" McCarthy's portrayal of a radically de-centered world.

> He tried to think of something to say but he could not . . . The world shrinking down about a raw core of parsible entities. The names of things slowly following those things into oblivion. Colors. The names of birds. Things to eat. Finally the names of things one believed to be true. More fragile than he would have thought . . . .. The sacred idiom shorn of its referents and so of its reality. Drawing down like something trying to preserve heat. In time to wink out forever. (88–89)

In several important ways, this passage relates synecdochically to the rest of the narrative. It begins by suggesting the man, or his consciousness, is himself/itself synecdochical of what remains, in that his being at a loss for words stands for the general trajectory of names and things moving toward "oblivion." By the end of the novel, readers will also see that the man, as "representative" of post-apocalyptic humanity, "winks out," so the loss of words, the contemplation of entropy, and the reference to life "cooling" foreshadow the climactic crisis of the familial plot, the death of the father, after which the son must recreate his world. The representativeness of the passage is also clear from the similarity of the diction used to describe the signs of the original cataclysm: what the man witnesses when "clocks stopped at 1:17" includes "A long shear of light" (52). The shear of light cuts through the sky as well as it cleaves time by inaugurating what the narrator refers to as the "new world" (cf. 161), a realm in which global annihilation precipitates the obliteration of meaning. Meaning, in general, is fading away, but the overall loss is figured as the excision of a language devoted to what is holy, an "idiom" with which to communicate "things one believed to be true." Critically, then, the account of knowing (what to say, what referents to use) is closely bound with notions of faith in what is true and, presumably, good.

What is good? While goodness is scarce, the narrative presents three main forms of it. The first two are basic and closely related: the principals' survival and anything that contributes to their well-being. As we might expect, there is relatively little mention of the goodness of

survival itself; if the stuff of their survival is itself good, the goodness of
their survival is self-evident. Conversely, much is made of the stuff of
survival, and some of the more satisfying passages for readers as well as
for characters are those that focus on the discovery and use of "goods."
The first description of a meal features a ham that is, despite its outward
desiccation, "Rich and good" (17). They also find morels in "a good
place" (41), and the boy deems the mushrooms "pretty good" (40).
At other crucial points, they "do good" at scavenging. Shortly after the
man announces that they are "starving" (110), he discovers apples and
a cistern with clean water, the latter prompting him to exult that there is
"Nothing in his memory anywhere of anything so good" (123). When
the man returns with the food and water, the boy concurs: "You did
good Papa" (124). The plot based on their search for "goods" ends with
the scavenging of a yacht on the coast but reaches a climax shortly after
the orchard and cistern episode when the man stumbles upon a backyard fallout shelter that contains "The richness of a vanished world,"
including "Crate upon crate of canned goods" (139, 138). Wherever
they can be found, usable commodities are "good" because they support
the good of survival.

The extraordinary richness of the fallout shelter points to how
the worth of goods overlaps with more abstract values. Specifically, in
addition to providing nutritional wealth, the shelter temporarily offers
a place in which the pair can partake of "civilized" normalcy that is
otherwise unavailable to them because it has vanished. The respite even
takes on sacral, ritual overtones. The father's invocation upon seeing
the underground cache, "Oh my God" (138), bespeaks its blessedness.
The boy is also affected by the miraculousness of the bunker and
wonders, "Is it real?" (139). Quickly, however, they embrace the tangible
goodness of domestic comfort and plenty that the mother-lode
provides. Somehow, instead of tearing into the food like the starved
mammals they are (though the man initially "clawed" a box open, 139),
the father commences a kind of tranquil picnic repast:

What would you like for supper?
Pears.
Good choice. Pears it is. (140)

Good choice, indeed—would a bad choice from the cornucopia of
cardboard boxes be possible? The shelter also makes available ordinary
domestic implements: the father uses a can opener, and they eat out
of "paperware bowls" with "plastic utensils and silverware" (140). The
routine meal completed, the father "put[s] the boy to bed," tucking in
his son as he would have done countless times in the milieu of his

former life (141). The bunks and the underground darkness afford long stretches of good rest, and the supplies also allow them to bathe properly with "soap and sponges" in "fresh warm water" (147), after which they wash their old clothes and don new ones from the cache (147, 148). To pass the time, they play checkers (148). Overall, even as the man worries about the bunker being a "dangerous" hideout (148), a potential trap, they both enjoy a brief period of home living, the "good life." Especially for the boy, underlying this find is a gift to be acknowledged, a goodness for which thanks are due. In fact, as soon as the boy sees the shelter, he questions their right to use its resources and is led by his father through a sort of end-time syllogism:

> Is it okay for us to take it?
> Yes. It is. They would want us to. Just like we would want them to.
> They were the good guys?
> Yes. They were.
> Like us.
> Like us. Yes.
> So it's okay.
> Yes. It's okay. (139–40)

Papa essentially makes this case: the guys with goods were good guys; good guys share with other good guys; wonder to relate, good guys discover the "tiny paradise" (150) into which the founding good guys could not descend: QED—rejoice and enjoy. That reasoning opens the door into the refuge for the boy, so to speak, but he later feels as if more should made of the goodness and says grace before they eat a second time: "Dear people, thank you for all this food and stuff . . ." (146). From the father's surprised oath to the son's blessing, it is evident that, in this new world, goods, those who "do good," and goodness itself are of a piece.

In addition to the initial two forms of goodness, then, the third type of goodness is basically the sense indicated by the intrinsic character of those who built and stocked the bunker, that they were decent in a way that transcends simply leaving stuff behind to be found by strangers. Such goodness might coincide with the first two senses, as with the fall-out shelter, but it is ultimately supplemental—as anything metaphysical would be for those beset by overwhelming worldly concerns—to the good of survival. Despite the limited opportunities for philosophical reflection, from the earliest passages of the novel, the narrative makes explicit that the protagonists do perceive their very survival as partaking of ethical and "civilized" goodness. As I remarked above, the father sees goodness as a quality of being embodied especially in his son, his "warrant." In this sense, the goodness of their survivalism relates metonymically to the traditional goodness of religion and the sacred. Not only is the boy "the word of God" (5), but he is "God's own fire-drake" (31), like a "tabernacle" (273), a "Golden chalice, good to house a god" (75). Paradoxically, as much as the sacred idiom is shorn of its referents, the father cannot help but think of his son in the holiest of terms: being with his son is a "blessing . . . no less real for being shorn of its ground" (31). The man accepts that there is no basis for belief; he believes anyway.

The man's discipleship requires total devotion, the observance of which entails an ethical imperative to protect his son. The narrative dramatizes acting on the imperative when the man defends his son by fatally shooting the roadrat. Afterward, the father deploys the boy's new knowledge to reaffirm the essence of their relationship.

> You wanted to know what the bad guys looked like. Now you know. . . . My job is to take care of you. I was appointed to do that by God. I will kill anyone who touches you. Do you understand?
>   Yes.
>   He sat there cowled in the blanket. After a while he looked up. Are we still the good guys? he said.
>   Yes. We're still the good guys.
>   And we always will be.
>   Yes. We always will be.
>   Okay. (77)

Cowled and questioning like a wavering novice, the boy seeks to reconcile the father's use of deadly force with his sense that they simply *are* good people. If the boy wonders whether it would have been some-how good to sacrifice himself in the clutches of the attacker, to turn the other cheek, as it were, then the father declares unequivocally the one commandment by which their micro-patriarchy functions—the father shall do anything needful (to protect the son), including killing. Their unalterable goodness stands distinct from the badness that would threaten them, personified by the roadrat. The father acts on and then explains the logical culmination of their survivalist consequentialism: the roadrat dies and they survive; goodness prevails over badness. Put another way, though the father knows the connection between language and the reality of religious belief has been shorn, his devotion to the boy, his warrant, shores his existence.

If the man and the boy are fundamentally good, so long as they have the goods to survive and avoid or thwart bad guys, how is goodness evident in other ways than the father's protective fervor? First, they adhere to a family ethical code, the initial reference to which occurs when the father abstains from drinking cocoa in an attempt to give all of it to his son (34). The boy catches him in his ploy and lectures him by recalling two of their shared precepts: one should not forego one's portion of food or drink and, more importantly, one should not go back on one's word ("You promised not to do that," 34). The boy concludes the homily: "If you break little promises you'll break big ones" (34). Based on this exchange, their code stresses honesty, fairness, constancy, and, given those values, we can well imagine many additional instances of their familial goodness. As I suggested above, however, insofar as they seem to reflect on their being, their image of themselves is largely based on what they are *not*, so their goodness is seen most easily in negative propositions. For example, they introduce themselves to Ely by declaring that they are "not robbers" (162). Most crucial to their ethics is a staunch rejection of cannibalism. To the question of surviving by eating other people, they say no, not us. In contrast, the characterization of the predatory roadrat helps establish the horror of cannibalism: a key detail about him is that his ". . . teeth . . . [are] . . . [c]laggy with human flesh" (75). The core value of their goodness is affirmed explicitly after they escape the house in which six men and women reside and confine other people in the basement as livestock. After they escape the house, in characteristic fashion, father and son debrief about the episode. The boy asks,

> We wouldnt ever eat anybody, would we?
> No. Of course not . . ..
> No matter what.
> No. No matter what.
> Because we're the good guys.
> Yes.
> And we're carrying the fire.
> And we're carrying the fire. Yes.
> Okay. (129)

The man justifies the initial negations with affirmations of goodness, "carrying the fire." The narrative order of confronting cannibalism directly and disavowing any possibility of indulging in it leads to two closely placed high points of their scavenging, finding the home with the cistern and the orchard and, most gloriously, uncovering the stocked bunker. Following so closely on the dialogue excerpted above, it is as if the boons reward them for reaffirming the cannibalism taboo. Just before they discover the bunker, the father offers a more general ethical precept that reinforces the notion of goodness rewarded. More particularly, he is trying to assure his son that the bunker door is truly different from the hatchway confining the human livestock and that there are likely to be "things in there," rather than people (137). "This is what the good guys do. They keep trying" (137). Though they realistically do not have any other option ("There's no place else to go," 137), they are rewarded for their good effort.

As the father's testimony on their aversion to eating people indicates, the intrinsic goodness of the pair is most explicitly figured as the carrying of fire, a metaphor that connotes civilization itself, civility as honorable behavior, and that which is sacred. The initial reference to their role as fire-carriers is made as they reassure themselves about their prospects following the violent encounter with the roadrat.

> We're going to be okay, arent we Papa?
> Yes. We are.
> And nothing bad is going to happen to us.
> That's right.
> Because we're carrying the fire.
> Yes. Because we're carrying the fire. (83)

On some level, even the boy, who is still recovering from the trauma of the skirmish with the roadrat, must know that something bad happening is a virtual certainty, that goodness cannot—with some prophylactic of mutual exclusivity—shield them from badness. Nonetheless, the story the two tell themselves is ostensibly necessary to provide a more elevated justification for persisting than animalistic survival. The enshrining of their survivalism in the phrase they repeat to each other about carrying the fire (the boy does not ask it as a question but seeks reaffirmation of the idea) suggests a form of providential protection that will see them through, despite all threatening evidence to the contrary. Here is the chink in the man's pragmatist armor, the small space he allows himself to believe in the sanctity of his son, the inevitability that the boy will be "lucky" after the man's death (278). That the man rightly intuits the luck of his son's eventual adoption into the veteran's family appears to validate the notion that the boy is special, that the faith of the father somehow trumps his pragmatism. In other words, there is no pragmatically satisfying answer to the question we might put to the father: how do you know? Throughout the novel, there is no experiential precedent for them to expect to encounter "good guys" with whom they (or, as it happens, the boy) can join. Every character other than the father and the son is either a threat or a likely burden, so, until the veteran appears, there is no model for the "good guys" besides the protagonists themselves. Somewhat like the way in which they project themselves onto the absent builders of the fallout shelter, they must imagine meeting versions of themselves to enlarge the good group, to continue carrying the fire. The idealism of their goodness therefore departs from the pragmatism that guides them but also serves as the ultimate goal, figured as fire-carrying, of their consequentialism.

Reckoning and Tottering in the Darkness

Long before the boy encounters the veteran, the good man of the adoptive family, the father and the son meet an aged man who calls himself Ely, and this meeting, which includes conversation, awkward companionship, and the sharing of food, is notable for depicting someone who complicates the dominant ethical scheme of the narrative and, subsequently, reveals himself to be insufficiently good to be a fellow traveler of the protagonists. As the only conventionally named character in the novel, the potential significance of "Ely" is hard to ignore. If he is a prophet, a post-apocalyptic Elijah, he is an anti-prophet, not unlike the man's wife, one who bears witness to the abyss, to nothingness. Thus speaks Ely: "There is no God and we are his prophets" (170). Later, he adds, "Things will be better when everybody's gone . . .. We'll all breathe easier" (172, 173). Insofar as he says puzzling things, he puts off the father, but in his actions he seems no less humane than the main characters. More significantly, Ely troubles the man mainly because the lone wanderer is unaccountable. In wondering how Ely supports himself, the father imagines the old man is "a shill for a pack of roadagents" (172), as if the father could brook someone openly hostile or completely sympathetic but not someone who is ambiguously foe and friend. While the boy wants to aid Ely, the father seems intent on proving that the inexplicable individual is not so good as to be a carrier of fire. The father prompts the old man to thank the boy for the food Ely accepts from them, but the old man equivocates: "Maybe I should and maybe I shouldnt" (173). Ely's gloominess, mysteriousness, and amorality amount to a troubling, frigid dousing of fire-carrying goodness. Until the father dies, the (false?) prophet is the only person to approximate the "good guy(s)" for whom they search, but he is not good enough. Initially, Ely claims to be "not anything," a formulation the good guys should understand. Ely is indeed *something*; we—the readers, the main characters—just do not know *what*. If nothing else, Ely is a figure who complicates the protagonists' binary model of good versus bad.

In addition to the moral ambiguity of Ely, other parts of the novel suggest that the conceptual barrier between good and bad is indistinct or permeable. For instance, as Kenneth Lincoln postulates (169), there is at least a modicum of tension between the good of the heroes and an act such as running away from the trapped people kept as livestock. Insofar as it makes perfect sense to ignore the appeals of the doomed people in the cellar or risk sharing their fate, the father's reaction conforms to his survivalist consequentialism. For the boy, knowing about the people in the cellar presents a major ethical dilemma that requires the father's confirmation of what the boy guesses: ". . . we couldnt help them because then they'd eat us too" (127). The ways in which both principal characters respond, implicitly and explicitly, to this episode raise questions about their identities, their goodness.

That the boy needs physical and moral comfort, as he rests "his head in the man's lap" (127), is unsurprising but nonetheless symbolic of undercutting, even momentarily, their being "upright." In spite of the obvious danger to them, the good son frames their reaction as an inability to help people in distress. In the context of the boy's other reactions to withholding aid in the novel, such as when he cries after his father insists "There's nothing to be done" for the lightning victim (50), there seems also to be a note of failure in his acceptance. If nothing else, helping implies that, under some more favorable circumstances, perhaps, liberating the imprisoned people would have been the good thing to do. In unpacking the thinking of the two, we might initially wonder how the boy is sure of their inability to help. As they flee the house, the boy observes the "masters" of the house, four men and two women, returning, so perhaps being outnumbered makes their inability to help obvious. Explicitly, the pair perceives the logical outcome of helping the human livestock would be to join their lot. More subtly, the pronoun references imply that the prisoners ("them") would be the attackers ("they'd eat us"). The man's initial reaction to the captured people suggests a view of them as threatening, or at least not good. The man cannot escape them fast enough. He drops his valuable lighter, but there is no time to retrieve it, though he does spend a little of their precious time to "slam down" the trapdoor, during which fleeting seconds the son identifies the more serious threat of the approaching figures (111). In short, for good guys on the lookout for other (potential) good guys, the father's response casts a slight ethical shadow, especially since the symbolic fire he carries, the lighter, is left behind with the damned men and women in the larder (cf. Lincoln 169). Some pages later, after they escape, after they acknowledge the fate of the people in the basement, after they reject, or negate, for themselves the very idea of subsisting on people, and after the father confesses to losing the lighter, it makes bleak sense that the elder sees "the absolute truth of the world" as "Darkness implacable" (130).

The ethical darkness of the father and the difference in the father's and the son's values are brought into relief by a revenge scenario involving a thief who loots all of their possessions while the protagonists are away from their campsite. Both are deeply distraught by the heist (the father swears, "Oh Christ," and the son cries, 253), and both are commited to finding the thief (254). The rift in their thinking about how to treat the man they are searching for is foreshadowed when the boy asks his father if they are going to kill whomever they track down; his father responds, "I dont know" (255). The question about punishment and the uncertainty of the response signal disequilibrium in their joint effort to "seek out the upright," here condensed in a crucial act of tracking, cutting for sign (in this case, sand fallen from the purloined cart, 254), and of enacting ostensible goodness to counter the badness of theft. The "outcast" (255) they catch evokes not only righteous indignation but also seething fury in the father, who threatens to "blow [the thief's] brains out" and leaves him not only without all of the pilfered property but also without his "vile rags" of clothing (256). The father claims to be leaving the thief as the thief left them, with nothing, so, for him, the punishment fits the crime—eye for an eye; tooth for a tooth. The thief, who had previously been punished by having his fingers cut off, is shocked by the father's severity (256). Initially, the boy is so upset that the thief realizes how determined the man is by merely looking at the son's eyes (256), which must reflect the worry hinted at with his original question about killing. The boy appeals for mercy on the thief's behalf (256), and, by the time they leave the outcast, he is "crying and looking back at the nude and slatlike creature" (258). Far from wanting to punish the culprit, the boy wants to "help him" (259). The vast difference in their attitudes toward the thief, the different conceptions of goodness to which the father and the son subscribe, is a more traumatic version of their disagreement "about what to give the old man," Ely: the father admits that, if not for the boy, Ely would receive nothing (173). As when the man yields to his son's graciousness with Ely, the father again relents, at least in attempting to relocate the outcast to return his clothes (260). After they fail to find the thief a second time, the father tries to assure his son of one thing: "I wasnt going to kill him . . ."; "But we did kill him," the boy counters (260). No one knows what becomes of the pilferer, but their contrasting notions of how to treat him serve the very clear purpose of differentiating the main characters' conceptions of goodness.

If the father's actual violence in killing the roadrat early in the novel leaves the boy bloodied and traumatized but safe, the father's threats of violence and stripping of the thief leave the boy physically safe but psychologically and morally devastated. Until the father is shot in the leg with an arrow some time after the thief episode (263), the boy seems unable to say more than two words to his father. Even after the man patches himself up and they agree to "start over" (267), the boy voices a kind of philosophical surrender when his father finally initiates an actual conversation. The child asserts:

> I'm talking.
> Are you sure?
> I'm talking now.
> Do you want me to tell you a story?
> No. . . .
> Why not?
> Those stories are not true.
> They dont have to be true. They're stories.
> Yes. But in the stories we're always helping people and we dont
>   help people.
> Why dont you tell me a story?
> I dont want to. . . .
> What about dreams? You used to tell me dreams sometimes.
> I dont want to talk about anything.
> Okay.
> I dont have good dreams anyway. (267–68, 269)

Even if we attribute some sullenness to the boy's youth and the fundamentally harsh life he leads, this exchange offers a striking rejection of what his father represents, which is to say that, as much as he loves Papa, he can no longer relate to him as a fellow traveler in the family narrative—good guys fighting for survival and helping those in need—which has sustained them. They do not help people (with one exception, Ely), and the boy's dreams are no longer worth sharing with the individual who is his "world entire" (6). The boy's defeatism regarding who they are reiterates doubt he voices a little earlier, when they are encamped on the beach. After his father confides that people "couldnt live anyplace else," specifically on another planet, the boy seems to despair of carrying the fire to any like-minded people: "I dont know what we're doing" (244). The father is initially speechless in the face of his son's dark night of the soul, though he finally counters somewhat weakly, "There are people and we'll find them. You'll see" (244). Immediately following his counterpoint, the man casts doubt on the likelihood of meeting good guys when he remarks that a message written in the sand would possibly be read by "the bad guys," a pragmatic point he instantly regrets making ("I shouldnt have said that," 245).

The very next passage lightens the mood with the shooting of a flare (245–46), a celebratory "highlight" that quite possibly alerted the thief to their position, since he steals what they have shortly after the flare pistol demonstration (253). There are people, to be sure, but the one person who shows up is not so good.

The thief is not the type of guy they hope to meet, but the son's over-all response to the encounter serves as a culmination to an ongoing argument with his father about how to treat other people. Throughout much of the novel, the son chafes at the father's survivalist insularity, imagining others as joining with them or by offering whatever aid they can provide. From the father's perspective, extending help to others compromises their safety, at least, ostensibly, until they encounter good guys who can carry their own weight and not make the pair more vulnerable. Oddly, it is as if the father must die for the boy to find what the father is seemingly unprepared to find: good guys, namely the veteran and his family. While the father lives, there is never a truly promising opportunity to expand the family by joining with others, such doubles of the protagonists who carry the fire, but the father's deathbed optimism—"You're going to be lucky" (279)—and the timing of the veteran's arrival, following closely on the father's death (in the subsequent paragraph, in fact), suggest that the veteran is a good guy, a figure to stand in for the father. Therefore, one question we can ask is this: in meeting the veteran, has the boy met a surrogate version of his deceased father? How do we know the veteran is good? The boy actually poses the question: "How do I know you're one of the good guys?" (to which the veteran honestly replies, "You dont," 283). For the boy's part, he does not seem to be in a frame of mind to discriminate between a good and a bad guy (the veteran suggests the boy is "kind of weirded out," 283), but the characterization of the man presumably assures readers and apparently impresses the boy favorably. One of the first signs of hope is that the veteran expresses regret upon hearing of the father's death (282). More significantly, the veteran declines the boy's offer to take his pistol (285). With all of his father's instilled distrust and avoidance of others, how does the boy know the man is honest, good? To interpret signs of the veteran's bona fides, the boy confirms that the man is "carrying the fire" (283), but nothing convinces the boy so much as the man's reporting that he has children and that his family members "dont eat people" (284). In addition to offering encouraging words, the veteran shows himself to be trustworthy, which the boy discovers when he returns to say a final farewell to his dead father and sees that his body is "wrapped in a blanket as the man had promised" (286). To recall the discussion of the protagonists' ethical code, keeping promises is fundamental to goodness, so readers and the boy can recognize that the veteran upholds comparable values. While neither a reader nor the boy can know absolutely that the veteran is good, the "signs" are providential.

As certain as the father is about his final resting place (277) and how his son will be lucky, the boy is unsure of how to act and what to think, even after joining the veteran's family. For all we know about what the boy thinks and believes to be true, he is like the pendulum continuing in its path, knowing and not knowing: how to survive, whom to trust, how to use the gun he holds distractedly when interviewing the veteran (282), how to speak with God/his father, et cetera. When the son relays the fact of his father's passing to the veteran, he confesses, "I dont know what to do" (282), and the few remaining pages of narrative do not suggest increasing certainty. Once the adoptive family embraces the orphan, in his thinking, the boy seems to chart a kind of parallel but separate course with his new kin. The maternal figure who has been absent since his earliest years, "the woman" (286), emphasizes bolstering the youth's religious instruction, but he mainly communes with his father, who would appear to remain the most important person in the boy's life, in spite of his absence. In other words, if the practice of religion is the prime feature of the family's fire-carrying, then the boy does and does not continue to act as such a bearer, for his father is still "his world," and talking to his dead father, the woman declares, involves him indirectly in spiritual fellowship: "She said that the breath of God was his breath yet though it pass from man to man through all of time" (286). In the truncated portrait of his new life, a brief paragraph sketching the fulfillment of what the boy had wanted all along and what his father had prophesied for him, there are three references to "God," but the boy seems unable to embrace the holy fire of religion to carry it. What is good to him is expressed in a culminating superlative claim, "the best thing was to talk to his father" (286), so the fire the boy carries is the memory of what had animated the "cold and stiff" form near the road (281). In not forgetting his father, the son harbors a ghostly flame, curiously inverting the living-in-the-moment survivalist practicality of his father. Without other information about the boy's new family, the life he is embarking on, his search for "the upright," as guided by a flame of mourning, appears much the same as "marching . . . into the nothingness" (15).

See the Trout?

The final description of the boy centers on remembering and reflection, and so too does the concluding paragraph of the novel focus on recollection. The last paragraph is a coda harking back to the lost world of natural beauty, with its immemorial forms and signs:

> Once there were brook trout in the streams in the mountains. You could see them standing in the amber current where the white edges of their fins wimpled softly in the flow. . . . On their backs were vermiculate patterns that were maps of the world in its becoming. Maps and mazes. Of a thing which could not be put back. Not be made right again. (286–87)

The image of the brook trout, like the bounteous bunker, signifies the "vanished world." Importantly, before arriving at this riparian end of the road, readers have already encountered the trout twice, as remembered from the father's precataclysm life. Early in the novel, as man and boy travel through territory familiar to the father, including a stop at the home in which he was raised (25), the man pauses to observe water pass below a bridge, "Where once he'd watched trout swaying in the current . . ." (30). Later, in the good place of morels and a river falls, the father remembers the trout again: "He'd stood at such a river once and watched the flash of trout deep in a pool . . ." (41). Taken together, the three passages about trout form a contemplative triptych. The first two clearly arise from the man's conscious recollection, but who is reflecting on the trout in the last paragraph of the novel? It is as if the narrator includes vital memories of the father after his death to sound the knell of a whole category of experiential knowledge. In the first two examples, the man had "watched" the trout, so the observation of the fish is something "known" by the man (but not known by the boy). The last example includes the same time signal, "once," but with a shift of reference: "You could see them." At this point, the man could not address someone or be addressed about the trout, so who is the targeted "second person"? On one hand, the second person pronoun could function idiomatically to ensure an active phrasing of "trout could be seen" (by someone). On the other hand, the last paragraph of the novel is "pronounced" not in the more idiomatic voice of the characters but in the manner of the omniscient narrator, the projection of McCarthy which is profound, philosophical, biblical, et cetera. In a way that is atypical of the rest of the work, then, the narrator addresses actual readers as if we were survivors in the novel, like the boy, who know firsthand the post-apocalyptic world but have no experience with the preapocalyptic world. This scenario makes for an awkward reading position. If there is one thing actual readers *cannot* know, it is the world after the kind of global cataclysm depicted in *The Road*, but readers *can* experience the scene of the final paragraph: trout still exist; they can be seen. Thus, the narrative concludes by putting readers in the position of *not* knowing what the narrator seems bent on making known to us *and* knowing what the narrator signifies cannot (any longer) be known.

To match the paradoxical narrative perspective of the last paragraph, the trout itself becomes an uncanny figure that evokes both the lost home of the father and the projected lost world of the audience. With its "Maps and mazes," the fish is a thing which we can *and* cannot know, that is *and* is not an inhabitant of our home, present-day earth. Some of the more evocative imagery of the final paragraph intensifies the imbrications of knowing and not knowing. The fish is at once graspable, "smell[ing] of moss in your hand" (286), and inscrutable, with "patterns" that resist reinscription, signification: "Not be made right again," "not be put back." The end of the novel offers maps of beginnings that are visible yet unreadable. The wimpling of the trout fins connotes additional obscurity if we consider another meaning of "wimple," an enveloping, a veiling ("Wimple," *v*. def. I.1). Puzzlingly, the symbol of the trout envelops a lost beginning in a veiled present to reveal "the end."

Curiously, too, the last paragraph veils the boy as a carrier of the fire. By the end, we know the boy is "alive and well," but of his own goodness, his blessed traits, we know nothing. In fairness, what revelation could the end disclose? The boy became a man much like his father but also guided those attracted to and edified by his fiery goodness? Perhaps it is "good" enough that the boy survives to join such benign others as he and his father had hoped to find, adopted rather than enslaved or eaten. Just so, the enfolding of the trout passage in the resolution of the boy's story returns our attention to the way in which "Everything [is] uncoupled" (11) and to the elegiac sentiments that the narrative succeeds so well in articulating and dramatizing. To recast T. S. Eliot, the world (of the narrative) ends not with a bang, such as the apotheosis suggested by a reviewer's phrase printed on the front cover, "the miracle of goodness," but with a wimple, the entropic earth enfolding "names" and "things into oblivion" (88). Could there be anything else at the end of the road/*The Road*? To revisit Ely's discourse, "Who would know such a thing?" (174).

CHAPTER 8

"Barren, silent, godless": Ecodisaster and the Post-abundant Landscape in *The Road*

Susan Kollin

Environmental crisis is no longer an apocalypse rushing toward a herd of sheep that a few prophets are trying to rouse. It is not a matter of the imminent future but a feature of the present. Environmental crisis is . . . a process within which individuals and society today dwell; it has become part of the repertoire of normalities in reference to which people construct their daily lives.
(Frederick Buell, From Apocalypse to Way of Life:
Environmental Crisis in the American Century *(76))*

[M]y fundamental epistemological starting points are from this enmeshment where the categorical separation of nature and culture is already a kind of violence, an inherited violence anyway.
(Donna Haraway, How Like a Leaf *(106))*

When hypochondriacs actually contract the plague of their worst fear their ontologies tend to be thrown out of kilter.
(Mike Davis, Dead Cities and Other Tales *(6))*

Environmental catastrophe is yesterday's news in Cormac McCarthy's Pulitzer-prizewinning book, *The Road,* a narrative that is part ecodystopian fiction and part American road novel. Published in 2006, the book features a father and son forced to scavenge a post-collapse landscape where the environment and the economy have both taken a decided nose-dive. As the pair travel south on their journey, readers are given glimpses of a possible twenty-first-century future where all recognizable social institutions are in ruins. Throughout the text,

McCarthy requires his characters and his readers to reconstruct belief systems, human relations and understandings of the self in this bewildering post-natural and post-capitalist world.

As a narrative deeply rooted in the concerns and debates of its time, *The Road* may be considered an apocalyptic revision of John Steinbeck's 1939 novel *The Grapes of Wrath*, which also won a Pulitzer. Both texts chronicle the plight of characters facing environmental and economic disaster in an America whose dreams of possibility and progress have been called into question. While Steinbeck's narrative features the dustbowl crisis that sends the Joad family west to California during the Great Depression, McCarthy's novel takes on the global environmental crisis, anticipating in the process the worldwide economic meltdown that unfolded shortly after his book was published. While Steinbeck's narrative pins its hope on the generosity and self-sacrifice of the sharecropping underclass and the family who recognize that their only means of survival is as a unified collective, McCarthy's novel offers limited promise. In *The Road*, the family provides only a temporary and uncertain sanctuary, the economy appears beyond repair, and the natural world seems to be forever altered for the worse.

As a document of Depression-era America, *The Grapes of Wrath* chronicles the social and economic upheaval arising out of human disconnection from nonhuman nature. Facing an increasingly competitive economy, landowners in the early twentieth century are pressured to modernize their agricultural practices, replacing their human workers with more efficient machines. For a short while it succeeds, as production increases and costs go down. The owners soon learn, however, that the system requires constant growth. As the narrator explains, the banks "don't breathe air," they "breathe profits . . . The bank—the monster has to have profits all the time. It can't wait. . . . When the monster stops growing, it dies. It can't stay one size" (32). In Steinbeck's novel, the emphasis on growth and profits has dire consequences for the land and the human populations who depend on it, with the environmental catastrophe that emerges revealed as the unintended consequences of rampant capitalism and hyper-development.

Likewise, the post-apocalyptic environment in *The Road* foregrounds a larger social order in crisis. Geographer David Harvey addresses these interlinking concerns, arguing that "all socio-political projects are ecological projects and vice versa," such that a conception of " 'nature' and of 'environment' is omnipresent in everything we say and do" (174). For Harvey, "critical examinations of the relation to nature are simultaneously critical examinations of society" (174). In both novels, the characters face what is clearly a natural as well as a human disaster, or what Donna Haraway calls a crisis of "nature-culture." Rather than keeping these entities separate, Haraway points to the intimate overlap that links the two. "Living inside biology is about living inside nature-cultures. It is about being inside history as well as being inside the wonder of the natural complexity" (26). A year before *The Road* was published, the United States experienced the worst natural disaster in its history in the form of Hurricane Katrina, where race and class were deciding factors in the level and type of misery that occurred. As the title of Chester Hartman and Gregory D. Squires' book succinctly puts it, "there is no such thing as a natural disaster." Human history certainly contributed to the scope of the catastrophe in New Orleans; from global warming and decades of haphazard urban planning before the crisis to government ineptitude and inaction after the catastrophe, Hurricane Katrina cannot simply be called a "natural" phenomenon (2–3).

Like *The Grapes of Wrath*, McCarthy's book is a novel of disaster, a horrifying account of environmental decline in the context of larger social failings. In *The Road,* the crisis in nature-culture is referenced at one point when the narrator describes the particularities of this post-apocalyptic landscape. "The bones of dead creatures sprawled in the washes," McCarthy writes, "All of it shadowless and without feature. The road descended through a jungle of dead kudzu. A marsh where the dead reeds lay over the water" (177). The scene offers some of the only descriptions of actual plant life in the text, with a telling reference to the overgrown "dead kudzu" that blocks the road and impedes the journey itself. This invasive weedy vine has a complicated history in the United States; according to Peter Goin, kudzu (*Pueraria lobata*) was introduced from either Japan or Korea in the 1870s and eventually became popular in the American South as a shade-producing plant for many domestic landscapes across the region. In the 1930s, kudzu was regarded as a way of controlling erosion on banks and fields throughout the South, with the U.S. Department of Agriculture even paying farmers to plant this "miraculous soil saver." Able to grow up to a foot a day, kudzu covered more than half a million acres by the 1940s, where it eventually proved to be too much of a good thing. As Goin points out:

> kudzu is extremely difficult to eliminate; it grows rapidly in nearly any kind of soil, and its roots sink deeply into the earth. Georgia folklore even warns that one should keep windows closed at night to keep out the kudzu . . .. by 1970 it was classified as a weed and money was appropriated for its eradication. By 1990 kudzu covered more than 2 million acres of forest land in the South. (5)

Drawing on the natural and social history of the invasive weed across the American South, McCarthy offers an instance of what might be called "environmental blowback," where human practices in the land—in this case, agricultural policies and economic pressures—end up creating unforeseen problems that may have actually exceeded the original concerns that were supposed to be resolved.

Post-abundant Realities

In *The Road*, the devastated landscape through which the characters journey is also littered with the accumulated debris of twenty-first-century consumer culture, a reminder of the excess and waste that marks daily life for many Americans. Throughout the narrative, McCarthy positions the supermarket shopping cart as a meaningful image to ponder in this context. While the Joad family travels from Oklahoma to California in their makeshift automobile in search of new lives, the father and son in *The Road* journey through the land pushing a series of derelict shopping carts that carry abandoned food items, clothing, household goods and other cast-off objects which they have collected during their travels.

Like the Joads' automobile, the shopping cart takes on a number of complicated meanings in *The Road*. Both the vehicle in *The Grapes of Wrath* and the cart in McCarthy's text represent the possibility of mobility and escape; without these objects, neither family will survive the wreckage. At the same time, both the vehicle and the shopping cart represent the system whose collapse has created such despair. In *The Grapes of Wrath*, for instance, the automobile is a product of the very hypermodernity that leads to the dispossession and displacement of the Oklahoma sharecroppers from the land. Steinbeck writes:

> The family met at the most important place, near the truck. The house was dead, and the fields were dead; but this truck was the active thing, the living principle. The ancient Hudson, with bent and scarred radiator screen, with grease in dusty globules at the worn edges of every moving part, with hub caps gone and caps of red dust in their places—this was the new hearth, the living center of the family. (99–100)

Ironically, the Joads place their hopes on the machine as a way out of the crisis, with the ancient truck positioned as nothing less than a family member, the new center of their collective survival. The Joads' belief that technology will somehow save them by solving their family's problems echoes a common refrain in the modern world. In *Collapse: How Societies*

Choose to Fail or Succeed, Jared Diamond addresses this belief as an "expression of faith" based on a faulty assessment that technology has somehow "solved more problems that it created in the recent past" (504). In *Fieldnotes from a Catastrophe: Man, Nature, and Climate Change*, Elizabeth Kolberg points to the bad faith that often circulates in popular assessments of science, arguing that there is always a close relationship between "what we know and what we refuse to know"(3). Modern optimism in scientific progress and new technologies often involves a willingness to not know, what Diamond calls "an assumption that, from tomorrow onward, technology will function primarily to solve existing problems and will cease to create new problems" (504).

In McCarthy's *The Road*, however, the automobile provides no such promise. Life in the aftermath of disaster cannot sustain technology, a point illustrated when the boy mishandles various pieces of scavenged equipment. Once he forgets to turn off the valve on the fuel container, which renders their scavenged stove useless; later the boy leaves their pistol behind on the beach and the father is forced to backtrack in order to retrieve it. McCarthy's novel views technology with some suspicion, replacing the Joads' automobile with the run-down grocery carts that offer a less than desirable means of transport (259). At one point after a delay in their travels, the boy asks his father if they can leave. The man responds by offering him a ride in the cart. The boy foregoes using the shopping cart as a means of transportation, treating it with mistrust (200). In a sense, the boy's response may be seen as a nod to his growing maturity, a gesture that shows his impatience with the father's fussing The boy's refusal to take the "ride" also points to a general suspicion in the text regarding the shopping cart as an object of aid for the characters. Positioned as a symbol of late-capitalist consumer culture in the larger text, the cart is a reminder of the irrational exuberance that characterized the economy of contemporary America, with its over-extended, debt-ridden citizenry, many of whose lives were threatened more by "hyperabundance" than by any kind of scarcity (Buell 202).

In *The Road*, the two main characters move through the landscape with their shopping cart, sifting through the detritus of a post-capitalist America, offering in turn what might be considered an ironic and belated take on "green consumerism." The two characters arrive at the edge of the city where they come upon a supermarket with a trashed parking lot. McCarthy writes:

> They . . . walked the littered aisles. In the produce section in the
> bottom of the bins they found a few ancient runner beans and
> what looked to have once been apricots, long dried to wrinkled

effigies of themselves . . .. In the alleyway behind the store a few shopping carts, all badly rusted. They went back through the store again looking for another cart but there were none. (22)

For McCarthy's characters, the automobile must be abandoned in the parking lot, the conditions of life having rendered this once ubiquitous possession now useless. The automobile no longer provides mobility and escape from crisis, just as the shopping cart does not carry the latest commodities from the marketplace, but only what can be sifted through and salvaged from the destroyed cities. The survivors must make do with less; one wheel on their cart starts making a "periodic squeak," but there is no means for them to fix it (186).

Even though they are in search of a better place, the father and son do not arrive at a new Eden, as the contemporary American road novel often promises. Instead, they are stuck with a fallen world that appears beyond redemption. There is no certainty of a return to a paradise or any assurance that they can remake life to resemble how it once was. At one point, McCarthy explains that the man realized he was keeping up a false front in the face of great doom. "He hoped it would be brighter where for all he knew the world grew darker daily" (213). The environment the characters inhabit has drastically changed, and the new task involves locating the basic elements that can make their current lives not only bearable, but meaningful.

They passed through towns that warned people away with messages scrawled on the billboards. The billboards had been whited out with thin coats of paint in order to write on them and through the paint could be seen a pale palimpsest of advertisements for goods which no longer existed. (127–28)

In this new landscape billboards no longer beckon consumers with enticing promises about their product. Instead, they repel and rebuke the viewer, offering only fading signs of a lost world.

In *The Road*, the environment thus features the ghostly remains of the commodities that previously fueled consumer culture but are now merely phantom reminders of what came before.

Odd things scattered by the side of the road. Electrical appliances, furniture. Tools. Things abandoned long ago by pilgrims enroute to their several and collective deaths. Even a year ago the boy might sometimes pick up something and carry it with him for a while but he didnt do that any more. (199–200)

While some Americans placed great hope in acts of consumption just as the boy himself once did, he no longer has faith that these acquisitions will serve a meaningful purpose in his new life. As Susan Stewart notes in her analysis of the "collection," while the practice of accumulating objects that we endow with value may promise to connect us to a prelapsarian past "beyond flux and history," she notes that the project of amassing a collection—here the abandoned consumer goods of a previous life—also links us to "the world of the dead" (57). These commodities are signs of what existed before and are thus reminders of the failure of that world. In *The Road*, the cities are "looted and exhausted," able to sustain only scores of foragers who move in "the rubble white of tooth and eye carrying charred and anonymous tins of food in nylon nets like shoppers in the commissaries of hell" (181).

Frederick Buell examines the ways a specter of crisis has become such a central aspect of contemporary American culture that it seems to have been domesticated into our everyday lives. At a time when many leaders resort to denial and self-delusion about the problems facing the environment and in an era when a powerful anti-science movement seeks to discredit current thinking on topics such as global warming, the belief that we inescapably face dire environmental problems nevertheless seems to have been folded into Americans' daily existence. As he explains, "even as it has been effectively contested and denied, a sense of unresolved, perhaps unresolvable, environmental crisis has become part of people's normality today" (xvii). Buell focuses on what he calls "crisis conceptualization," the means by which societies try to make sense of and manage catastrophe. Typically, the focus has appeared on the "end" itself and on the elements leading up to the crisis. Yet, as he explains:

> The prospect of these "ends" does not mean that people confront an onrushing apocalypse, the end of humanity. These foreseeable "ends" are something that people are in the process of living through. Apocalypse, by contrast, almost seems too easy; with a big bang—with prophesy, revelation, climax, and extermination—it and we are over and done with. Living on through loss seems by contrast as bad or even worse; it means experiencing environmental deterioration, steady decline in human well-being, and increasing constraint on future human action consciously and slowly while realizing that they are likely to continue for generations after one is gone. (78)

McCarthy's novel takes up the project of "living on through loss," following the main characters' journey through a devastated landscape as they learn to make sense of what survival might entail. In this way, McCarthy writes beyond "the end" as a way of meditating on the meanings of disaster and what has been lost, producing what critic

Kenneth Lincoln calls "philosophy at ground zero" (165). In *The Road*, environmental collapse is not some future event looming over America, but a disaster that has already taken place. The task for both the readers and the characters then, is to imagine what comes next, what may be salvaged and what must be left behind in order to rebuild society and reconceptualize human relations to nature and to each other.

In doing so, McCarthy's novel contributes to the "imagination of disaster" that Susan Sontag located in post-World War II science fiction novels and disaster films. For Sontag, literary and cinematic disaster narratives make visible the larger social paranoia of the cold-war era in a way that allows readers and audiences to "participate in the fantasy of living through one's own death and more, the death of cities, the destruction of humanity itself" (212). Such disaster fantasies carry tremendous cultural and psychological power as she explains:

> one job that fantasy can do is to lift us out of the unbearably humdrum and to distract us from terrors—real or anticipated— by an escape into exotic, dangerous situations which have last-minute happy endings. But another of the things that fantasy can do is to normalize what is psychologically unbearable, thereby inuring us to it. In one case, fantasy beautifies the world. In the other, it neutralizes it. (224–25)

While nuclear paranoia and cold-war fears typically shape these disaster narratives, Sontag notes that most of them offer only limited social critique and instead supply audiences with an "extreme moral simplification" of the problems at hand (215). These disaster narratives tend to feature the improper use of technology as something that may be alleviated by the "savior-scientist" in a utopian gesture that restores the fate of the world. In doing so, however, the stories generally leave intact elements of the very technology and hypermodernity that contributed to the crisis (223).

Geographer Mike Davis extends Sontag's observations about cold war social paranoia by examining the imagination of disaster at the millennium. In *Dead Cities and Other Tales*, Davis notes an "acute hypochondria" afflicting many Americans, a culture of hysteria that has contributed to the emergence of "Fear Studies" as a new area of academic interest at the turn of the century. Davis notes that by the late twentieth century,

> [d]ozens of pundits were raving about the "mainstreaming of conspiracy culture," the arrival of "risk society," the "hermeneutic

of suspicion," the "plague of paranoia," "the mean world syndrome," or the newly discovered role of the amygdala as the "center of the [brain's] wheel of fear". (4)

The problem for Davis and other social critics is that many Americans have misdirected their fears in constructing these new terrors, with such displacement part of a larger "refusal to reform real conditions of inequality" (5). He thus focuses on the interplay between rapid modernity and social inequity, as well as the Freudian uncanny and its return of the repressed. Using the work of twentieth-century Marxist philosopher Ernst Bloch, Davis discusses the much greater hidden concerns facing American life. For Bloch, a close relationship exists between the anxieties of the modern world and "urban-technological" developments, with the uncanny emerging out of modern "non-integration with Nature" or the mechanized world's "detachment and distance from the natural landscape" (8). In his study of "dead cities," Davis extends these discussions, showing how a repressed nature in the aftermath of an uneven hypermodernity poses dire consequences, especially for less privileged classes and races.

Buell likewise focuses on the contemporary American culture of fear, particularly as it impacts recent environmental narratives. He argues that the "environment wars" that rage today may be regarded as the unfinished work of the social movements of the 1960s and 70s and as a legacy of the 1980s "culture wars." As Buell explains, the contemporary environmental movement itself could not exist without a larger and ongoing national critique, the sense that the United States had recently "entered a rapid decline—that the nation was rapidly losing pride and position externally and affluence and stability internally" (8). He points to how the "decline seems to show up in a wide variety of areas; in global power and prestige; in global economic strength; in internal economic strength; in social stability and morality; in cultural unity and educational excellence" (8). Recent bestsellers such as economist Thomas Friedman's *Hot, Flat, and Crowded: Why We Need a Green Revolution and How it Can Renew America* capture this sentiment. With the aid of a new green revolution, he proposes that keeping America on-track environmentally will necessarily also restore the nation's overall economic health as well as its political standing in the world. Ecological concerns have a social basis for Friedman, whose imagination of disaster calls for a team of savior-economists that can bring forth a renewed environmentalism as key to American global power, and as a means of countering the overall threat of national decline.

As an allegory of a hyperabundant America, *The Road* calls into question various master narratives of national identity, particularly notions of US exceptionalism. During the post-9/11 war on terrorism and at a time when the economy and the environment face a number of compelling challenges, many Americans are struggling to redefine national identity as well as the country's role in the world. In McCarthy's novel, the United States is no longer an outlier, a national model to uphold or an exceptional player in the history of nations. Instead, the author places the country in human history as a nation playing out a familiar story in a long line of civilizations that have come and gone. In this way, *The Road* recasts narrative time, with the setting of the novel at once seemingly ancient and yet also quite contemporary. McCarthy writes, for instance, that the man and the boy are like "pilgrims in a fable" (3) or the "last host of christendom" (16), forever moving through the "ashes of the late world carried on the bleak and temporal winds to and fro in the void" (11), while struggling to make sense of the "[f]ossil tracks in the dried sludge" (12) and "the mummied dead everywhere" (24). McCarthy places the American landscape of *The Road* alongside the prehistoric and the pharaonic; his environment is thus Homeric, biblical as well as contemporary.

Lincoln examines *The Road* for the ways it locates the anxieties of modern America alongside ancient stories about "end-times." For him, the novel pits current "industrial-military blowback against mean survival," while detailing "the charred aftermath of denied global consequences" (164). The language of *The Road* is incantatory in its repetitions and fragmentations, like an ancient text exhumed from the desert in bits and pieces, as if the narrative itself did not quite survive the catastrophe in full form. Lincoln suggests that the "writing settles into a postholocaust grammar of scree, shards, smoke, fractals, bits and pieces of charnel, dead flesh and sallow bone . . . .. Is this a survivor's handbook, barely numbered, unstructured observations of the days after?" (165). As he explains, given the gruesome scenes of violence, suffering and torture, language itself faces an enormous task in the novel. McCarthy's "words must set up with edge, heft, rhythm, and resilience against the despoliation of the setting, the despair of the characters, the reader's fatigue. The language labors epically to redeem a fallen world, a humanity gone rabidly insane," Lincoln argues. "How else could a reader get through the story?" (164). In *The Road*, McCarthy's strangely poetic writing enables readers to maintain the journey even through the devastating revelations. Something has to sustain them, for as the man tells the boy, the images we put in our minds "are there forever" (12).

Re-Routing the Road Story

The continuous movement of the characters in the novel links *The Road* to the larger tradition of the road story. With a setting that is both ancient and contemporary, the novel employs conventions that may be traced to Homer, Chaucer, and Cervantes, as well as to twentieth-century American literature. Even as the man and the boy undergo an archetypal journey where they confront various hazards and assorted enemies along the way, *The Road* may also be examined in the context of recent developments in the modern American road novel. David Laderman examines the dual nature of the road as a symbol in both contexts. For him, the road is at once a central "element of American society and history, and also a universal symbol of the course of life, the movement of desire, the lure of both freedom and destiny" (2). In these contexts, the road itself embodies divided meanings. Laderman explains:

> Like the wheel, the road expresses our distinction as human, embodying the essential stuff that makes human civilization possible. Conjuring an array of utopian connotations (most generally, "possibility" itself), the road secures us with direction and purpose. And yet, the road also can provoke anxiety: We take the road, but it also takes us . . .. Often the road provides an outlet for our excesses, enticing our desire for thrill and mystery. The horizon beckons both auspiciously and ominously. Exceeding the borders of the culture it makes possible, for better or for worse, the road represents the unknown. (2)

McCarthy's road also contains both possibilities; while stasis is not an option for the two characters because life cannot be sustained in the devastated ecologies of this new world, the journey itself provides no guarantee that a future exists. Even at the end of the narrative, it is not clear what the boy's fate will be once the father dies, leaving his son with substitute parents who may or may not carry "the fire."

The Road provides an ironic take on the road story in other ways as well. Katie Mills examines what she calls the "democratization of mobility" in the post-World War II period as more Americans gained the economic means to purchase their own automobiles and thus took to the road in greater numbers than ever before (2). She argues that in the process, road novels and movies employed "automobility as a metaphor to champion the significant social rebellions of the postwar period" such that these stories became positioned "as vehicles for Americans' sense of the self as autonomous and mobile, two linked qualities that [can be found] in the term "automobility" (2–3). McCarthy's text, however, is a road novel without an automobile. The promise of technology has withered away in this world. The only sign of car culture to be found here appears in a landscape littered with various abandoned and useless vehicles visible along the interstate. "The raw rims of the wheels sitting in a stiff gray sludge of melted rubber, in blackened rings of wire" (273).

Mills points to the ways American subcultures after World War II have used the tradition of the road novel as a means of imagining new possibilities outside mainstream culture. In the post-collapse world of *The Road*, McCarthy likewise revises the genre along lines of class and economy, with the grocery cart replacing the automobile as a new means of transportation. Like the "tricked-out cars created in postwar barrios and suburban garages" that Mills addresses (3), the man in McCarthy's novel cleverly alters a grocery cart to fit his new needs:

> When the cart was loaded with all that it could hold he tied a plastic tarp down over it . . . they stood back and looked at it . . .
> He thought that he should have gotten a couple of extra sets of wheels from the other carts in the store but it was too late now. He should have saved the motorcycle mirror off their old cart too. (155)

Here the man regrets not salvaging the motorcycle mirror from their previous cart in a gesture that references other forms of motorized transportation sometimes featured in the road story. In an interesting way too, the cart the man rigs up is reminiscent of the makeshift vehicles that homeless people often build for themselves in order to survive life on the streets. Recently, urban business owners have begun complaining about the fate of their stray carts, many of which may be found far from the parking lots that originally stored them. These shopping carts seem to have taken on a new life via homeless craftsmen who face forced mobility and have resorted to using the cart as a home-on-wheels as well as a means of transporting reclaimed items that were previously cast-off as useless.

American road stories, according to Mills, offer opportunities for "philosophical meditation" (18) as they typically address questions of "autonomy, mobility, and identity," with the road itself providing the means for the characters' reflection and thought (12). Mills points to the ways road stories "usually narrate a conflict, some disruption in a preexisting power dynamic, which motivates a character to go on the road" (12). These tales have taken various forms throughout American literary history. The 1930s tales of migration and dislocation that came out of the Depression, for instance, were central to the development of the genre, such that the Beat writers of the postwar era of prosperity would find it necessary to radically alter *The Grapes of Wrath* and other "tragic narratives of the Dust Bowl migration into optimistic postwar transformations" (15). Thus in *The Road*, the chrome mirror from the abandoned motorcycle that the father forgets to mount on his last reclaimed shopping cart serves perhaps as a reference to popular counter-culture road stories that featured motorcycles, such as the 1969 film *Easy Rider*. Yet rather than taking its lead primarily from the revisionist Beats, McCarthy's post-disaster road novel appears to revert back to the sensibilities of the 1930s, when mobility was largely not a choice, but a requirement for survival, and the journey was undertaken with less exuberance.

Some critics of the genre focus less on its promise of emancipation through the freedom of the road, and instead comment on the ways the form contains potentially reactionary elements. Stephen Cohan and Ina Rae Hark, for instance, have examined the American road story for the ways it "promotes a male escapist fantasy linking masculinity to technology" and as a narrative tradition that has an uneasy yet dependent relationship to domesticity and its gendered confinements (3). Timothy Corrigan likewise examines what he regards as a telling female absence in many American road stories. For him, the genre is often shaped by a "male hysteria" that emerged as a response to feminism and the new gender formations of the post-Vietnam War era. In this way, the genre often serves as a reactionary narrative to the decentering of male power through the "hysterical but impossible need to stabilize male identities within history" (138).

Rather than merely participating in these larger tendencies of the road novel, McCarthy's text may be offering a critique of such male hysteria. While *The Road* contains only a few female characters who themselves serve only a minor role in the story, the text provides insights into how the road tale might in fact differ for men and women, and why some characters might wish to forego the journey itself. In *The Road,* the mother of the boy appears briefly at the beginning of the story before she kills herself. She tells the man that she cannot see herself as a survivor, but instead regards them as "the walking dead in a horror film" (55). Here the woman speaks her own version of the truth about their gruesome situation to the man, telling him that sooner or later they will be caught and killed: "They are going to rape us and kill us and eat us and you wont face it," she tells him (56).

While the father and son end up taking to the road without female companionship, they do so as a result of the woman's agency rather than her passivity. The woman's decision to kill herself and forego the journey comes not from some post-traumatic response, but from having a different set of embodied experiences that have provided her with a different knowledge and understanding of what the future might entail. The woman tells the man that her heart "was ripped out" of her the night their son was born, "so don't ask for sorrow now. There is none" (57). Recognizing herself within a different film script and storyline, she chooses the terms of her own death over what she believes will be a more dehumanizing and tortuous ending.

In some ways, the woman's assessment of what the future might hold may in fact be more accurate than the man's. Life on the road is full of misery and suffering, with some people facing greater torment than others. At one point, the man and boy hide and watch as a group of armed men "passed two hundred feet away, the ground shuddering lightly. Tramping. Behind them came wagons drawn by slaves in harness and piled with goods of war and after that the women, perhaps a dozen in number, some of them pregnant" (92). The implication, we learn from a horrific scene later in the novel, is that their babies will be eaten soon after they are born. While the man and the boy largely manage to escape these fates on the road, most of the characters they encounter along the way experience horrendous suffering in the form of cannibalism, slavery, starvation and torture.

American Futures

Ultimately, *The Road* may also be read as a companion piece to McCarthy's earlier novel, *No Country for Old Men*. Both narratives function as contemporary road novels that treat many of the same issues facing modern America. *No Country for Old Man,* along with its 2007 Oscar-winning adaptation directed by Ethan and Joel Coen, has been understood as an allegory for the dilemmas recently facing the United States during the Iraq War and as a tale of contemporary America gone astray. *No Country for Old Men* is set in West Texas in the early 1980s and features small-town sheriff Ed Tom Bell, whose traditional ways of law and order cannot adequately cope with the new threat he now faces. The social terrain he was once familiar with has radically changed, and the character is left struggling to keep up with this mystifying new world. Bell's search for a renegade hit man ultimately proves unsuccessful as the enemy is always beyond his reach and the lawman is always one step behind in his understanding of the crimes. The sheriff's investigative skills and ability to understand the situation around him thus no longer work in tracking down the threat, and he is eventually resigned to giving up his search.

As the villain, Anton Chigurh embodies a seemingly incomprehensible threat; he is a perplexing outlaw who does not operate according
to any of the old rules. Instead, Chigurh continually finds new,
inventive means of eliminating his targets while getting around the
law. The other characters in the story keep marveling at the hit man's
incomprehensible ways. He can't be caught, made to back down through
threats, or outsmarted. Yet in mocking national ideals and regional
conventions, Chigurh is nevertheless regarded as a man with principles.
The problem is that the sheriff and the other characters in the text
do not understand those principles. The narrative itself is an odd tale
with a rather quirky outlaw, and its genre classification is as perplexing
as the problem of the threat itself. Is *No Country for Old Men* a horror
tale, a noir, a thriller, a road story, a crime narrative, a comedy or a
modern-day Western?

In *No Country for Old Men*, the characters are left as perplexed about
these changes as Americans are left confused about national identity
itself in the new millennium. Just as readers must make sense of this
new type of threat in *No Country for Old Men,* so they must adjust to a
new reality in McCarthy's post-disaster account in *The Road*. In that
sense, McCarthy's text builds on the critique offered by Steinbeck's
earlier novel for a contemporary era that nevertheless faces similar
economic and social crises. Like the characters in *The Road*, the Joads'
predicament is dire—the capitalist machine refuses to die, the bosses
have little sympathy for the plight of laborers and the sharecroppers
have few alternatives at their disposal. With even less of the guarded
optimism that shaped Steinbeck's text, McCarthy takes readers on a
complicated journey through a drastically changing social and natural
landscape; the rules have shifted, and the environment has been forever
altered. What is left is the struggle of rethinking America and our own
place in the world in an era where problems about national identity,
globalization, and the environment are all rapidly transforming what
we thought we once knew.

CHAPTER 9

"He ought not have done it": McCarthy and Apocalypse

Dana Phillips

Introduction: On *The Road*

Here is one way to describe *The Road*:

> In Cormac McCarthy's latest novel, apocalyptic firestorms have destroyed cities, towns, villages, crossroads, fields, and woods. Clouds of ash cloak the skies. Cows are extinct; even kudzu is no more. Inevitably, society has collapsed: troops of cannibals rigged out in barbaric battle-gear roam crumbling byways in search of flesh. But the lonely pair at the center of the novel remains fully human as they journey from the broken heart of Appalachia to the ruined coast. They are "carrying the fire," the father and son tell each other, and for once McCarthy seems to agree wholeheartedly with his characters. He gives their emotion its due, and does not kill them off with a flick of his pen, as he has done so often in the past. Elegiac and tragic, muted yet lyrical, The Road *marks a return to form for contemporary American fiction's most debated stylist. The novel may be regarded, someday, as a masterwork to be shelved near Hemingway's* In Our Time *and Faulkner's* As I Lay Dying.

Readers of *The Road* will agree that this description makes sense, perhaps even good sense, of the text. It should seem familiar to those readers who also consulted reviews of the book upon its publication in 2006, or have sampled the spurt of criticism it began to produce shortly thereafter. Nevertheless, this description, which is my own, is far from conclusive: to speak plainly, I think it is mistaken. But I have produced it here so that I may begin addressing the first question *The Road* and its reception seem to me to raise, which is this: *why* write about apocalypse now? The second question the book and its reception seems to me to raise follows from the first. Simply put, it is this: *has* McCarthy written about apocalypse now? I want to consider both questions in this chapter, before offering an alternative description of *The Road* by way of a conclusion.

The End of the World—But Not the Apocalypse

As every schoolboy should know if he has pursued his schooling to completion at the graduate level, descriptions determine cases. In this respect, the first description of *The Road* offered here is unexceptional, despite being a pastiche—and something of a spoof—generated by my survey of blurb-worthy responses to the book so far. I have been surprised to see how readily, and how *readerly*, discussion of *The Road* was opened under the sign, and not just the rubric, of Apocalypse: as if McCarthy, having entered the Last Days of his career, had broken the fateful Seventh Seal and the Trump of Doom had sounded, penultimately, in his fiction. "Apocalyptic" is not how I would have described the book, had I remembered I was already describing it even as I was reading it for the first time.

Over the course of his career, McCarthy has been nothing if not consistent, because consistency is an entailment of the point of view he adopts, or more accurately—since there is no question of its being personal—constructs in his work. Such consistency has the effect of enlivening well-worn clichés and genre conventions, such as those a writer of fictions set in the American South and Southwest may have no choice but to employ. But this enlivening does not require that McCarthy wants or needs to offer an affirmation or a verdict of the sort novelists have long been thought to want or need to offer in order to resolve their densely plotted narratives. Bearing this in mind, I find (impressionistically) and want to argue (critically) that while in *The Road* the world may have come to an end, the world is also the same as it ever was: filled with mortal peril, because it is shaped by causes the advent of which is pure chance, while the effects of these causes seem more or less deterministic.

Now, I am aware that *The Road* is dedicated to its author's very young son, John Francis McCarthy. I also notice that the father and son protagonists of *The Road* speak to each other more tenderly than has been the norm in McCarthy's recent fiction, at least in scenes in which neither party is a whore or a horse. I appreciate as well the fact that the pair avoids the gruesome deaths usually meted out to McCarthy's characters: neither is eaten by a bear, for example, if only because there do not seem to be any bears left to eat them. But I cannot see that the book differs in kind from, say, *Blood Meridian* or *Child of God*. As those books do, it takes violence and beauty as given, as natural; and like those books it also refuses to comfort its reader by positing a difference, much less admitting a contradiction, between the violence and the beauty it depicts. In *The Road*, sometimes the violence simply is the beauty. Early in the book, as the father and son make their way southward out of the mountains of Tennessee, the father recollects the following:

> In that long ago somewhere very near this place he'd watched a falcon fall down the long blue wall of the mountain and break with the keel of its breastbone the midmost from a flight of cranes and take it to the river below all gangly and wrecked and trailing its loose and blowsy plumage in the still autumn air. (*The Road*, 17)[1]

The lack of comfort in McCarthy's fiction, as well as its uncanny ability to locate the beauty in violence—in acts of predation, for instance, like the taking of a crane by a falcon—while neither glamorizing nor apologizing for the violence, helps explain why, when I told a friend that I was going to write about *The Road*, he looked crestfallen and replied, "He ought not have done it." This glum response was expressive, I thought, of both a moral and an aesthetic judgment. And I don't need to rehearse the premises (which, by the way, I'm sure my friend understands fully) that would support the claim that moral and aesthetic judgments always already overlap and intertwine. Book reviews and McCarthy scholarship provide all the evidence one needs to accept at face value, or at least close to it, the imbrication of moral and aesthetic judgments—and illustrate the trouble that the terrible beauty of McCarthy's fictional world makes for both. Here I will limit myself to a synopsis, and pointed discussion, of what has been said about *The Road*.

But before I do that, I want to suggest that the most important task facing those interested in McCarthy does not involve placing his work in a tradition, as readers who imagine the course of literary history as a seamless continuum have tried to do, but articulating its *singularity* (a concept I borrow from Derek Attridge). For me, this means coming to terms with McCarthy's point of view, which as has been often noted is (among other things) Melvillean. Yet it is Melvillean in a very particular and delimited way. McCarthy—the author, that is, and not the man—is like the title character in Melville's celebrated short story "Bartleby, the

Scrivener," who repeatedly tells his employer that he prefers not to do any writing even though that is his job as a copyist, and who may have been driven mad by the sad spectacle of undelivered mail when he formerly worked in the US Post Office. Except that McCarthy, all questions of preference to one side, continues writing even though any stories he tells now are likely (especially if they are couched in literary prose) to be composed precisely of "dead letters," and he thus seems to be an even more perverse character, and more of a cipher, than the original. Never more so, perhaps, than in *The Road*, where McCarthy presents the following scene, in which the father has what amounts to a moment of posthumanist awakening, or rather disillusionment:

> he'd stood in the charred ruins of a library where blackened books lay in pools of water. Shelves tipped over. Some rage at the lies arranged in their thousands row on row. He picked up one of the books and thumbed through the heavy bloated pages. He'd not have thought the value of the smallest thing predicated on a world to come. It surprised him. That the space which these things occupied was itself an expectation. He let the book fall and took a last look around and made his way out into the cold gray light. (157–58)

I take it that this scene puts the scattered bands of present-day humanists on notice: if you are still placing bets on the power of the book, of any book (including *The Road*), to prevent or at least ameliorate the end of the world, you ought to hedge those bets now, while you still can.

The end of the world must be like that: it must force us to hedge, or call off, our bets. And it must make our arguments seem failed, too: perhaps most especially those arguments which intend to take the end of the world into account—*to game it out*, as in the doomsday scenarios concocted by military strategists at the Pentagon and at so-called think-tanks, scenarios enacted with the aid of armies of software programmers in a virtual world to which access is gained via play-stations and computer terminals instead of books. We keep imagining the end of the world, but inadequately (so far) thanks to certain technological and intellectual shortcomings. I doubt *The Road* does much to compensate for our inadequacy in this area, but reviewers and a few critics have responded to the book as if it might—or, more to the point, *should*. Reading it, as I suggested earlier, under the sign of apocalypse, they have characterized *The Road* as a contribution to a well-established genre of futuristic but dystopian fiction, a genre stretching back to such post-nuclear holocaust novels as Nevil Shute's 1957 *On the Beach* and Walter M. Miller, Jr.'s 1960 *A Canticle for Leibowitz*, novels in which the future is either radically and woefully foreshortened, or just as radically but still more woefully prolonged. But *The Road* is said to differ from its progenitors in that it takes its dystopia neat, without the tonic water of hopefulness that characterizes other dystopian novels, or with just a splash of that tonic water, depending on how one reads the book's conclusion—or rather conclusions, as there seems to be more than one.

So how, exactly, does the world comes to an end in *The Road*? You might think it scarcely matters: surely one way of ending the world is just as good or bad as another. But you would be wrong, as is illustrated by the way in which critical discussion of *The Road* has been skewed by an impression, possibly erroneous, that in it the end of the world is brought on, and not merely exacerbated, by human agency: specifically, by all-out nuclear warfare. If this were indeed the case, then the narrative would be, so to speak, *solemnized*, and in precisely the way these readers assume it to be. *The Road* would be, as Elizabeth Hand says it is, "a cautionary tale" (46). It would, of course, still be ironic. But its irony would have an especially bitter flavor that might be lacking if, in the book, the world's end were owing to a different sort of cause, say to cosmic accident. In the latter case, readings of the novel as an antinuclear cautionary tale would echo each other a bit hollowly.

I don't mean to suggest that reviewers and critics have entirely failed to note the ambiguity of the world's end in *The Road*. Many have noted it, and for good reason. Here is how McCarthy describes the unnerving event that initiates the world's last days:

> The clocks stopped at 1:17. A long shear of light and then a series of low concussions. He got up and went to the window. What is it? she said. He didnt answer. He went into the bathroom and threw the lightswitch but the power was already gone. A dull rose glow in the windowglass. He dropped to one knee and raised the lever to stop the tub and then turned on both taps as far as they would go. She was standing in the doorway in her nightwear, clutching the jamb, cradling her belly in one hand. What is it? she said. What is happening?
> I dont know.
> Why are you taking a bath?
> I'm not.
>
> (*The Road*, 45)

This scene fills in some of the back-story, and explains why the father and son find themselves on the road some 8 or 10 years later. In it, the father and the boy's soon-to-be-mother (she is pregnant) are awakened by the cataclysmic event that initiates the firestorms, the ash-choked skies, and the breakdown of society. It seems likely that readings of this scene have been informed by pessimism with regard to nuclear disarmament, and by the perverse flipside of this pessimism: by awe at nuclear might.

It also seems likely that McCarthy, as is his habit, underplays this scene partly in order to tease out this pessimism and its perverse flipside. That is, he may be baiting his readers into misreading, and into ignoring the fact that not all the details here are strictly consistent with the detonation of nuclear weaponry. The "long shear of light," for example, seems a doubtful precursor to such an event: nuclear warfare does not begin with a fireworks show. The "long shear of light" argues more for the entry into the atmosphere of a massive meteor than for the descent of multiple warheads, as does the "dull rose glow in the windowglass" that follows the "series of low concussions." And if the world-shattering event does involve the impact of a massive meteor and not the detonation of multiple warheads, then certain scenes in the novel take on a quality they would otherwise lack: the scene in which father and son take refuge in a backyard fallout shelter, for example, becomes darkly comic. Having heeded cold-war era propaganda and prepared for one kind of death from above, the homeowners seem to have been blindsided by another. This sort of thing happens all the time in McCarthy's fiction.

But sifting the text of *The Road* in this realist fashion—fact-checking it—is probably imprudent, since the book is a work of fiction not bound by strictures of verisimilitude. So I will settle for troubling the notion that its author portrays a post-nuclear world, and instead will turn my attention to the immediate reaction to the "long shear of light" and those "low concussions" on the part of the book's protagonists. This reaction is purely pragmatic: the wife simply wants to know what has happened, and the husband, though unable to answer her question, senses that now is a good time to fill the tub with tap water, as the clock has stopped, the power is out, and the future seems much in doubt. The husband intuits, in other words, that now is not the moment to engage in formal deliberations on the validity of all the different doomsday scenarios that have been proposed, or prophesied, down the ages. Nor is it the moment for long-winded answers to simple questions. "Why are you taking a bath?" "I'm not." Enough said.

Primal Fiction

Reviewers and critics can afford to take a more time-consuming, leisurely approach, and many of them have wondered about the precise nature of McCarthy's doomsday scenario while fretting over its moral and aesthetic implications, which as I have already indicated are generally (and rightly) taken to be mutually reinforcing if not quite identical. Possibly no other reader's take on McCarthy's work has been so fretful, in this respect, as that of the critic and novelist James Wood. He identifies *The Road*, as does almost everyone else, as a post-apocalyptic novel, and hints that it also may be a "9/11 novel pretending not to be one" ("Getting to the End," 44). Thus Wood begins tightening a string around the book and limning its significance in terms of genre. He next suggests that stylistically it is "both the logical terminus, and a kind of ultimate triumph, of the American minimalism that became well-known in the 1980s under the banner of 'dirty realism,'" a form of minimalism that Wood observes was steeped in a variety of anti-sentimentality "so pronounced as to constitute a kind of male sentimentality of reticence" ("Getting to the End," 45). He is preparing to concede that *The Road*, for a book by McCarthy, is rich in pathos, and next admits that in it the "dirty minimalism" he has just disparaged—as almost everyone does nowadays—"comes alive" ("Getting to the End," 45).

Wood realizes something other readers of *The Road* have tended to miss, and that is the book's sheer peculiarity—its identity, or lack thereof, as something of a literary misfit and oddball. "*The Road* is not a science fiction, not an allegory, and not a critique of the way we live now," Wood writes. "It poses a simpler question, more taxing for the imagination and far closer to the primary business of fiction-making: what would this world without people look like, feel like? From this, everything else flows" ("Getting to the End," 46). The valuable insight here has to do with "the primary business of fiction-making," and I want to follow up on this insight by noting that in McCarthy's work as a whole, and in *The Road* in particular, this business is more "primary"— more minimal, too—than Wood allows. By constructing what we might call, following Wood, "primal fictions" (and "primal" should be read as a portmanteau word: *primary* + *minimal* = *primal*), McCarthy does not so much shirk some of the entailments associated with genre conventions as he, in effect, strangles those entailments in their beds— character development comes most immediately to mind here. It is as if McCarthy's writing were simultaneously postmodern (otherwise he could not avail himself of the stylistic resources of Hemingway and Faulkner, nor could he deploy all the riches of his vocabulary) and premodern at once, or epic, rather than novelistic, in design and effect.

As Wood writes with regard to *The Road*, "The narrative is about last-ditch practicality, and is itself intensely practical" ("Getting to the End," 46). Something of the sort is only to be expected in a primal fiction, where building a world—or shoring up the still usable fragments of a ruined world—is the chief task, maybe the only task, at hand. Attending to this task often lends McCarthy's work an almost documentary flavor, as he focuses on the details of the quotidian for their own sake:

> they left their packs and went back to the station. In the service bay he dragged out the steel trashdrum and tipped it over and pawed out all the quart plastic oilbottles. Then they sat on the floor decanting them of their dregs one by one, leaving the bottles to stand until at the end they had almost a half quart of motor oil. He screwed down the plastic cap and wiped the bottle off with a rag and hefted it in his hand. Oil for their little slutlamp to light the long gray dusks, the long gray dawns. You can read me a story, the boy said. Cant you, Papa? Yes, he said. I can. (*The Road*, 6–7)

Here it seems that the writer may not even be aware that these details, and the dialogue that ensues (such as it is: more about this in a moment), might be made to bear allegorical, metaphorical or symbolic weight, in addition to the freight it already carries as one of many plot points composing the narrative line. As Wood puts it, in *The Road* McCarthy's style is "sagely humdrum" ("Getting to the End," 46). I don't think Wood means the compliment to be in the least backhanded.

Yet Wood does have reservations about McCarthy's fiction. Much as he admires "McCarthy's remarkable effects," he has concerns about "the matter of his meaning," and by "meaning" Wood intends to gesture toward something transcendent. He thinks McCarthy "manipulates his theological material" and that his fiction "has always been interested in theodicy, and somewhat shallowly." "A post-apocalyptic vision," Wood writes, "cannot but provoke the dilemmas of theodicy, of the justice of fate" ("Getting to the End," 47). So having provided a hint about the way in which McCarthy seems to obviate some of the entailments of both literary history and the novel as a genre—by writing primary or primal fictions—Wood puts him right back on the hook.

Wood's judgment is baffling on two counts. He seems not to have explored the full implications of his own identification of McCarthy as a writer of primary or primal fictions. Nor does he seem to have considered how weakly—how absurdly—an attempt at a theodicy (classically, a defense of the goodness of God in the light of the reality of evil) would figure in any of the work McCarthy has published to date, since in this work realities, and not deities, are the plenipotentiary entities. Of course one also has to consider the fact that Oprah Winfrey, like Wood, is concerned with theodicy, too. In her June 5, 2007 interview with McCarthy (which can be viewed online at www.youtube.com), Oprah asks him if he has "worked out the God thing." He tells her that it can be good to pray, even if you are "quite doubtful about the whole business."

The answer is evasive, and it may be paradoxical, too (since it seems likely that praying when you are doubtful is only going to make you feel disingenuous and shabby). But it is in line with McCarthy's fiction, which often features atheists who believe in God.

In *The Road*, for example, Ely—the only character identified by name—tells the father and son, "There is no God and we are his prophets" (143). Ely also tells them that he predicted the end of the world long ago. "I knew this was coming," Ely says. "This or something like it. I always believed in it" (142). Some readers take Ely to be a figure of the prophet Elijah, and thus part of the thread of biblical allusion McCarthy has woven into his text. But interpretation of *The Road* as allusive fails to consider its setting: in the south, biblical names are still common, and all one needs to do in order to hear open-ended speculation about the end of the world like Ely's ("this or something like it") is visit a grocery store, take a seat on a neighbor's porch, or listen to AM radio. Amateur eschatology is a southern pastime (while theodicy is taken for granted: God can do or not do whatever he pleases without fear of contradiction). This makes Ely's words artifactual, like the arrowheads and the Spanish coin the father finds in the furrows of an old field near the coast. They do not mean—cannot mean—what they once might have meant.

If I haven't taken care of the task already, I would like to suggest, as a way of meeting the challenge posed by Wood (and resolving the paradox teased out of McCarthy by Oprah), that Wood's disappointment in McCarthy has to do, first of all, with the critic's preference for focusing on genre at the expense of overlooking the particularities of point of view, which in McCarthy's case has everything to do with his being an author of primary or primal fictions in which the narrators are not merely "impersonal" but radically unpersoned. And, secondly, I think Wood's disappointment has to do with what Frank Kermode long ago called "the sense of an ending," and the multiple ways in which that sense shapes both authorial design and readerly response.

One of the traits of McCarthy's fiction that has long been both a signature feature of his style and one of the implications of his authorial point of view is his treatment of dialogue, and thus of not only the words but also the thoughts and emotions of his characters. And hence of the characters themselves, too, none of whom are privileged, however much time we may spend with them as readers. This continues to be the case in *The Road*, in which the father and son and their utterances are treated with considerable objectivity.

McCarthy's habit of eschewing quotation marks and other forms of punctuation has the effect of rendering the speech (and thoughts and emotions) of his characters as, well, a matter of words. These words

(Ely's, for example) are caught up in the flow of other words, many, if not all, of which are produced by a narrator who keeps close at hand and who hears what the characters say, knows what they think, and senses what they feel, yet remains sufficiently at a distance to perform the task of narration in a properly professional manner. Wood describes this sort of thing as "a kind of secret sharing," which is made possible by "free indirect style," also known as "close third person" and "going into character," among other things (*How Fiction Works*, 8). Typically, novelists have used free indirect style as a means of generating sympathy for their protagonists and ironic detachment from their antagonists, or vice versa. As Wood's formulation of free indirect style as a matter of "going into character" suggests, it may be a strategy of representation borrowed from the theater—a sort of "method" writing—or from more folkloric forms of storytelling. But McCarthy's use of free indirect style is less dramatic and more neutral, and it manages to be ironic even when being ironic is not the best of manners—and may seem like a subtle form of aggression. According to J. Hillis Miller, "In either oral or written forms indirect discourse is an artifice of language. It is always at a remove from speech used in its own immediate context" (*Reading Narrative*, 164). Sharpening the point, he puts it in more deconstructionist terms: "A supplementary ironizing displacement redoubles an already acentered and duplicitous language" (169).

Consider the following passage of *The Road*, from very early on in the book:

> When it was light enough to use the binoculars he glassed the valley below. . . . Looking for anything of color. Any movement. Any trace of standing smoke. . . . Then he just sat there holding the binoculars and watching the ashen daylight congeal over the land. He knew only that the child was his warrant. He said: If he is not the word of God God never spoke." (4; my ellipses)

The father's utterance here, and others like it elsewhere in the book, has been taken to mean that for McCarthy, in this fictional outing more so than in others, theological concerns have not been taken off the table and are actively under consideration. But notice something: the father's words are in effect being "glassed" by the impersonal narrator just as "the valley below" is being glassed by the father. The scene, and the broader context, in which the father utters these words (defiantly or in despair: who can tell?) is scarcely a hopeful one. And we should recall McCarthy's knack of setting his characters up for a fall just at the moment they begin to betray symptoms of optimism, much less a vainglorious hope of redemption.

"If he is not the word of God God never spoke." McCarthy does not have to comment on this statement's dismal implications, much less complete the syllogism. His use of free indirect style thus seems to be as much, if not more, a matter of "distant third person" and of "withdrawing from character" as it is the reverse. Besides, his treatment of the father's son in other, later scenes makes it apparent that the boy is just a boy: one of the last boys on earth, and therefore precious, but just a boy for all that. In one scene, the duo approaches a ruined plantation house, which the boy is afraid to enter. In the following conversation, he is the first to speak:

> Can we wait a while?
> Okay. But it's getting dark.
> I know.
> Okay.
> They sat on the steps and looked out over the country.
> There's no one here, the man said.
> Okay.
> Are you still scared?
> Yes.
> We're okay.
> Okay.
>
> (*The Road*, 172)

This is typical of the dialogue between father and son throughout the book. Now, it would be glib to dismiss their conversation on grounds of its falling short of being a free and equal exchange of ideas, or a full expression of the contents of consciousness in the manner, say, of Henry James. Yet it also would be a mistake to take this conversation as evidence of a Hemingway-like reticence when it comes to the expression of emotions on the part of McCarthy's narrator. In fact, such conversations become increasingly fraught with tension, even dread, as *The Road* progresses and the odds against the protagonists grow longer. The narrator approaches this tension and dread in a somewhat clinical fashion—he treats it, in effect, like data—but then so do McCarthy's characters. "Okay," as anyone who has ever had occasion to use it as an affirmative knows, can be uttered noncommittally and even evasively. And noncommittal utterance, along with tactical neutrality, must be the order of the day once the world has come to an end. For this reason, and others, plumbing the motives of McCarthy's characters—especially if that means psychoanalyzing them—is like mesmerizing stones: it seems doable only because it is impossible. There is no way to tell whether it is successful or not.

The End of *The Road*

So much, then, for character in *The Road*: let me return to McCarthy's plot. Generically, the arc of the narrative of The End is the arc of a story foretold, less because The End has been prophesied and more because it has been described and projected—even, in some cases, planned and plotted—so often and from so many points of view: utopian, dystopian, strategic, religious, environmental, . . . and so on. And this means that to tell a story, any story, of apocalypse is to set in motion all manner of subroutines or, if you prefer, subplots. But in *The Road*, many of these subroutines or subplots do not seem to be running or unfolding, in large part because the world is too shattered, and the cast of characters too small and too traumatized, to support such rich and varied activity. What counts in *The Road*, therefore, is not how the narrative resolves or what surplus or transcendent "meaning" it makes, Michael Chabon argues. "The only true account of the world after a disaster as nearly complete and as searing as the one McCarthy proposes," Chabon writes, "would be a book of blank pages, white as ash" ("Dark Adventure," 101–02). So in this instance closure, and surplus or transcendent "meaning," are nonstarters. What signifies—makes particular and delimited meanings, that is—in *The Road* is the source of the fiction, or as I have suggested, the point of view. Chabon makes a similar claim: "For naturalism operating at the utmost extremes of the natural world and of human endurance, a McCarthy novel has no peer" ("Dark Adventure," 98).

Minimalism, pragmatism, or naturalism—call it what you will: these labels may come close to identifying McCarthy's stock in trade in *The Road*, but none are likely to stick for long. For in the latest work of this writer, the labeling impulse itself is called into question, and naming has become a quaint activity. (This accounts for the namelessness of McCarthy's protagonists, and may account as well for the acute damping-down of what some critics regard as McCarthy's trademark stylistic excess: his bursts of Faulknerian High Modernist prose.) The assignment of nouns to persons, places, and things, of verbs to actions and states of being, and of modifiers to either nouns or verbs, is and can only be a nostalgic indulgence once the world itself has come, or is rapidly coming, to an end. After describing yet another instance of the necessities of survival (the father sets up camp and builds a fire), McCarthy writes:

> they sat there in silence with their hands outheld to the flames. He tried to think of something to say but he could not. He'd had this feeling before, beyond the numbness and the dull despair.

> The world shrinking down about a raw core of parsible entities. The names of things slowly following those things into oblivion. Colors. The names of birds. Things to eat. Finally the names of things one believed to be true. More fragile than he would have thought. How much was gone already? The sacred idiom shorn of its referents and so of its reality. Drawing down like something trying to preserve heat. In time to wink out forever. (*The Road*, 75)

The passage is telling in more ways than one. It suggests that for McCarthy, minimalism, pragmatism, and naturalism are not stylistic choices he may or may not employ as he sees fit or as the occasion merits, nor are they philosophical positions that might underwrite his fiction and lend it gravitas (or, to again use the word Wood prefers, transcendent "meaning"). They are, instead, endgames. They are what one must play out, once one's worst doubts have been confirmed and one's cynicism, skepticism, and nihilism have been validated, and one's mortality confirmed, not philosophically but traumatically: then one might "try to think of something to say," and find one cannot. When that happens, if one is a father or a writer, one might find oneself—instead of telling one's son a story or writing a novel—conducting an inventory of one's dwindling stock in trade: first the "raw core of parsible entities" goes by the board, then the "names of things" begin to slip away, and finally the "sacred idiom" itself—the Word—seems exhausted, and will soon "wink out forever."

This is not a context in which a theodicy will be persuasive, or even seem plausible. In this context, a theodicy might even strike one's auditors, or readers, as obscene. The world McCarthy describes in *The Road* seems better suited to archaeological than theological treatment (another reason it seems to me to be continuous with the world he described in *Blood Meridian* and earlier work). Whatever was going to happen in this world has happened, and therefore speculation about its larger meaning (if any) can only be offered in hindsight and retrospectively. On the day after, or at any rate on the page after, the scene in which the father muses over his inability to think of anything to say, he and his son come across a "tableau of the slain and the devoured."

> Shapes of dried blood in the stubble grass and gray coils of viscera where the slain had been field-dressed and hauled away. The wall beyond held a frieze of human heads, all faced alike, dried and caved with their taut grins and shrunken eyes. They wore gold rings in their leather ears and in the wind their sparse and ratty hair twisted about on their skulls. The teeth in their sockets like

dental molds, the crude tattoos etched in some homebrewed woad faded in the beggared sunlight. Spiders, swords, targets. A dragon. Runic slogans, creeds misspelled. (*The Road* 77, 76)

One effect of scenes like this (and several others are equally gruesome) is to complicate our "sense of an ending" by means of complicating our sense of history. Frank Kermode, writing 40 years before the publication of *The Road*, argued that in the postwar era, "apocalypse" ceased to be *imminent* and became *immanent*, or ongoing and universal, which radically redefined the historical condition itself as sheer presence—and thus drained the very notion of the apocalyptic of most of its meaning. "We no longer live in a world," according to Kermode, "with an historical *tick* which will certainly be consummated by a definitive *tock*" (*The Sense of an Ending* 64). Paradoxically, this makes it difficult, if not impossible, to write about apocalypse *now*.

Thus it is unsurprising that for a fiction supposedly set in the future, in *The Road* the signs of futurity are few, if any. What are we to make of McCarthy's "tableau of the slain and devoured," for instance, as an index of time and place? It is as if an entire local chapter of the Society for Creative Anachronism had actually met the sort of gruesome end its members had long fantasized about, all of them dying on the points of crudely forged blades wielded by barbarians. In *The Road*, the future seems outdated in more ways than one. Witness the technologies McCarthy describes: the father and son push a shopping cart with a rearview mirror salvaged from a motorcycle strapped to it; they light their evenings with a slutlamp, whatever that is; the fallout shelter where they take refuge is stocked with canned hams; the father is armed with a six-shot revolver; he is wounded in the leg by a man armed with a bow and arrow; and when he boards a wrecked yacht in yet another of his many attempts at scavenging, he finds a brass sextant (a navigator's tool that helped delineate the Age of Discovery) and an EPIRB (a radio beacon: a device that only gets used when all seems lost). But in the absence of satellites the EPIRB is now as useless to the father as the sextant is in the absence of the sun; besides, he doesn't *want* anyone to find him and his boy. So perhaps the chief irony in *The Road*, and of its reception, is that everything McCarthy describes might well have happened many years ago, say sometime in the mid-1980s. The father and his son are lost in time as well as space.

If "the sense of an ending" is bound up with the sense of time, of history, and of place, then the end described in *The Road* is less definitive than it may seem to certain readers. At the conclusion of the book, and after his father's death, the son is taken in by a family of survivors, who tell him that they "dont eat people" (239) and who speak to him reassuringly, if vaguely, of "the breath of God" (241). Given the status quo, we can assume they are folk of what passes for sterling moral quality and devout spirituality. But what we cannot tell is how pragmatic their dietary strictures and faith will prove to be in the long term, or—more to the point—if there will be a long term, insofar as they and their scant few fellow human beings are concerned. Having seen the boy to safety, however precarious, McCarthy then closes out his text with a lyrical paragraph that seems likely to strike his readers as more hopeful than it actually is:

> Once there were brook trout in the streams in the mountains. You could see them standing in the amber current where the white edges of their fins wimpled softly in the flow. They smelled of moss in your hand. Polished and muscular and torsional. On their backs were vermiculate patterns that were maps of the world in its becoming. Maps and mazes. Of a thing which could not be put back. Not be made right again. In the deep glens where they lived all things were older than man and they hummed of mystery. (*The Road*, 241)

While this may be the most beautifully written passage in the book, it is also the most damning (which is saying a lot). Once there were brook trout, and now there are not. You could see them, and now you cannot. They smelled of moss, and now not even moss smells of moss anymore. Maps of the world in its becoming are indecipherable in a world that has come and gone, that cannot be put back or made right again. It is hard to see an upside here.

But I suppose this paragraph will seem redemptive to many readers nonetheless, because placed as it is—at "the end"—it appears to hold forth a promise of a new beginning, provided one reads the brook trout as, say, allegorical, symbolic, mythic or otherwise charged with greater meaning. So perhaps in this one instance McCarthy really "ought not have done it," given the ways in which both readerly expectations and genre conventions operate. Kermode's reflections on novelistic form seem apposite here. "Somewhere along the line it will join what Sartre calls 'bad faith'," Kermode writes. "The novel has, for all that may be said in theory against such a possibility, 'a priori limitations'" (*The Sense of an Ending*, 137), because it gives shape, even at the price of bearing false witness, to sheer contingency—and thus it effects closure anyhow and creates greater meaning willy-nilly. It is with Kermode's description of novelistic form as "bad faith" and of the novel's "a priori limitations" in mind that I have sedulously avoided referring to *The Road* as a "novel" throughout this chapter: I suspect it may not be one!

Given this suspicion—that is, given my hunch that McCarthy is not guilty of the "bad faith" that Kermode describes, nor answerable to the strictures of novelistic good faith that James Wood has charged him with ignoring—I would counter my friend's complaint that McCarthy "ought not have" written an apocalyptic novel by claiming that, in fact, *he has not done so.* And thus I would prefer to interpret the brook trout one encounters at the end of *The Road* simply as brook trout. But not because interpreting these fish that way—by reading literally—makes me feel any better about the book's apparent foreclosure of the future on its final page. For what McCarthy describes there is not a (new) new beginning, but an old (new) beginning: the foreclosure of the future, yes, but also the foreclosure of the past. Brook trout are survivors from another era and another place. Holed up in refuges from southern Appalachia northward, they rode out the end of the last ice age, which had driven them from their arctic home (they are actually char, not trout) and then, as the glaciers receded, left them high—but not dry— and lonesome, isolated in pockets of high-country watershed, where they have been playing out their endgame ever since. If once they "hummed of mystery," it was the sort of mystery posed by the deep time explored by the geologist and the paleontologist, and not the deep space imagined by those who hope that someday there might be, even if it is only described in a book, a heaven on earth.

Conclusion

So here at the end, and with all that I have argued in this chapter in mind, let me offer you another way to describe *The Road*:

> *In Cormac McCarthy's latest book, the most recent in a long line of fictions produced by this author, not a lot has changed. The setting has shifted from the American southwest back to the American southeast; and the world, or at least a considerable portion of it, seems to have come to an end. Yet the shift of setting and the end of the world must be counted as only so much detail. For McCarthy, writing fiction has long been a matter of "T for Texas, T for Tennessee"—of deconstructing that culturally and historically minimal pair. He is, for someone who is nominally a novelist, unusually impartial when it comes to the divagations of time and space, and the ripples in that continuum made by human actors. The tendency of his fiction is toward a phenomenological reduction that renders narration almost solely as point of view: as perspective given content by a writerly vocabulary and dimension by the basic elements of story (chiefly, duration and description of events).*

The attenuated but haunting result is a form of cosmic irony—if there can be such a thing—that remains largely uninterpreted despite the richness, or the sparseness, of McCarthy's prose. Thus to read The Road *for signs of hope and redemption is to misread it, and worse: it is to miss the boat not by an hour or a day, but by an epoch or even an era. In* The Road, *there is no boat: all boats have been sunk. This is not so much the book's conclusion—in which a shattered yacht, the "Bird of Hope" or Pájaro de Esperanza, makes an appearance—as its premise. Yet in* The Road *there has been no apocalypse: the end of the world is simply the end of the world, and McCarthy describes the scene as if he were a policeman dispatched by who knows what agency: There is nothing new to see here, folks. Now move along. There can be no rubbernecking on the road.*

Notes

Chapter 2

1. Typescript, first draft. Heavily corrected, 441 pp. (501 leaves). Irregular pagination. Cormac McCarthy Papers, Southwestern Writers Collection, The Wittliff Collections, Texas State University-San Marcos. Collection 91, Box 46, Folder 9.
2. Materials relating to *Cities of the Plain* in the Cormac McCarthy Papers include a film treatment titled "El Paso/Juarez." The title page of this treatment reads "a treatment for a film written by Cormac McCarthy" and "© copyright Cormac McCarthy 1978." Typescript, 16 leaves. Collection 91, Box 69, Folder 2.
3. Typescript draft with holograph corrections. Incomplete, numbered 1–17; 63–127 (83 leaves). Labeled by McCarthy as an "early draft." The scene I refer to here occurs on pages numbered 14–17. Cormac McCarthy Papers. Collection 91, Box 69, Folder 6.

Chapter 3

1. All subsequent quotations from the novel in this essay come from this edition.

Chapter 7

1. In this chapter, I have referred to two primary works by Cormac McCarthy: the (October 2007) Vintage Movie Tie-in edition of *No Country for Old Men* and the First Vintage International (2006) edition of *The Road.*

Chapter 9

1. All quotations are from the first edition of Cormac McCarthy, *The Road* (New York: Knopf, 2006).

Works Cited

Acting McCarthy: The Making of Billy Bob Thornton's All the Pretty Horses. Dir. Peter Josyph and Raymond Todd. Perf. Bruce Dern, Julio Merchoso, Matt Damon, Henry Thomas, Lucas Black, Miriam Colon, Barry Markowitz, Ted Tally, Sally Menke. DVD. Lost Medallion Productions, 2001.

Alarcón, Daniel Cooper. "All the Pretty Mexicos." *Cormac McCarthy: New Directions.* Ed. James D. Lilley. Albuquerque, NM: University of New Mexico Press, 2002. 141–52.

All the Pretty Horses. Dir. Billy Bob Thornton. Perf. Matt Damon, Henry Thomas, Penelope Cruz, Lucas Black, Julio Oscar Mechoso, Bruce Dern. Columbia Pictures, 2000, DVD. Miramax/Columbia, 2005.

Allen, Christian M. *An Industrial Geography of Cocaine.* New York and London: Routledge, 2005.

Allen, William Rodney. *The Coen Brothers: Interviews.* Oxford, Mississippi: University Press of Mississippi, 2006.

Alleva, Richard. "The Haunting: *No Country for Old Men.*" *Commonweal* 134.22 (21 December 2007): 14–16.

Aquinas, Thomas. "The Harmony of Reason and Revelation." Trans. A. C. Pegis. *Philosophy of Religion: Selected Readings.* Second Edition. Eds. Michael Peterson, William Hasker, Bruce Reichenbach, and David Basinger. New York: Oxford University Press, 2001. 67–71.

Arendt, Hannah. *Eichmann in Jerusalem: A Report on the Banality of Evil.* Revised Edition. 1965; reprint. New York: Penguin, 1994.

Aristotle, *Nicomachean Ethics.* Trans. David Ross, rev. J. L. Ackrill and J. O. Urmson. Oxford: Oxford University Press, 1980.

Arnold, Edwin T. "The Last of the Trilogy: First Thoughts on *Cities of the Plain.*" *Perspectives on Cormac McCarthy.* Second Edition. Eds. Edwin T. Arnold and Dianne C. Luce. Jackson, MS: University Press of Mississippi, 1999. 221–47.

Arnold, Edwin. "'Go to sleep': Dreams and Visions in the Border Trilogy." *A Cormac McCarthy Companion: The Border Trilogy.* Eds. Edwin Arnold and Dianne Luce. Jackson, MS: University Press of Mississippi, 2001. 37–72.

Augustine. "Evil is Privation of Good." Trans. Albert C. Outler. *Philosophy of Religion: Selected Readings.* Second Edition. Eds. Michael Peterson, William Hasker, Bruce Reichenbach, and David Basinger. New York: Oxford University Press, 2001. 251–55.

Baum, Dan. "The Price of Valor." *The New Yorker* 12 and 19 July 2004: 44–52.

Beck, Bernard. "Cold, Cold Heart: Who's Afraid of *No Country for Old Men*?" *Multicultural Perspectives* 10.4 (2008): 214–17.

Bell, Madison Smartt. "A Writer's View of Cormac McCarthy." *Myth, Legend, Dust: Critical Responses to Cormac McCarthy*. Ed. Rick Wallach. Manchester, UK: Manchester University Press, 2000. 1–11.

"Billy Bob's Filmography: *All the Pretty Horses* (2000)." *BillyBobapalooza: The Official Billly Bob Thornton Website.* www.billybobthornton.net/film%20 alltheprettyhorses.htm, 10 December 2010.

Blair, Robert. "A Cognitive Developmental Approach to Morality: Investigating the Psychopath." *Cognition* 57 (1995): 1–29.

Bloom, Harold. *How to Read and Why*. New York: Scribner, 2000.

—, ed. *Modern Critical Views: Cormac McCarthy*. Philadelphia, PA: Chelsea House Publishers, 2001.

Bluestone, George. *Novel into Film*. Baltimore, MD: Johns Hopkins University Press, 1957.

Bordwell, David. *Narration in the Fiction Film*. Madison, WI: University of Wisconsin Press, 1985.

Box Office Guru. *All the Pretty Horses*. www.boxofficeguru.com/, 20 March 2009.

Braudy, Leo. "Whose Country?" *Film Quarterly* 61.4 (2008): 10–11.

Brickner, R. "A Hero Cast Out, Even by Tragedy." *New York Times Book Review*. 13 January 1974: 6.

Brown, Royal. "No Exit in Texas." *Cineaste* 33.3 (2008): 9–10.

Buell, Frederick. *From Apocalypse to Way of Life: Environmental Crisis in the American Century*. New York: Routledge, 2004.

Bulter, Judith. *Precarious Life: The Powers of Mourning and Violence*. London and New York: Verso, 2006.

Cant, John. *Cormac McCarthy and the Myth of American Exceptionalism*. New York and London: Routledge, 2008.

Carlson, Thomas A. "With the World at Heart: Reading Cormac McCarthy's *The Road* with Augustine and Heidegger." *Religion & Literature* 39.3 (2007): 47–71.

Carroll, Noël. "Art and Mood: Preliminary Notes and Conjectures." *The Monist* 86 (2003): 521–55.

—. "Film, Emotion, and Genre." *Passionate Views: Film, Cognition, and Emotion*. Eds. Carl Plantinga and Greg Smith. Baltimore, MD: Johns Hopkins University Press, 1999. 21–47.

Castillo, Debra A. *Easy Women: Sex and Gender in Modern Mexican Fiction*. Minneapolis, MN: University of Minnesota Press, 1998.

Chabon, Michael. "Dark Adventure: On Cormac McCarthy's *The Road*." *Maps and Legends: Reading and Writing across the Borderlands*. New York: HarperCollins, 2009. 95–108.

Chollier, Christine. " 'I aint come back rich, that's for sure' or The Questioning of Market Economies in Cormac McCarthy's Novels." *Southwestern American Literature* 25.1 (Fall 1999): 43–49.

—. "Autotextuality, or Dialogic Imagination in Cormac McCarthy's Border Trilogy." *A Cormac McCarthy Companion: The Border Trilogy*. Eds. Edwin

T. Arnold and Dianne C. Luce. Jackson, MS: University Press of Mississippi, 2001. 3–36.

Cohan, Steven and Ina Rae Hark. "Introduction." *The Road Movie Book*. Eds. Steven Cohan and Ina Rae Hark. New York: Routledge, 1997. 1–16.

Cooper, Lydia R. "'He's a Psychopathic Killer, But So What?' Folklore and Morality in Cormac McCarthy's *No Country for Old Men*." *Papers in Language and Literature* 45 (2009): 37–59.

Corrigan, Timothy. *A Cinema Without Walls: Movies and Culture after Vietnam*. New Brunswick, NJ: Rutgers University Press, 1991.

"Cuatro Ciénagas Coahuila." *Explorando México*. www.explorandomexico.com/about-mexico/11/52, 9 Mar. 2009.

Darwall, Stephen. *Impartial Reason*. Ithaca, NY: Cornell University Press, 1983.

Davis, Mike. *Dead Cities and Other Tales*. New York: The New Press, 2008.

Desmond, John M. and Peter Hawkes. *Adaptation: Studying Film and* Literature. New York: McGraw-Hill, 2006.

Diamond, Jared. *Collapse: How Societies Choose to Fail or Succeed*. New York: Viking, 2005.

Do the Right Thing. Dir. Spike Lee. Perf. Danny Aiello, Ossie Davis, and Ruby Dee. 40 Acres and a Mule Filmworks, 1989.

Dimock, Wai Chee and Michael T. Gilmore. "Introduction." *Rethinking Class: Literary Studies and Social Formations*. New York: Columbia University Press, 1994. 1–11.

Dow, William. *Narrating Class in American Fiction*. New York: Palgrave Macmillan, 2009.

Ebert, Roger. "*No Country for Old Men*: Good Country for Dead Men." *Chicago Sun-Times*, 8 November 2007. www.rogerebert.suntimes.com, 19 December 2008.

—. Review of *All the Pretty Horses*. 22 December 2000. http://rogerebert.suntimes.com/apps/pbcs.dll/article?AID=/20001222/REVIEWS/12220301/1023, 20 March 2009.

Edberg, Mark Cameron. *El Narcotrafficante: Narcocorridos and the Construction of a Cultural Persona on the U.S.-Mexico Border*. Austin, TX: University of Texas Press, 2004.

Egan, Jennifer. "Men at Work: The Literary Masculinity of Cormac McCarthy." *Slate*. 10 October 2006, www.slate.com/id/2151300/, 10 December 2010

Ellis, Jay and Natalka Palczynski. "Horses, Houses, and the Gravy to Win: Chivalric and Domestic Roles in The Border Trilogy." *Sacred Violence: Cormac McCarthy's Western Novels*. Second Editon, Volume 2. Eds. Wade Hall and Rick Wallach. El Paso, TX: Texas Western, 2002. 105–25.

—. "The Rape of Rawlins: A Note on *All the Pretty Horses*." *Cormac McCarthy Journal* 1 (Spring 2001): 66–68.

—. *No Place for Home: Spatial Constraint and Character Flight in the Novels of Cormac McCarthy*. New York and London: Routledge, 2006.

Evans, Nicholas. *The Horse Whisperer*. New York: Dell Publishing, 1996.

Faulkner, William. *Requiem for a Nun*. New York: Garland, 1987.

Fischer, John Martin and Mark Ravizza. *Responsibility and Control: A Theory of Moral Responsibility*. Cambridge; New York: Cambridge University Press, 1998.

Fisher-Wirth, Ann. "Abjection and 'the Feminine' in *Outer Dark*." *Cormac McCarthy: New Directions*. Ed. James D. Lilley. Albuquerque, NM: University of New Mexico Press, 2002. 125–40.

Fleming, Michael. "Jones, Jackson Ride into 'Sunset.'" *Variety*, 20 August 2009. www.variety.com/article/VR1118007539.html?categoryid=14&cs=1&query =sunset+limited, 7 September 2009.

Flory, Dan. *Philosophy, Black Film, Film Noir*. University Park, PA: Penn State University Press, 2008.

Foote, Horton. "Writing for Film." *Film and Literature: A Comparative Approach to Adaptation*. Eds. Wendell Aycock and Michael Schoenecke. Lubbock, TX: Texas Tech University Press, 1988. 5–20.

Franco, Jean. "Killing Priests, Nuns, Women, Children." *On Signs*. Ed. Marshall Blonsky. New York: Johns Hopkins University Press, 1985. 414–20.

Freeland, Cynthia. *The Naked and the Undead: Evil and the Appeal of Horror*. Boulder, CO: Westview Press, 2000.

Friedman, Thomas. *Hot, Flat and Crowded: Why We Need a Green Revolution and How It Can Renew America*. New York: Farrar, Strauss, and Giroux, 2008.

Gayon, Jean. "Realism and Biological Knowledge." *Knowledge and the World: Challenges beyond the Science Wars*. Eds. Martin Carrier, Johannes Roggenhofer, Philippe Blanchard, and Gunter Kupper. Berlin: Springer, 2004. 171–90.

Gilmore, Richard. "*No Country for Old Men*: The Coens' Tragic Western." *The Philosophy of the Coen Brothers*. Ed. Mark Conard. Lexington, KY: University Press of Kentucky, 2009. 55–78.

Goin, Peter. *Humanature*. Austin, TX: University of Texas Press, 1996.

Goldie, Peter. *The Emotions: A Philosophical Exploration*. Oxford: Clarendon Press, 2000.

Grossman, Dave. *On Killing: The Psychological Cost of Learning to Kill in War and Society*. Revised Edition. New York: Back Bay Books, 2009.

Guillemin, George. "'As of Some Site Where Life Had Not Succeeded': Sorrow, Allegory, and Pastoralism in Cormac McCarthy's Border Trilogy." *A Cormac McCarthy Companion: The Border Trilogy*. Eds. Edwin T. Arnold and Dianne C. Luce. Jackson, MS: University Press of Mississippi, 2001. 92–130.

—. *The Pastoral Vision of Cormac McCarthy*. College Station, TX: Texas A&M University Press, 2004.

Hall, Wade and Rick Wallach, eds. *Sacred Violence: A Reader's Companion to Cormac McCarthy*. El Paso, TX: Texas Western Press, 1995.

Hardt, Michael and Antonio Negri. *Empire*. Cambridge, MA: Harvard University Press, 2001.

—. *Multitude: War and Democracy in the Age of Empire*. New York: Penguin, 2005.

Hartman, Chester and Gregory D. Squires, eds. *There is No Such Thing as a Natural Disaster: Race, Class, and Hurricane Katrina*. New York: Routledge, 2006.

Harvey, David. *Justice, Nature, and the Geography of Difference.* Cambridge: Blackwell Press, 1996.

Hedgpeth, Don. *They Rode Good Horses: The First Fifty Years of the American Quarter Horse Association.* Amarillo, TX: American Quarter Horse Association, 1990.

Henry: Portrait of a Serial Killer. Dir. John McNaughton. Perf. Michael Rooker, Tracy Arnold, and Tom Towles. Maljack Productions, 1990.

Herrera-Sobek, Maria. "The Theme of Drug Smuggling in the Mexican Corrido." *Revista Chicano-Riqueña,* 7 (1979): 49–61.

Hitchcock, Peter. "They Must Be Represented? Problems in Theories of Working-Class Representation." *PMLA* 115 (January 2000): 20–32.

Hodge, Roger. "Blood and Time: Cormac McCarthy and the Twilight of the West." *Harper's.* 2 January 2006: 65–72.

Holloway, Carson. "*No Country for Old Men*: Demonic Evil and the Limits of Tradition." *First Principles,* 3 November 2008. www.firstprinciplesjournal. com, 19 December 2010.

Holloway, David. *The Late Modernism of Cormac McCarthy.* Westport, CT: Greenwood, 2002.

Hunt , Alex and Martin M. Jacobsen. "Cormac McCarthy's *The Road* and Plato's *Simile of the Sun." Explicator* 66.3 (2008): 155–58. *Academic Search Complete.* EBSCOHost. http://search.ebscohost.com/login.aspx?direct=true&db=a9h& AN=33648961&site=ehost-live, 3 June 2009.

'Hubris.' *Oxford English Dictionary.* Second Edition. 1989.

Jarrett, Robert L. "Cormac McCarthy's Sense of an Ending: Serialized Narrative and Revision in *Cities of the Plain." Cormac McCarthy: New Directions.* Ed. James Lilley. Albuquerque, NM: University of New Mexico Press, 2002. 313–40.

Jarrett, Robert L. *Cormac McCarthy.* New York: Twayne, 1997.

Johnson, Bradley A. "Review of *No Country for Old Men* by Joel and Ethan Coen." *Political Theology* 9.2 (2008): 212–14.

Johnson, Chalmers. *Blowback: The Costs and Consequences of American Empire.* New York: Henry Holt, 2004.

Johnson, Gary. Review of *All the Pretty Horses. Images Journal.* www. imagesjournal.com/issue09/reviews/horses/, 20 March 2009.

Jones, Cindy. "Privett, Samuel Thomas, Jr. [Booger Red]." *The Handbook of Texas Online.* The Texas State Historical Association, 1999. www.tshaonline. org/handbook/online/index.html, 10 June 2009.

Josyph, Peter. "Losing Home: A Conversation with Ted Tally about *All The Pretty Horses." The Southern Quarterly* 40.1 (2001): 132–46.

—. "Tragic Ecstasy: A Conversation with Harold Bloom about Cormac McCarthy's *Blood Meridian." Southwestern American Literature,* 26.1 (2000): 7.

Kant, Immanuel. *Grounding for the Metaphysics of Morals.* Trans. James W. Ellington. Third Edition. Indianapolis, IN: Hackett, 1993.

—. *Religion within the Limits of Reason Alone.* Trans. T. M. Greene and H. H. Hudson. New York: Harper Torchbooks, 1960.

Kaplan, Temma. "Final Reflections: Gender, Chaos, and Authority in Revolutionary Times." *Sex in Revolution: Gender, Politics, and Power in Modern Mexico.* Eds. Jocelyn Olcott, Mary Kay Vaughan, and Gabriela Cano. Durham, NC and London: Duke University Press, 2006. 261–76.

Kermode, Frank. *The Sense of an Ending: Studies in the Theory of Fiction.* New York: Oxford University Press, 1968.

Kitses, Jim. "Bloodred Horizons." *Sight and Sound* 11.3 (2001): 12–15.

Knox, Bernard M. *Oedipus at Thebes: Sophocles' Tragic Hero and His Time.* New Haven, CT: Yale University Press, 1957.

—. "Introduction" to *Oedipus the King* in Sophocles. *The Three Theban Plays: Antigone, Oedipus the King, Oedipus at Colonus.* Trans. Robert Fagles. New York: Penguin, 1982. 131–53.

Kolbert, Elizabeth. *Fieldnotes from a Catastrophe: Man, Nature, and Climate Change.* New York: Bloomsbury, 2006.

Korsgaard, Christine. "Skepticism about Practical Reason." *Journal of Philosophy* 83 (1986): 5–25.

Kristeva, Julia. "Women's Time." *The Kristeva Reader.* Trans. Alice Jardine and Harry Blake. Ed. Toril Moi. New York: Columbia University Press, 1986. 187–213.

Kundera, Milan. *The Unbearable Lightness of Being.* Trans. Michael Henry Heim. New York: Harper & Row, 1985.

Laderman, David. *Driving Visions: Exploring the Road Movie.* Austin, TX: University of Texas Press, 2002.

Leitch, Thomas M. *Film Adaptation and its Discontents: From Gone with the Wind to The Passion of the Christ.* Baltimore, MD.: Johns Hopkins University Press, 2007.

Limón, José E. "La Llorona, The Third Legend of Greater Mexico: Cultural Symbols, Women, and the Political Unconscious." *Between Borders: Essays on Mexicana/Chicana History.* Ed. Adelaida R. Del Castillo. Encino, CA: Floricanto, 1990. 399–432.

—. *American Encounters: Greater Mexico, the United States, and the Erotics of Culture.* Boston, MA: Beacon Press, 1999.

Lincoln, Kenneth. *Cormac McCarthy: American Canticles.* New York: Palgrave Macmillan, 2009.

Luce, Dianne C. "'When You Wake': John Grady Cole's Heroism in *All the Pretty Horses.*" *Sacred Violence: A Reader's Companion to Cormac McCarthy.* Eds. Wade Hall and Rick Wallach. El Paso, TX: Texas Western Press, 1995. 155–67.

Lyman, Rick. "'*All the Pretty Horses*': After Choppy Seas, a Film Nears Port." *The New York Times,* 23 December 2000: B11.

Macías, Anna. *Against All Odds: The Feminist Movement in Mexico to 1940.* Westport, CT and London: Greenwood, 1982.

Marx, Samuel. "A Mythical Kingdom: The Hollywood Film Industry in the 1930s and 1940s." *Film and Literature: A Comparative Approach to Adaptation.* Eds. Wendell Aycock and Michael Schoenecke. Lubbock, TX: Texas Tech University Press, 1988. 21–32.

McCarthy, C. J. Jr. "Wake for Susan." *The Phoenix,* (1959): 3–6.

McCarthy, Cormac. "A Drowning Incident." *The Phoenix*, (1960): 3–4.

—. *The Orchard Keeper*. New York: Random House, 1965.

—. *Outer Dark*. New York: Random House, 1968.

—. *Child of God*. New York: Random House, 1973.

—. *Suttree*. New York: Random House, 1979.

—. *Blood Meridian: Or, The Evening Redness in the West*. New York: Random House, 1985.

—. *All the Pretty Horses*. New York: Knopf, 1992.

—. "All the Pretty Horses." Unpublished typescript. Cormac McCarthy Papers, Southwestern Writers Collection, The Witliff Collections, Texas State University-San Marcos.

—. *The Crossing*. New York: Knopf, 1994.

—. *Cities of the Plain*. New York: Knopf, 1998.

—. "Cities of the Plain." Unpublished, incomplete typescript for a screenplay. Cormac McCarthy Papers, Southwestern Writers Collection, The Witliff Collections, Texas State University-San Marcos.

—. *No Country for Old Men*. New York: Knopf, 2005.

—. *The Road*. New York: Knopf, 2006.

—. "Cormac Country." *Vanity Fair* (August 2005) : 98–104.

—. "El Paso / Juarez." Unpublished film treatment. Cormac McCarthy Papers, Southwestern Writers Collection, The Witliff Collections, Texas State Univesrity-San Marcos.

—.Interview, Oprah Winfrey. "The Cormac McCarthy Interview." 22 February 2009. www.oprah.com/oprahsbookclub/Oprahs-Exclusive-Interview-with-Cormac-McCarthy-Video. 10 December 2010. 1.

Mele, Alfred R. 'Testing Free Will.' *Neuroethics*. 2 December 2008. www.springerlink.com/content/?k=Mele%2c+Alfred+R.+++%e2%80%98Testing+Free+Will.%e2%80%99+++Neuroethics. 10 December 2010

Mellen, Joan. "Spiraling Downward: America in *Days of Heaven, In the Valley of Elah*, and *No Country for Old Men*." *Film Quarterly* 61.3 (2008): 24–31.

Mills, Katie. *The Road Story and the Rebel: Moving through Film, Fiction, and Television*. Carbondale, IL: Southern Illinois University Press, 2006.

Monsiváis, Carlos. Foreword. *Sex in Revolution: Gender, Politics, and Power in Modern Mexico*. Eds. Jocelyn Olcott, Mary Kay Vaughan, and Gabriela Cano. Durham, NC and London: Duke University Press, 2006. 1–20.

Morrison, Gail Moore. "*All the Pretty Horses*: John Grady Cole's Expulsion from Paradise." Revised Second Edition. *Perspectives on Cormac McCarthy*. Eds. Edwin T. Arnold and Dianne C. Luce. Jackson, MS: University Press of Mississippi, 1999. 175–94.

Morton, Adam. *On Evil*. New York: Routledge, 2004.

Nagel, Thomas. *The Possibility of Altruism*. Princeton, NJ: Princeton University Press, 1970.

Natale, Richard. "How'd They Saddle up the Novel?" Review of *All the Pretty Horses. Los Angeles Times* 25 December 2000. http://articles.latimes.com/keyword/all-the-pretty-horses-movie, 20 March 2009.

Negri, Antonio. "Art and Culture in the Age of Empire and the Time of the Multitudes." 2003. *Empire and Beyond*. Trans. Ed Emery. Malden, MA: Polity, 2008. 63–71.

Nichols, Shaun. "How Psychopaths Threaten Moral Rationalism: Is It Rational to be Amoral?" *The Monist* 85 (2002): 285–303.

—. "Norms with Feelings: Towards a Psychological Account of Moral Judgment." *Cognition* 84 (2002): 221–36.

—. *Sentimental Rules: On the Natural Foundations of Moral Judgments.* New York: Oxford University Press, 2004.

Nietzsche, Friedrich. *The Will to Power.* Trans. Walter Kaufmann and R. J. Hollingdale. Ed. Walter Kaufmann. New York: Vintage, 1968.

No Country for Old Men. Dir. Joel and Ethan Coen. Ed. Roderick Jaynes. Music: Carter Burwell. Perf. Javier Bardem, Tommy Lee Jones, Kelly Macdonald, Tess Harper, and Gene Jones, 2007, DVD. Miramax and Paramount Vantage, 2008.

"*No Country for Old Men*: Pro and Con Reviews of Hollywood's 'Best Picture of the Year.'" *Cineaste* 33:3 (2008): 8.

O'Connor, Flannery. *Wise Blood.* New York: Farrar, Straus and Cudahy, 1962.

—. "A Good Man is Hard to Find." *A Good Man is Hard to Find and Other Stories.* New York: Harcourt, Brace, 1955.

Ong, Walter J. *Orality and Literacy: The Technologizing of the Word.* 1988. London and New York: Routledge, 2002.

Pablos, Julia Tuñón. *Women in Mexico: A Past Unveiled.* Trans. Alan Hynds. Austin, TX: University of Texas Press, 1987. (1999).

Paz, Octavio. *The Labyrinth of Solitude: Life and Thought in Mexico.* Trans. Lysander Kemp. New York: Grove, 1961.

Persona. Ingmar Bergman, dir., prod., United Artists, distributor, 1967.

Plantinga, Carl. *Moving Viewers: American Film and the Spectator's Experience.* Berkeley, CA and Los Angeles, CA: University of California Press, 2009.

Plato. *Apology.* In Apology *Euthyphro, Apology, Crito, Phaedo.* 38a. Perseus Online. 29 July 2009 www.perseus.tufts.edu/hopper/text?doc=Perseus:text: 1999.01.0170, 10 December 2010.

—. *Meno.* Trans. W. K. C. Guthrie. *Plato: The Collected Dialogues.* Eds. Edith Hamilton and Huntington Cairns. Princeton, NJ: Princeton University Press, 1963. 353–84.

Quiñones, Sam. *True Tales from Another Mexico: The Lynch Mob, the Popsicle Kings, Chalino, and the Bronx.* Albuquerque, NM: University of New Mexico Press, 2001.

Ramachandran, V. S. *A Brief Tour of Human Consciousness.* New York: Pi Press, 2004.

The Road. Dir. John Hillcoat. Music: Nick Cave, Warren Ellis. Pref. Viggo Mortenson, Kodi Smit-McPhee, Charlize Theron, Robert Duvall. Dimension Films, 2009.

Roberts, Monty. *The Man Who Listens to Horses.* New York: Random House, 1996.

Rodriguez, Ileana. *House/Garden/Nation: Space, Gender, and Ethnicity in Postcolonial Latin American Literatures by Women.* Trans. Robert Carr and Ileana Rodriguez. Durham, NC and London: Duke University Press, 1994.

Rosenbaum, Jonathan. "All the Pretty Carnage." Review of *No Country for Old Men* by Joel and Ethan Coen. *Chicago Reader* 8 November 2007. www. chicagoreader.com/features/stories/moviereviews/2007/171108, 9 June 2009.

Rothfork, John. "Cormac McCarthy as Pragmatist." *Critique* 47.2 (2006): 201–14. *Academic Search Complete*. EBSCOHost. 7 March 2009. http://search.ebscohost.com/login.aspx?direct=true&db=a9h&AN=20024570&site=ehost-live, 10 December 2010.

Saccarelli, Emanuele. "The Banality of Evil: *No Country for Old Men*." *World Socialist Web Site*, 24 November 2007. www.wsws.org 19 December 2008.

Sanborn, Wallis. *Animals in the Fiction of Cormac McCarthy*. Jefferson, NC: McFarland & Co., Publishers, 2006.

Sánchez, Rosaura. "The History of Chicanas: A Proposal for a Materialist Perspective." *Between Borders: Essays on Mexicana/Chicana History*. Ed. Adelaida R. Del Castillo. Encino, CA: Floricanto, 1990. 1–29.

Sarris, Andrew. "Just Shoot Me! Nihilism Crashes Lumet and Coen Bros." Review of *No Country for Old Men* by Joel and Ethan Coen. *New York Observer*, 23 October 2007. www.observer.com/2007/just-shoot-me-nihilism-crashes-lumet-and-coen-bros 13 May 2009.

Schocket, Eric. *Vanishing Moments: Class and American Literature*. Ann Arbor, MI: University of Michigan Press, 2006.

Scott, A. O. "'All the Pretty Horses': Lost Souls Adrift Across a Barren Mesa." *New York Times* 25 December 2000: E1.

Scott, Jacqueline. "The Price of the Ticket: A Genealogy and Revaluation of Race." *Critical Affinities: Nietzsche and African American Thought*. Eds. Jacqueline Scott and A. Todd Franklin. Albany, NY: SUNY Press, 2006. 149–71.

Scott, Ridley. "Interview: The Great Ridley Scott speaks with *Eclipse*." 3 June 2008. http://eclipsemagazine.com/hollywood-insider/interview-the-great-ridley-scott-speaks-with-eclipse-by-scott-essman/5812/

Sepich, John and Christopher Forbis. "A Concordance to *The Road* by Cormac McCarthy." *Cormac McCarthy Resources*. 2 July 2007. http://www.johnsepich.com/a_concordance_to_the_road.pdf, 12 June 2009.

Sharrett, Christopher. "Comic Dread in the Modern Frontier." *Cineaste* 33:3 (2008): 11–13.

Shaw, Patrick W. "Female Presence, Male Violence, and the Art of Artlessness in the Border Trilogy." *Myth, Legend, Dust: Critical Responses to Cormac McCarthy*. Ed. Rick Wallach. Manchester, UK and New York: Manchester University Press, 2000. 256–68.

Shay, Jonathan. *Achilles in Vietnam: Combat Trauma and the Undoing of Character*. 1994; reprint. New York: Scribner, 2003.

Shay, Jonathan. *Odysseus in America: Combat Trauma and the Trials of Homecoming*. New York: Scribner, 2002.

Silence of the Lambs. Dir. Jonathan Demme. Perf. Jodie Foster, Anthony Hopkins, and Scott Glenn. Orion Pictures/Strong Heart/Demme Productions, 1991.

Simonett, Helena. "Narcocorridos: An Emerging Micromusic of Nuevo L.A." *Ethnomusicology*, 45 (2001): 315–37.

Singer, Peter. *How Are We to Live*. Buffalo: Prometheus Books, 1995.

Sinnott-Armstrong, Walter. "Consequentialism." *The Stanford Encyclopedia of Philosophy*. Ed. Edward N. Zalta. August 2008. Stanford University.

http://plato.stanford.edu/archives/fall2008/entries/consequentialism/, 12 June 2009.

Smith, Greg M. *Film Structure and the Emotion System*. New York: Cambridge University Press, 2003.

Snyder, Phillip. "Cowboy Codes in Cormac McCarthy's Border Trilogy." *A Cormac McCarthy Companion: The Border Trilogy*. Eds. Edwin T. Arnold and Dianne C. Luce. Jackson, MS: University Press of Mississippi, 2001. 198–227.

Sontag, Susan. *Against Interpretation and Other Essays*. New York: Farrar, Strauss, and Giroux, 1966.

Sophocles. *The Three Theban Plays: Antigone, Oedipus the King, Oedipus at Colonus*. Trans. Robert Fagles. New York: Penguin, 1982.

Spurgeon, Sara L. "'Pledged in Blood': Truth and Redemption in Cormac McCarthy's *All the Pretty Horses*." *Western American Literature* 34 (1999): 24–47.

Steinbeck, John. *The Grapes of Wrath*. 1939. Reprint. New York: Penguin, 2006.

Stewart, Susan. *On Longing: Narratives of the Miniature, the Gigantic, the Souvenir, the Collection*. Durham, NC: Duke University Press, 1993.

Stoehr, Kevin L. *Nihilism in Film and Television*. Jefferson, NC: McFarland, 2006.

'Squander.' *Oxford English Dictionary*. Second Edition. 1989.

Sullivan, Nell. "Boys Will Be Boys and Girls Will Be Gone: The Circuit of Male Desire in Cormac McCarthy's Border Trilogy." *A Cormac McCarthy Companion: The Border Trilogy*. Eds. Edwin T. Arnold and Dianne C. Luce. Jackson, MS: University Press of Mississippi, 228–55.

—. "The Evolution of the Dead Girlfriend Motif in *Outer Dark* and *Child of God*. *Myth, Legend, Dust: Critical Responses to Cormac McCarthy*. Ed. Rick Wallach. Manchester, UK: Manchester University Press, 2000. 68–77.

Tatum, Stephen. *Cormac McCarthy's All the Pretty Horses: A Reader's Guide*. New York and London: Continuum, 2002.

—. "Spectrality and the Postregional Interface." *Postwestern Cultures: Literature, Theory, Space*. Ed. Susan Kollin. Lincoln, NE and London: University of Nebraska Press, 2007: 3–29.

The Horse Whisperer. Dir. Robert Redford. Perf. Robert Redford, Kristen Scott Thomas. Touchstone Pictures, 1998.

Thornton, Niamh. *Women and the War Story in Mexico: La Novela de La Revolución*. Lewiston, ID: Mellen, 2006.

Todd, Raymond. "Kafka's Mountain: Notes Passed During a Screening of All the Pretty Horses." *Sacred Violence: Cormac McCarthy's Western Novels*. Second Edition Volume 2. Eds. Wade Hall and Rick Wallach. El Paso, TX: Texas Western Press, 2002. 189–204.

Travers, Peter. Review of *No Country for Old Men* by Joel and Ethan Coen. *Rolling Stone*, 1 November 2007. www.rollingstone.com, 19 December 2008.

Wald, Elijah. *Narcocorrido: A Journey into the Music of Drugs, Guns, and Guerrillas*. New York: Rayo, an imprint of HarperCollins, 2002.

Wallach, Rick, ed. *Myth, Legend, Dust: Critical Responses to Cormac McCarthy.* Manchester, UK: Manchester University Press, 2000.

Walters, Ben and J. M. Tyree. "Cash and Carrion." Review of *No Country for Old Men* by Joel and Ethan Coen. *Sight and Sound* 18:2 (2008): 48–49.

Wegner, John. "'Mexico para los Mexicanos': Revolution, Mexico, and McCarthy's Border Trilogy." *Myth, legend, dust: Critical Responses to Cormac McCarthy.* Ed. Rick Wallach. Manchester, UK: Manchester University Press, 2000. 249–55.

Williams, Raymond. *Keywords: A Vocabulary of Culture and Society.* Revised Edition. New York: Oxford University Press, 1983.

"Wimple." *The Oxford English Dictionary.* Second Edition. 1989. http://dictionary.oed.com/, 15 June 2009.

Witek, Terri. "'He's hell when he's well': Cormac McCarthy's rhyming dictions." *Myth, legend, dust: Critical responses to Cormac McCarthy.* Ed. Rick Wallach. Manchester, UK: Manchester University Press, 2000. 78–88.

Wood, James. "Getting to the End." *The New Republic* 21 May 2007: 46.

—. *How Fiction Works.* New York: Farrar, Straus and Giroux, 2008.

Woodward, Richard B. "Cormac McCarthy's Venomous Fiction." *New York Times Magazine* 19 April 1992: 28–31. www.nytimes.com/books/98/05/17/specials/mccarthy-venom.html, 13 Mar. 2009.

—. "Cormac McCarthy's Venemous Fiction." *New York Times Magazine* 19 April 1992, sec. 6: 28–31+.

—. "Cormac Country." *Vanity Fair* August 2005, 98–104.

Xenophon. *The Art of Horsemanship.* Trans. Morris H. Morgan. Mineola, NY: Dover Publications, Inc., 2006. (Originally published by Little, Brown and Company, Boston, 1893).

Further Reading

McCarthy's Work

Short Fiction
McCarthy, C. J. Jr., "Wake for Susan." *The Phoenix,* (1959), 3–6.
McCarthy, Cormac. "A Drowning Incident." *The Phoenix,* (1960), 3–4.

Novels
—. *The Orchard Keeper.* New York: Random House, 1965.
—. *Outer Dark.* New York: Random House, 1968.
—. *Child of God.* New York: Random House, 1973.
—. *Suttree.* New York: Random House, 1979.
—. *Blood Meridian: Or, The Evening Redness in the West.* New York: Random House, 1985.
—. *All the Pretty Horses.* New York: Knopf, 1992.
—. *The Crossing.* New York: Knopf, 1994.
—. *Cities of the Plain.* New York: Knopf, 1998.
—. *No Country for Old Men.* New York: Knopf, 2005.
—. *The Road.* New York: Knopf, 2006.

Screenplay
The Gardener's Son. New York: Ecco Press, 1996.

Plays
The Stonemason. New York: Ecco Press, 1994.
Sunset Limited. New York: Vintage International, 2006.

Studies of McCarthy

Books and Special Issues
This section contains book length studies, reader's guides and handbooks, and special issues of scholarly journals dedicated exclusively to Cormac McCarthy's works. A recent explosion in books published on the author have greatly enriched the depth and breadth of research available to readers interested in pursuing research on McCarthy and his writing.

Arnold, E. and Luce, Dianne, eds. *Perspectives on Cormac McCarthy:* Revised Edition. Jackson, MS: University Press of Mississippi, 1999.

—. *The Southern Quarterly. Special Issue: Cormac McCarthy's Border Trilogy,* 38.3 (2000).

—. *A Cormac McCarthy Companion: The Border Trilogy.* Jackson, MS: University Press of Mississippi, 2001.

Bell, Vereen. *The Achievement of Cormac McCarthy.* Baton Rouge, LA: Louisiana State University Press, 1988.

Bloom, Harold. *Cormac McCarthy.* New York: Chelsea House Publishers. 2002.

—. *Cormac McCarthy's* All the Pretty Horses. New York: Chelsea House Publishers. 2003.

Cant, John. *Cormac McCarthy and the Myth of American Exceptionalism.* New York and London: Routledge, 2008.

—, ed. *The Cormac McCarthy Society Journal. Special Issue: No Country for Old Men* 5 (2006).

Ellis, Jay. *No Place for Home: Spatial Constraint and Character Flight in the Novels of Cormac McCarthy.* New York and London: Routledge, 2006.

Frye, Steven. *Understanding Cormac McCarthy.* Columbia, SC: University of South Carolina Press, 2009.

Graulich, Melody, ed. *Western American Literature. Special Issue: Cormac McCarthy.* 44.2 (2009).

Guillemin, Georg. *The Pastoral Vision of Cormac McCarthy.* College Station, TX: Texas A&M University Press, 2004.

Hage, Erik. *Cormac McCarthy: A Literary Companion.* New York: McFarland. 2010.

Hall, Wade and Wallach, Rick, eds. *Sacred Violence:* Second Edition, Volume 1. *Cormac McCarthy's Appalachian Works.* El Paso, TX: Texas Western Press, 2002.

—. *Sacred Violence:* Second Edition, Volume 2. *Cormac McCarthy's Western Novels.* El Paso, TX: Texas Western Press, 2002.

Holloway, David. *The Late Modernism of Cormac McCarthy.* Westport, CT and London: Greenwood Press, 2002.

Jarrett, Robert L. *Cormac McCarthy.* New York: Twayne, 1997.

Josyph, Peter. *Adventures in Reading Cormac McCarthy.* Lanham, MD: Scarecrow Press, 2010.

King, Lynnea Chapman, Rick Wallach and Jim Welsh, eds. *No Country for Old Men: From Novel to Film.* Lanham, MD: Scarecrow Press, 2009.

Lilley, James. *Cormac McCarthy: New Directions.* Albuquerque, NM: University of New Mexico Press, 2002.

Lincoln, Kenneth. *Cormac McCarthy: American Canticles.* New York: Palgrave Macmillan, 2009.

Luce, Dianne. *Reading the World: Cormac McCarthy's Tennessee Period.* Columbia, SC: University of South Carolina Press, 2009.

Owens, Barcley. *Cormac McCarthy's Western Novels.* Tucson, AZ: University of Arizona Press, 2000.

Sanborn, Wallis. *Animals in the Fiction of Cormac McCarthy*. Jefferson, NC: McFarland & Co., Publishers, 2006.

Sepich, John. *Notes on Blood Meridian*. Louisville, KY: Bellarmine College Press, 1993. Print.

Tatum, Stephen. *Cormac McCarthy's All the Pretty Horses: A Reader's Guide*. New York and London: Continuum, 2002.

Wallach, Rick, ed. *Southwestern American Literature: Special Issue, Cormac McCarthy*. 25.1 (1999).

—, ed. *Myth, Legend, Dust: Critical Responses to Cormac McCarthy*. Manchester, UK: Manchester University Press, 2000.

Wegner, John, ed. *The Cormac McCarthy Journal*. 1.1 (2000).

The section below provides a selected list of journal articles, essays from anthologies and book chapters dealing mainly with *All the Pretty Horses*, *No Country for Old Men*, and *The Road*, although individual selections from books or collections already listed above are not included.

Journal Articles and Book Chapters

All the Pretty Horses

Chollier, Christine. "Exporsure and Double Exposure in Cormac McCarthy's Baroque Trilogy." Ed. David Holloway. *Proceedings of the first European Conference on Cormac McCarthy*. Miami: Cormac McCarthy Society, 1998. 49–56.

Clark, B. "Art, Authenticity and Social Transgression in Cormac McCarthy's *All the Pretty Horses*." *Southwestern American Literature*. 25.1 (1999): 117–23.

Ellis, Jay. "The Rape of Rawlins: A Note on *All the Pretty Horses*." *Cormac McCarthy Journal* 1 (Spring 2001): 66–68.

Josyph, Peter. "Losing Home: A Conversation with Ted Tally about *All The Pretty Horses*." *The Southern Quarterly* 40.1 (2001): 132–46.

Lyman, Rick. "'*All the Pretty Horses*': After Choppy Seas, a Film Nears Port." *The New York Times* 23 December 2000: B11.

Spurgeon, Sara L. "'Pledged in Blood': Truth and Redemption in Cormac McCarthy's *All the Pretty Horses*." *Western American Literature* 34 (1999): 24–47.

Sullivan, Nell. "Boys will be Boys and Girls will be Gone: The Circuit of Male Desire in Cormac McCarthy's Border Trilogy." *The Southern Quarterly*, 38.3 (2000): 167–187.

No Country for Old Men

Alleva, Richard. "The Haunting: *No Country for Old Men*." *Commonweal* 134.22 (21 December 2007): 14–16.

Beck, Bernard. "Cold, Cold Heart: Who's Afraid of *No Country for Old Men*?" *Multicultural Perspectives* 10.4 (2008): 214–17.

Cooper, Lydia R. "'He's a Psychopathic Killer, But So What?' Folklore and Morality in Cormac McCarthy's *No Country for Old Men.*" *Papers in Language and Literature* 45 (2009): 37–59.

Gilmore, Richard. "*No Country for Old Men*: The Coens' Tragic Western." *The Philosophy of the Coen Brothers.* Ed. Mark Conard. Lexington, KY: University Press of Kentucky, 2009. 55–78.

Hodge, Roger. "Blood and Time: Cormac McCarthy and the Twilight of the West." *Harper's.* 2 January 2006. 65–72.

Holloway, Carson. "*No Country for Old Men*: Demonic Evil and the Limits of Tradition." *First Principles* 3 November 3, 2008. www.firstprinciplesjournal. com, 19 December 2008.

Mellen, Joan. "Spiraling Downward: America in *Days of Heaven, In the Valley of Elah*, and *No Country for Old Men.*" *Film Quarterly* 61.3 (2008): 24–31.

Rothfork, John. "Cormac McCarthy as Pragmatist." *Critique* 47.2 (2006): 201–14. *Academic Search Complete.* EBSCOHost. http://search.ebscohost.com/login. aspx?direct=true&db=a9h&AN=20024570&site=ehost-live, 7 March 2009.

Saccarelli, Emanuele. "The Banality of Evil: *No Country for Old Men.*" *World Socialist Web Site,* 24 November 2007. www.wsws.org 19 December 2008.

The Road

Carlson, Thomas A. "With the World at Heart: Reading Cormac McCarthy's *The Road* with Augustine and Heidegger." *Religion & Literature* 39.3 (2007): 47–71.

Gray, Richard. "Open Doors, Closed Minds: American Prose Writing at a Time of Crisis," American Literary History, 21.1 (2009): 128–48.

Hunt , Alex and Martin M. Jacobsen. "Cormac McCarthy's *The Road* and Plato's *Simile of the Sun.*" *Explicator* 66.3 (2008): 155–58. *Academic Search Complete.* EBSCOHost. http://search.ebscohost.com/login.aspx?direct=true&db=a9h& AN=33648961&site=ehost-live, 3 June 2009.

Kunsa, Ashley. "Maps of the World in Its Becoming: Post-apocalyptic Naming in Cormac McCarthy's *The Road.*" *Journal of Modern Literature* 33.1 (2009): 57–74.

Mizruchi, Susan. "Risk Theory and the Contemporary American Novel," *American Literary History,* 22.1 (2010): 109–35.

Websites and Interviews

Concordance for all McCarthy novels: www.johnsepich.com/cormac_mccarthy/ index.html, 3 December 2010

Cormac McCarthy.com: The Official Webpage of the Cormac McCarthy Society. www.cormacmccarthy.com/, 3 December 2010

Map of Blood Meridian: www.googlelittrips.com/GoogleLit/Hi_Ed/Entries/2007/ 4/18_Blood_Meridian_by_Cormac_McCarthy.html, 3 December 2010

Santa Fe Institute. www.santafe.edu/, 3 December 2010

Winfrey, Oprah. "The Cormac McCarthy Interview." 22 February 2009. www. oprah.com/media/20080601 obc 267033502CORMACWEBEA O VIDEO 1.

Woodward, Richard B. "Cormac McCarthy's Venomous Fiction." *New York Times Magazine* 19 April 1992, sec. 6: 28–31.
—. "Cormac Country." *Vanity Fair* August 2005: 98–104.

Related Studies

The works in this section provide interested readers with helpful historical, literary, regional, filmic and other contextual background. Some of the works included mention McCarthy, although none focus on his writing exclusively.

Acting McCarthy: The Making of Billy Bob Thornton's All the Pretty Horses. Dir. Peter Josyph and Raymond Todd. Perf. Bruce Dern, Julio Merchoso, Matt Damon, Henry Thomas, Lucas Black, Miriam Colon, Barry Markowitz, Ted Tally, Sally Menke. DVD. Lost Medallion Productions, 2001.

Aycock, Wendell and Michael Schoenecke, ed. *Film and Literature: A Comparative Approach to Adaptation.* Lubbock, TX: Texas Tech University Press, 1988.

Conard, Mark, ed. *The Philosophy of the Coen Brothers.* Lexington, KY: University Press of Kentucky, 2009.

Desmond, John M, and Peter Hawkes. *Adaptation: Studying Film and Literature.* New York: McGraw-Hill, 2006. Print.

Kollin, Susan, ed. *Postwestern Cultures: Literature, Theory, Space.* Lincoln, NE and London: University of Nebraska Press, 2007.

Limón, José E. *American Encounters: Greater Mexico, the United States, and the Erotics of Culture.* Boston, MA: Beacon Press, 1999.

Parrish, Timothy. *From the Civil War to the Apocalypse: Postmodern History and American Fiction.* Amherst, MA: University of Massachusetts Press, 2008.

Paz, Octavio. *The Labyrinth of Solitude: Life and Thought in Mexico.* Trans. Lysander Kemp. New York: Grove, 1961.

Simonett, Helena. "Narcocorridos: An Emerging Micromusic of Nuevo L.A." *Ethnomusicology,* 45 (2001): 315–37.

Spurgeon, Sara L. *Exploding the Western: Myths of Empire on the Postmodern Frontier.* College Station, TX: Texas A&M University Press, 2005.

Wald, Elijah. *Narcocorrido: A Journey into the Music of Drugs, Guns, and Guerrillas.* New York: Rayo, an imprint of Harper Collins, 2002.

Notes on Contributors

Jay Ellis teaches in the Program for Writing and Rhetoric and the English Department at the University of Colorado in Boulder. His publications on Cormac McCarthy include *No Place for Home: Spatial Constraint and Character Flight in the Novels of Cormac McCarthy* (Routledge), "Identity across *Blood Meridians*" in *Rhetorical Democracy: Discursive Practices of Civic Engagement* (Hauser and Grim, eds. Erlbaum), and "Another Sense of Ending: The Keynote Address to the Knoxville Conference" in *The Cormac McCarthy Journal*. Current projects include completing a second novel and an interdisciplinary study of poems, a long-arc television series (*Deadwood*) and novels and films concerned with domesticity, particularly in putatively masculine narratives: *Don't Fence Me In: Spatial Ambivalence in American Literature and Culture.*

Dan Flory is Associate Professor of Philosophy at Montana State University, Bozeman, and in 2007–2008 served as Visiting Associate Professor of Philosophy at American University in Cairo, Egypt. He is author of *Philosophy, Black Film, Film Noir* (Penn State University Press, 2008) and has published essays in *Film and Philosophy*, *Journal of Aesthetics and Art Criticism*, *American Quarterly*, and *The Routledge Companion to Philosophy and Film*.

Donovan Gwinner is Assistant Professor of English and teaches composition, literature, and interdisciplinary studies at Aurora University, in Aurora, Illinois. His research interests include contemporary US historical fiction and ethnic studies. He has published recently on the film "Brokeback Mountain," and his scholarship has focused on the work of Leslie Marmon Silko, William T. Vollmann, and Sherman Alexie.

Andrew Husband is a doctoral student in English and a member of the Literature, Social Justice, and Environment (LSJE) Initiative at Texas Tech University. He has published articles in *Texas Theatre Journal* and *ISLE: Interdisciplinary Studies in Literature and Environment* and presented papers on Stephen Crane, Nuruddin Farah, and Cormac McCarthy.

Susan Kollin is Associate Professor of English at Montana State University where she teaches courses on Western American literature and film, feminist theory, and environmental studies. Her work has appeared in *American Literary History*, *Modern Fiction Studies*, *Contemporary Literature*, *Arizona Quarterly* and *ISLE (Interdisciplinary Studies in Literature and Environment)*. She is the author of *Nature's State: Imagining Alaska as the Last Frontier* and editor of *Postwestern Cultures: Literature, Theory, Space*. She is past president of the Western Literature Association.

Stacey Peebles is Assistant Director of the Lloyd International Honors College at the University of North Carolina, Greensboro. Her research focuses on the representation of war and violence in literature and film. She has published a number of articles on Cormac McCarthy that have appeared in *Sacred Violence* (2002), *No Country for Old Men: From Novel to Film* (2009), *Texas Studies in Literature and Language*, and *Southwestern American Literature*. Other publications have addressed the work of Terrence Malick, Michael Herr, and Flannery O'Connor. In 2009 her article on Anthony Swofford and Colby Buzzell appeared in *PMLA*'s special issue "War." She is completing a book titled *Battle Rattle in the Suck: Narrating the American Soldier's Experience in Iraq*.

Dana Phillips is Assistant Professor of English at Towson University. He also has taught at the University of Pennsylvania, Princeton University, Bryn Mawr College, Brown University, the Bread Loaf School of English in Juneau, Alaska, and—as a Fulbright Senior Specialist—at the University of the Witwatersrand in Johannesburg, South Africa. His publications include articles on Whitman, Thoreau, Emerson, McCarthy, DeLillo, and ecocriticism, and a book, *The Truth of Ecology: Nature, Culture, and Literature in America*, which was published by Oxford University Press in 2003 and won the Modern Language Association prize for best book by an independent scholar in 2004. The book was republished by Oxford Scholarship Online in 2007.

Stephen Tatum is Professor of English and Director of Environmental Humanities at the University of Utah, where he teaches courses in the literatures and cultures of the American West, critical theory, and environmental writing. Among his publications are the co-edited (with Melody Graulich) collections, *Reading The Virginian in the New West* (2003), and *Cormac McCarthy's All the Pretty Horses: A Reader's Guide* (Continuum, 2002). His most recent book, *In the Remington Moment*, is forthcoming in 2010 from the University of Nebraska Press. He is a two-time recipient of the Don D. Walker Prize for best article or essay in Western American literary studies and is a past president of the Western Literature Association.

Linda Woodson is a professor at The University of Texas at San Antonio where she teaches courses in the literatures of Texas and the Southwest, American literature, rhetoric, and composition. She has previously served as department chair and as coordinator of the composition program. She is the author of numerous articles on Cormac McCarthy and of articles and books on rhetoric and composition.

Index

Printed in Great Britain
by Amazon

35861730R00126